Mastering

Fashion Buying and Merchandising Management

Tim Jackson
and
David Shaw

palgrave
macmillan

First published 2001 by
PALGRAVE MACMILLAN
Houndmills, Basingstoke, Hampshire RG21 6XS
and London
Companies and representatives
throughout the world

ISBN-13: 978–0–333–80165–9
ISBN-10: 0–333–80165–2

A catalogue record for this book is available
from the British Library.

This book is printed on paper suitable for recycling and made from fully
managed and sustained forest sources. Logging, pulping and manufacturing
processes are expected to conform to the environmental regulations of the
country of origin.

13
10   09

Printed and bound in Great Britain by the MPG Books Group, Bodmin and King's Lynn

■ Ⅴ   Contents

■ ⊻ Preface

The idea behind this book emerged from the authors' need for a suitable textbook on fashion buying and merchandising management to support their lecturing and course development at The London College of Fashion. With the increasing interest among students in higher education studying fashion-related subjects, the need for such a textbook became obvious. Tim Jackson and David Shaw, having both been previously employed in the fashion business, were surprised to find a dearth of European literature on the area of fashion buying and merchandising management.

This book will be of practical interest to all types of fashion and business students, especially those undertaking fashion design, fashion retailing, fashion management or fashion product-related courses. For those already employed in the fashion business, it is envisaged that it will widen and deepen their knowledge base, as well as support both individual and corporate career development programmes. It will also give the general fashion-interested reader a clear insight into these most important aspects of the fashion industry.

Using their own original teaching materials, and with the support of many current practitioners within the fashion trade, the authors set out to write this first clearly structured textbook on the subject. All material contained within this text, other than where specifically referenced, comes from original research conducted by the authors in conjunction with major fashion retailing organisations based in the United Kingdom.

Significant primary research has been undertaken with middle and senior management across a wide spectrum of fashion businesses. In-depth interviews and documentary evidence provided the substantive details. A great deal of information contained in this book is not accessible within the public domain. The unique and mainly uncharted subject matter of this book has meant that most of the material used in the text is original. Unlike most textbooks, there has been little cross-referencing to other academic texts. The authors felt that this is a rather unique approach to the writing of a text book, and therefore must take full responsibility for any omissions that may exist. This work makes an original contribution to the field of knowledge in this area by presenting and synthesising many hitherto unpublished conceptual frameworks.

We would like personally to thank all those people who have helped make the writing of this book possible. The majority we have listed below in alphabetical order, although there are some contributors who requested to remain unnamed. Many are current practitioners in the trade who gave up their valuable spare time to help with the project. We would also thank all our lifelong associates within the industry for helping us along the fashion pathway. To all readers, we hope that you find this book both interesting and helpful. A glossary of terms has been included at the back of this book for quick reference.

■ ☑ Acknowledgements

We acknowledge the following for helping us with material for the book:

Helen Anstey (London College of Fashion)
David Beattie (Retail Systems and Services)
Clare Boulton (London College of Fashion)
Maurice Bennett (Oasis)
John Bovill (Oasis)
Joanna Bowring (Courtaulds)
Andrew Brundle (Jaeger)
Sarah Crawford (Warehouse)
Exposure (PR)
Tim Gulbride (London College of Fashion)
Kate Hardy (Hermès)
Ros Hibbert (Line)
Tony Hines (London College of Fashion)
Nick Hollingworth (Arcadia)
Matthew Jeatt (Promostyl)
Kim Mannino (Promostyl)
Virginia McKeown
Bridget Miles (Marks & Spencer)
Claire Morgan
Colin Porter (House of Fraser)
David Riddiford (Selfridges)
Michael Talboys (London College of Fashion)
Catherine Thomas
Alison Thorn (B&Q)
Chris Webb (Jaeger)

Special thanks also go to Karen Jackson and Lynn Levy for helping us in the final production and proof-reading of this book.

■ ⩔ Introduction

Many people have a perception of what the job of a fashion buyer is like and believe that it is predominantly concerned with selecting designer labels and attending glamorous catwalk shows. This may be true of some boutique buying and it may reflect the experience of buyers for certain department stores and catalogues stocking Designer ready-to-wear items. However, it is not true for most fashion which is bought and sold through well known high street fashion retail brands. The job of a buyer in most high street fashion retailers is more hard work than glamour and requires strong commercial ability as much as it does knowledge of fashion design.

Given the wide assortment of literature about fashion design and the deficit of material concerning fashion buying, the authors believe the job of this book is to explain the diversity of issues surrounding the subject. A major aim of the book is to prepare those wishing to enter or develop careers in fashion retail buying and merchandising for the tough commercial reality of the job. This book has been written to explain the business of buying and merchandising in fashion retailing and consequently takes a very vocational perspective about what is a frequently discussed but often misunderstood subject.

Another key aim of this book is to explain the vital role of marketing in the process of designing and buying a range of products. Unfortunately the term 'marketing' is widely used by people to refer to different things. It is in fact as much concerned with the design and delivery of fashion product benefits as it is with the promotion of those benefits. Interestingly, many fashion retailers regard it as an operational function which has a very specific role of promoting the company and its products through a combination of advertising and PR. The responsibilities for product and price decisions are given to the separate functions of design, buying, merchandising and garment technology. These teams are made up of people who are not necessarily trained in marketing but in reality are making real marketing decisions every day. It is the view of the authors that many past product range mistakes made by fashion retailers could have been avoided had buyers taken marketing-led as opposed to design-led decisions. These issues are specifically tackled in Chapters 3 and 4 of the book.

A definition of fashion

The word 'fashion' has been defined in a variety of ways over the years. Perna (1987)[1] refers to it as 'the style of dressing that prevails among any group of persons . . . which may last for a year or two or a span of years'. In a general sense it is concerned with a contemporary style that has traditionally been reflected through individuals' clothing, accessories, hair styling and cosmetics. These are characteristics of individuals' appearance. Wilson and de la Haye (1999)[2] make the point that fashion clothing has become central to mass culture as a means through which individuals express themselves and create identities. However, a consumer who wishes to use fashion as a means of projecting an image to others can do so in an increasing number of ways, as lifestyle messages in the media extend opportunities for people to manipulate their appearance in society. A key attribute of something that is fashionable is that it is visible when being 'consumed' or used. As such, a fashion statement is as likely to be made these days by a person's car, the terminology they use, mobile phone, computer game and even garden as it is through their clothing.

Fashion is no longer only for the rich and thanks to the development of fashion retailing it is available for the majority at affordable prices. In turn this has seen the evolution throughout Europe of many national, international and now global fashion retailers. The emphases on design throughout every aspect of our every day lives are increasing, as businesses appreciate the price premium that can be commanded from 'designed' products. Fashion forecasters have long been advising industry sectors such as car and electrical goods on trends including shape and colour, but are now also advising plant growers about trends in demand for plant styles and shades. Fashion clothing is fast moving from a once utilitarian and functional product towards an aspirational and more psychologically uplifting aspect of consumer purchasing.

Fashion is not only to be found at *haute couture* fashion shows, but can be found on the street or even in charity or second-hand shops. Good fashion buyers leave no stone unturned as to where they seek inspiration for the next fashion trend. Being out and about looking in clubs, street markets, parks and beaches – in fact, most public places – is part of the daily life of the best fashion buyers. There is no one reference book that contains all the fashion answers – not even this one!

The growth of fashion retailing

Fashion retailing has enjoyed considerable growth throughout both the industrialised and the developing world. The increasingly affluent global society, combined with faster international communications, has created the reality of global fashion. A more international wardrobe from such famous names and brands as Bennetton, Levi's, The Gap and Nike is now replacing national costume. We are also seeing fashion consumers segmenting into smaller and more fragmented social groups, which are being influenced by an increasing variety of stimuli such as sport, music, film, TV and dance. In marketing terms, this is sometimes known as 'tribalism', and is explained by the fact that as society becomes more uncertain, crowded and confused, the individual seeks comfort by becoming aligned to smaller societal groupings with clear values and symbols. Fashion forms part of that tribal symbolism. Increasingly the individual is using fashion as a vehicle for making a personal statement about their self-image, in an endeavour to elevate them both physically and psychologically. Throughout Europe it is interesting to note that in some countries, dressing smartly and fashionably is seen as a societal norm for all classes; in other European countries, clothing and fashion are low down on the agenda of societal importance.

The ability of fashion retailers quickly to deliver the latest fashion look to the shop floor is now an imperative as fashion styles and trends change at increasing speed and regularity. Such a fast-moving trade requires the fashion buyer to make faster and faster product decisions, if they are to stay ahead of their competitors. In the final analysis the fashion buyer who gets the latest look into their shop first, and successfully sells it all is going to have the most profitable business. Unlike other more stable retail commodities, fashion products are by their very nature complex and difficult to understand. Another aim of this book is to clearly explain to the reader how the role of both the fashion buyer and fashion merchandiser work together to deliver products to retail outlets.

The glamorous world of fashion as generally portrayed by the media is only the thin veneer on top of a very complex range of business decision-making activities. By the end of the book the reader will acquire a clear understanding of how European fashion retailing works. In today's competitive market place, it is difficult to claim that any industry works only in one way or another. Throughout the book the authors have consulted across a wide range of international retailers, in an endeavour to clearly document best practice as it happens at the turn of a new millennium. The fashion industry is a major employer throughout Europe and the world. Very often the economic significance of the fashion industry to society as a whole is trivialised, probably as result of the 'catwalk' imagery, so often the public's only view into what is an important part of the economy.

Fashion retailing and profit

It is important to realise that fashion buying and merchandising are probably the most important management functions of any fashion retailing business. If the business does not buy the goods that the customers demand, or if they fail to get the right goods to the right place at the right time, then the business will suffer. No matter how good the sales team is in the shops or the accountants in the back office, without the right goods they will not be able to generate enough sales, and ultimately enough profit. It is for these reasons that fashion retailers put such importance on the role of buyer and merchandiser, going to great lengths to select the right calibre of staff and to remunerate them well.

Fashion buying is not simply about the buyer buying what she personally likes, or necessarily about buying the latest fashion trends – it is about supplying the businesses customer with what they want. The fashion trade is littered with businesses that have gone or are going bust. While some were once at the frontiers of 'trendiness', they failed or are failing to deliver adequate bottom-line profit on a regular basis. Regular and sustainable profits are vital for the survival of any fashion business. Observation of your local shops over a relatively short time, will reveal the unforgiving dynamics of fashion retailing – closed shops, changed retail formats, lost fashion names and vanished brands. These are all clues to the tough and dynamic nature of fashion retailing. Ask anyone over the age of thirty-five about the names of the fashion shops they once used – a large number will have been consigned to fashion history.

Fashion retailing and marketing

As with any other form of business activity, fashion buying requires a sound marketing approach if it is to succeed. It is important for readers to understand that marketing has an increasingly important role to play throughout all aspects of fashion retailing. The unique nature and speed of fashion retailing requires marketing to be used in more innovative, subtle and faster ways than before. Historically the marketing function in fashion retailing has been concerned with the promotion of the product range and the brand. Chapter 4 examines how the entire marketing mix, rather than promotion alone, can be harnessed to create a powerful and holistic approach to fashion marketing. Marketing in the fashion industry is developing quickly and a clear understanding and successful application will be vital for many fashion retailers struggling at the start of the new millennium.

Marketing is a business philosophy that ensures any business or organisation delivers to the customer what they want, rather than forcing them to accept what the business thinks they want. It is no use guessing what the fashion consumer wants; smart fashion businesses use a combination of detailed design research and marketing techniques to ensure they know what is required. The importance of segmenting customer needs and the best segmentation methods for fashion retailers are explained in Chapter 4.

Fashion retailers and society

The widespread availability and interest in mass-market fashion is now creating new problems for fashion retailers. Apart from increasing global competition and increasing price competitiveness, we are for the first time seeing the development of an ageing population that is maintaining an interest in fashion. Historically fashion was normally associated with youth; now as the post-Second World War 'baby-boomers' enter middle age with high levels of affluence and spare time, fashion interest is being retained much later in life. It is clear that many European fashion retailers are not reacting to this new demand. A majority of European fashion retailers still seem locked in time, determined to try and maintain their sales to a contracting and increasingly less important youth market. With the exception of a handful of developed countries, the population is getting older and wealthier than ever before. The new challenge of re-aligning and successful marketing to this older target group seems to be eluding a majority of fashion retailers.

Is fashion buying a glamorous job?

There is a popular misconception that the life of a fashion buyer is the ultimate glamorous career. The job generally involves extensive international travel, attendance at star-studded fashion shows and the power to use one's personal influence over the seasonal range selection. While the job does have its glamorous moments, by the end of the book the reader will realise that the job is tough and complex, requiring hard work and stamina. To work as a fashion buyer or merchandiser requires highly motivated and flexible individuals, able to work under pressure. Interpreting what the fashion consumer wants well ahead of the season is a vital part of the work. It is not simply about buying clothes that a buyer or merchandiser likes to wear themselves: professional buyers may well buy clothes for their organisation that they themselves would never consider wearing. The consumer is always king in fashion buying, not the buyer. Many young people believe that a career in fashion buying will enable them to buy the clothes that they themselves would like to wear. Generally, this is not the case.

International travel is accompanied by extensive preparations, busy meeting schedules with little or no time to relax; foreign travel must not be confused with an annual foreign holiday. Fashion shows are often fast, furious and uncomfortable, allowing the buyer only a fleeting glance to take note of the latest trends. After the show, there is the need to try and distil those trends relevant to mass market consumers. Not everything that is shown at *haute couture* fashion shows can be applied to future seasons in mainstream fashion markets. The buyer is under intense pressure to quickly and efficiently analyse the key trends. There is no scientific methodology or formulae to help; this is where experience, intuition and foresight come together in the form of 'fashion wisdom'.

The fashion buyer has increasingly to cope with a great deal of information as a result of the developing computer technologies being utilised in retailing. The 'information deluge' is in many respects forcing the buyer and merchandiser to become more systematic, and possibly less creative than in the past. In Chapters 1 and 2, the changing dynamics of the buying role and its relationship to merchandising is fully explained. Fashion buying and merchandising across all types and sizes of fashion retailer are increasingly requiring more developed IT skills and understanding. IT within fashion retailing, used innovatively, will be one of the most important competitive weapons of the future. The implications of the Internet for fashion retailing generally are discussed at length in the final chapter of the book (Chapter 10). The fast pace of technological change is creating significant threats and opportunities for fashion businesses. Whether retailing in shops – 'bricks and mortar retailing' (as it is now known) – will decline as result of Internet retailing is currently the big question facing conventional fashion retailers. Whatever the answer, the fashion buyer and merchandiser will still be required to provide the right goods for whichever market dominates. It seems unlikely that the fashion buyer will ever be replaced by technology, although computing innovation may challenge the future role and scope of merchandising.

Buyers past and present

Fashion retailing was historically a small-scale enterprise, with the owner or manager often making stock buying decisions at the same time as running the shop. In the very early days, fashion was always made to measure, with mass-produced garments becoming widely available only as a result of the Industrial Revolution. Small-scale fashion retailing worked successfully for many years, until dynamic economic development heralded mass production and multiple outlet retailing.

As fashion retailers have got larger, so has the quantity of each garment being purchased. With higher quantities have come higher values of stock investment: getting the style wrong becomes more and more financially dangerous. As fashion retailers became larger and carried wider and more diverse ranges of products, the need for a series of specialist garment buyers rather than one individual became inevitable. Soon large fashion retailers needed a team of specialist buyers, thus giving them time to develop their specialist skills and understanding of a specific garment type. Today, it is often the case that a fashion buyer may remain buying a limited range of garment types throughout her career, simply as result of having gained expertise early on in one or two garment types. Knitwear buyers are often very specialised as result of their need to fully understand yarns and knitting processes. Women's underwear and swimwear buyers also need specialist fabric and garment construction knowledge, but additionally need a good understanding of human anatomy to ensure the best garment fit for the customer. A number of products such as bras and shoes need careful design and sizing to ensure their fit is perfect.

The modern buyer needs to adapt to a strategy of life-long learning if they are to keep abreast of fashion and technological development. The role of the buyer has changed dramatically over time, and will continue to do so. The recent growth in undergraduate, postgraduate and in-service fashion courses shows clear evidence of a need for growing professionalism in fashion buying and mechandising.

The development of the fashion buyer

The fashion buyer's role has very greatly been affected by the structural changes that have occurred, and that are still occurring, in the market place. As result of changing consumer affluence, habits and preferences, we can see in the Table I.1 how fashion retailing and the products that it has had to sell has changed over time. The impact upon the work of the fashion buyer is also examined. Throughout the history of fashion retailing, fashion shops have evolved and

Table I.1 Changing shops, products and their impact on fashion buying

Decade	Type of outlet	Type of product	Influences and impact on buyer
1910s	Individual	Exclusive made to measure/self-made	Individual knowledge of customer Customers mainly wealthy
1920s	Department stores develop	Wider ranges – ready-made + made to measure	Wider range of customers and products
1930s	Multiple chains start	Affordable clothes for all + some aspirational brands	Cheaper ready-made clothes selling in volume
1940s	Mixture of outlets	Wartime utility	Limited supply, quality and quantity – rationing
1950s	Most fashion shops in decline	General shortage	Basic – rationing continues
Mid-1950s	Halt in decline	Fashion awakes	French + American design influences
1960s	Boutiques evolve	Teen 'baby boomers' need young fashion	Continued American influence + influence of pop culture on fashion
1970s	Young fashion multiples	Mass disposable youth fashion Start of brand awareness	Increasing competition + keener prices
1980s	Branded chains evolve	Youth market seeks aspirational brands + power dressing	Mass-multiples face brand growth
1990s	Brands + 'new-value' retailers grow	Market polarises into brands and value retailers + tech fabrics	Middle-market fashion retailers face hyper competition
2000–	Brands + value continue Bland retailers in difficulty Internet + catalogue retailers grow	Continued polarisation of market Fashion demand from older customers Fundamental garment + fabric developments – hi-tech evolves	Customers seek the unique or value Older customers catered for Customers aware of global prices Garments with 'screen' appeal essential

developed to keep up with changing consumer tastes, the economy and fads within different types of retailing. The major developments that have occurred during the last hundred years of the previous millennium are shown in Table I.1.

As is shown in the Table I.1, fashion retailing has metamorphosed over the last century. At each stage there have been several key influences from both home and abroad that have fundamentally forced retailers to buy new products, in new markets, using new approaches. There has been a rapid decline of home-produced merchandise in most European countries, and that has also had a major bearing on where fashion buyers source products. The reader can only speculate as to how the market will develop in the next millennium. Needless to say, it is probable that there will be many casualties amongst those 'bland' or middle-ground retailers who fail to face up to increasing international competition and smarter customers. More importantly a major issue for them will be whether they will be able to sustain the costs of renting expensive shops and stores in main shopping areas. Most fashion pundits believe that fashion will always need to be seen, felt and tried on by the consumer, although there is a strong argument that more basic, easy fitting or utilitarian garments can and are already bought remotely through mail order purchasing. The doubters about Internet fashion purchasing should look hard at the substantial market share currently held by mail order companies.

Fashion buying and merchandise management – a warning!

A senior manager of a fashion buying office of one of Britain's leading fashion retailers, once commented to one of the (then young) authors of this book: 'The day you think you have a full and complete understanding of the fashion industry, book yourself into the local lunatic asylum. Nobody can ever fully understand everything that there is to know about the entire business and never will!' The authors, while writing this book, have reflected at length over this comment, and have come to the conclusion that there is a great deal of truth in it. Fashion is continually moving and changing; it is sometimes like a mirage in the desert – there one minute and gone the next. Nothing is guaranteed in fashion except its continuity: from the start till the end of time there will always be fashion.

The authors having spent many years lecturing fashion students, and have been disappointed with the paucity of literature available on the subject of fashion buying and merchandising. We have endeavoured to embody both our own commercial experience, the best practice currently available from our many and generous advisers and mentors, together with our own academic marketing knowledge. Rather than writing a book simply putting theory into practice, we have approached it from a standpoint of blending practice into theory. Hopefully, it will give our readers a clear understanding of the work of the fashion buyer and fashion merchandiser, within the context of European retailing; the book will need updating in the future to reflect the undoubted changes of the fashion industry.

Notes

1. Perna, R. (1987) *Fashion Forecasting*, Fairchild Publications.
2. De la Haye, A. and Wilson, W. (1999) *Defining Dress: Dress as Object Meaning and Identity*, Manchester University Press.

▣ ꙍ ▮ The roles of the fashion buyer and garment technologist

Buying and merchandising

Chapters 1 and 2 are concerned with the roles of buyers, garment technologists and merchandisers, and the industry context in which they operate. For the purposes of this book we are concerned with the issues relating specifically to buyers, merchandisers and garment technologists of fashion clothing and accessories: it is important for the reader to understand that fashion retailing has many unique aspects that are quite different from general retailing.

The jobs of a buyer and a merchandiser, although complementary, are fundamentally different and have different entry requirements and career pathways. Traditionally buyers have been more visually creative, often skilled in both garment construction and design, whereas merchandisers have tended to be more numerate and analytical. Now though IT, analytical and negotiation skills are considered equally important for both. The job of technologists varies among retail businesses but has become more significant and standardised in the last five years. This chapter looks in detail at the roles of buyer and technologist, with Chapter 2 focusing on merchandising.

Terminology

Not only are the jobs of buyers and merchandisers different but the job of a buyer varies from company to company according to the type of business it is. For example, there are differences in the role of a buyer for a manufacturer, wholesaler and a retailer and within the retail industry there are marked differences between the scope of activities and range of responsibilities at different levels of the market.

A women's wear buyer at Selfridges may well be responsible for stocking the store with well known brands of Designer clothing, whereas a buyer for a multiple retail brand, such as Top Shop, will be responsible for overseeing the complete product development process before arranging delivery of the finished products. Similarly the owner of a boutique or independent clothes retailer will also be involved in 'buying' stock, often from wholesalers, to sell in their shop. This chapter looks at the roles from a *multiple retailer* perspective but the issues raised have a wider application to fashion retailing.

In addition to buying and merchandising the two other functions that play a vital role in the development of a seasonal range include garment technology and design, both of which are explained in this book. However, before we look in more detail at the buying and merchandising roles, it will be helpful to provide some simple definitions and briefly identify the boundaries of responsibilities that exist between these very interdependent functions.

Table 1.1 Buying, merchandising and related function: Brief definitions

Buyer	Decides on the styles to be bought and negotiates production with suppliers
Merchandiser	Works with buyers planning stock mix according to trend analysis, manages budget and controls stock deliveries and allocation to stores
Designer	Provides creative direction and produces product designs for buyers to select from
Garment technologist	Provides technical (fabric and construction) advice and controls sample development

For convenience this book will refer to the buyer as female and merchandiser as male although fashion retail buying offices are traditionally female-dominated.

Structures

A typical fashion retail buying office will locate all these functions close to one another as the day-to-day activities, concerned with managing the current season, combined with developing the next and planning for the one after that, require inputs from all four functions (Table 1.1). Indeed, one of the difficulties of being a buyer is the need to be planning for or dealing with issues relating to three or four different fashion seasons simultaneously.

Unsurprisingly, with so much going on and the complexity surrounding the processes in range development, buying and merchandising teams need to be located together enabling them to communicate efficiently and make informed decisions about the ranges for which they are jointly responsible.

The buying office structure model

Modern buying offices are 'open-plan', with buying and merchandising teams working together on different product areas. Design and garment technology are smaller teams, working across a number of product areas, and are located nearby. A model of the layout of a typical buying office indicating where the buying, merchandising, garment technology and design functions are commonly positioned relative to each other is shown in Figure 1.1.

The buying team

The structure of buying and merchandising teams will vary according to the size and kind of business involved. Figures 1.2 and 1.3 are structures based on

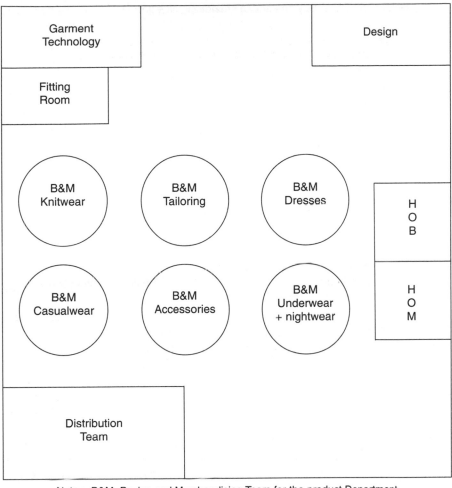

Notes: B&M: Buying and Merchandising Team for the product Department.
HOB: Head of Buying
HOM: Head of Merchandising

Figure 1.1   A typical open plan buying office in fashion retailing

a multiple fashion retailer or chain store business that has its buying and merchandising operations centralised. Most of these centralised operations are located in London, with a few exceptions like Next (Leicester), New Look (Weymouth) and Littlewoods (Liverpool). The two models show both the traditional and more modern structures generally adopted by such companies.

The traditional structure (see Figure 1.2)

In this kind of structure there is a buying team and a merchandising team for a particular product area, with a buying and merchandising controller overseeing

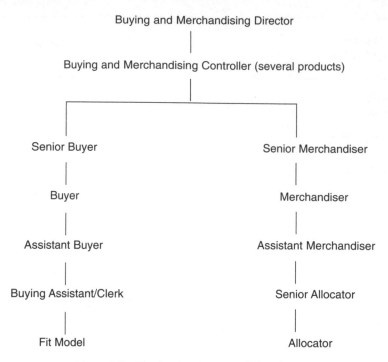

Figure 1.2   The buying team: traditional structure

teams across a number of different areas. Buying teams can be categorised in different ways by product area (e.g. separates, underwear, accessories, etc.), or by company division (men's wear, women's wear), or even sometimes by fabric (jersey wear, knitwear, etc.). Ultimately the size and history of the fashion retailer business will influence how teams are organised.

However, buying office structures in many companies have adapted (see Figure 1.3) to accommodate the need for technical specialists in garment construction, which is in itself a reflection of consumers' increased quality expectations. The change has the added advantage of relieving buyers of some of responsibility for many repetitive and technical tasks like fitting sessions.

Sample fittings or 'fit sessions' are part of the process of range development, and are covered in more detail in Chapter 7. They are normally run by a garment technologist, although a member of the buying team is also required to attend. In the old structure a house 'fit model' would often have been under the line management of the buyer. It is more common now for the fit model to be under the management of the technologist. Some fashion retailers do not employ in-house fit models, preferring to source them from specialist agencies, or to use a buying assistant/clerk who is of the right size.

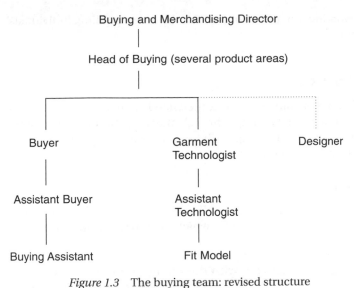

Figure 1.3 The buying team: revised structure

The role and responsibilities of a buyer

This section aims to explain the responsibilities of a buyer and examine the activities of those working in a centralised buying environment. As the functions are different they will be discussed separately.

Buying

The principal objective of the buying function is to ensure that the products bought for sale by the retailer are appropriate for the target market and can sell in sufficient quantities to achieve the profit margin expected by the business. This sounds like a simple task but is in fact very complex and difficult to achieve in a competitive market where consumers are fickle, choice is great and fashion trends fast-moving. Many retailers that are selling fast-moving, low-priced, up-to-the-minute fashion sell and replace their entire stock every six weeks.

The buyer

A buyer is a manager who has overall responsibility for the selection, sales and profitability of the product range within a particular category (garment type), e.g. skirts. This is the substantial part of her job, but a point which is often overlooked by people writing on this subject is that she is also the manager of the buying team. Consequently she will be involved in recruitment for the team, together with Human Resources, and have line management responsibility for those working on the team, which includes guiding individuals' career development.

Responsibilities

The overall responsibility is to select merchandise that maximises the sales and profitability of a product range, through meeting the target customers' exact product needs. This overall responsibility can be explained more easily through looking at the main issues in detail.

Main responsibilities

Success in each of these areas makes a critical contribution to the overall profitability of the product range for which the buyer is responsible.

1   To develop and buy a range of merchandise that achieves the profit margin and is consistent with the retailer's buying strategy

Each garment type will have to achieve an *overall level of profit*, which is sometimes referred to as a 'target margin' or 'net achieved margin after discount' (NAMAD). This is the profit achieved at the end of a season after all mark-downs, discounts and unsold stock (terminal stock) has been accounted for. The buyer's task therefore is to maximise full price sales of stock bought and minimise the quantity of unsold stock at the end of a season.

To do this she must work with the merchandiser in planning the stock mix and understand how the seasonal fashion trends generally adopted by other fashion businesses need to be interpreted for the target customer.

Preferred supplier lists are popular with big retail groups as supplier performance can be measured against specific criteria set by the retailer (e.g. on-time delivery). Monitoring supplier performance enables the company to reduce its overall number of suppliers, improving general efficiency, and provides the buyers with a list of effective suppliers who can contribute to maximising profits.

2   To source and develop products from an effective supplier base

Not only do buyers have to be aware of the effect that inefficient suppliers have on profits (see Chapter 7) but they have to get the right balance between *cost* and *quality* on the products they buy. The buyer always has to keep in mind the profit that each product is intended to contribute to the season. The company will not thank her for providing the customer with a wonderful product at a competitive selling price but which achieves only a very small profit margin because it cost so much to make.

Another important consideration in the selection of suppliers is the bad publicity that can arise for a retailer from using unethical manufacturers. The media is sensitive to this issue and can generate very bad PR for a fashion retailer if it is discovered using suppliers that exploit their workforce. Ethical issues surrounding the use of suppliers include poor working conditions, low wage rates and the use of child labour. Cynics might say that companies are only ever concerned about the issues if and when the media run stories or documentaries about the subject.

The sourcing of suppliers is one of the many reasons why a buyer will be required to travel a great deal both within the UK and overseas. It is important for the buyer to visit a new supplier to evaluate whether or not they are capable of meeting the stringent requirements of the product order and meet the preferred supplier criteria.

3   To be responsible for the negotiation of product prices including delivery and payment terms

When the buyer has decided on the final product design, after inputs from merchandising, design and garment technology, she will begin the process of meeting suppliers and discussing *cost prices*. This is a complex area which is examined later in the chapter and requires the buyer to be skilled in negotiation. Successful negotiation is partly dependent upon the use of various negotiation 'levers' to trade with the other person. In negotiating a product cost price there are many levers over and above specific product construction issues, including who pays for delivery and in what form and when the payment is to be made.

4   To research and evaluate all relevant product and market trends

The buyer is the individual who has to evaluate all the information surrounding the development of a range. The information is diverse but falls into two main categories relating to current and past sales and future fashion trends, issues which are discussed in Chapters 3, 4 and 6, and underline the buyer's need for close understanding of the work undertaken in merchandising and design. In addition to the sources of specialist design and merchandising data, buyers also evaluate competitor ranges through regular visits to their stores.

5   To communicate effectively with suppliers, product teams and senior management within the company

Effective communication with a variety of different people and businesses is a key skill for a buyer and will require her to master different techniques for different situations. For example, effective communication with suppliers is mainly concerned with being clear, realistic and accurate about the specific terms of the order to be placed. However, effective range presentations or product reviews in which a new season's designs are shown within the business will involve other more creative skills which have to be combined with confident presentation techniques. *Product reviews* are a crucial part of the buyer's job and are discussed in Chapter 8.

6   To work within the constraints of merchandise planning

Buyers have to operate within *very controlled parameters* that include financial budgets, available selling space, and specific commercial considerations such as historical sales performance and key fashion trends like colour. As such, the degree of creativity and autonomy in fashion buying role is more limited than many people think.

7 To effectively manage and develop the buying team

The overall success of a particular garment type or department is very dependent upon the combined team's effort. The sheer volume and complexity of the work requires the team to be flexible, self-motivated and have a good understanding of what each other is doing so that information can be communicated effectively and decisions made quickly and accurately.

A 'day in the life' of a fashion retail buyer

Figure 1.4 is designed to provide the reader with an insight to the multi-task nature, complexity and long hours associated with the job of a buyer in a fashion multiple retailer.

Unlike many jobs, there is very little in the way of a routine for a buyer, although Mondays are fairly predictable as they are traditionally 'figures day' in a buying office. This is the day when Saturday's sales for the product area are calculated, providing a complete picture of the sales for the previous week. Sales performance will be measured against a number of targets (e.g. last year's equivalent) and the necessary action planned in response.

The 'snapshot' of a day in Figure 1.4 does not reflect any of the travelling commitments that buyers have and which are over and above these kind of day-to-day activities. Travelling is often perceived to be glamorous or a perk of the job but in reality it is a time-consuming activity resulting in office work building up while the buyer is away. This in turn leads to greater pressure and

---

Current season is Autumn/Winter (a typical Monday)

8.00 a.m. (Arrive in office)
- Review figures with merchandiser
- Refer to on-line management information system (MIS), showing sales performance of current season
- Review schedule for day (mostly meetings)
- Meet with assistant buyer to delegate tasks
- Meeting with senior management over response to last week's sales
- Meet with designer and buying controller to discuss colours three seasons ahead
- Continue meeting with buying controller to discuss overseas trips
- Back to desk chase up phone calls to suppliers/make fabric selections
- **Lunch break** – buy a sandwich/do comparative shopping on the way (maybe 20 minutes)
- Back at the office for a meeting with a supplier, negotiating cost prices
- Work on products two seasons ahead – decisions on trimmings, re-costing products
- Continue meeting with merchandiser, planning stock deliveries two seasons ahead
- Phone call from marketing who need current season samples for publicity, delegate to buying assistant

7.00–7.30 p.m. leave

Figure 1.4 A 'day in the life' of a buyer in a fashion multiple retailer

longer hours on her return. Furthermore, meeting schedules on overseas trips are intensely packed with between four and six appointments in a day, to maximise use of time, and the six–eight weeks of the year taken up with trips can wreak havoc on her social life.

Buying competencies

Some of the larger retail groups have developed specific job-related competencies for buyers and merchandisers, in order to help define their responsibilities more clearly, and so structure the training needs and career development pathways associated with each of the functions. The following is based on the different competencies identified for buyers within a high street fashion retail brand. Although it is specific to one particular business, the issues identified are common to many other large fashion retailers where buying and merchandising operations are centralised.

1 Personal characteristics

These relate to the personal qualities considered to be important to becoming an effective buyer:

- Commercial with creative flair
- Multi-tasking flexibility
- Retentive memory
- Mental agility
- Energetic
- Positive approach to problems/criticism
- Self-motivated
- Consistent temperament
- People/action oriented
- Tough but fair
- Creative.

2 Awareness

This can be divided into specific fashion awareness and general commercial awareness:

a Fashion awareness
- Understands customers' changing fashion requirements
- Anticipates future looks
- Interprets relevant future looks in new ranges
- Can develop coordination opportunities in new ranges
- Can improve perceived garment quality
- Anticipates and plans for gaps in ranges.

b Commercial awareness
- Can accurately judge cost and selling prices on seeing garments
- Can predict sales potential of a product
- Understands the different contributions to sales targets of mark-down and repeats

- Actively seeks and develops new suppliers
- Coordinates buying with other garment types where appropriate
- Understands target customers' buying behaviour
- Understands and evaluates data in broad market context.

3   Planning

- Tracks and knows status of all orders for a season through a critical path
- Understands the need to prioritise the critical path according to stock needs
- Has contingency plans in place
- Manages time of self and team through effectively sharing and prioritising work
- Prepares thoroughly for meetings, negotiations and presentations.

4   Action

- Accepts responsibility for own and team's decisions and actions
- Picks up bargain buying potential for out-of-season products
- Ensures commercial balance of new fashion and core best selling lines
- Reacts to poor sales while minimising price reductions
- Stays calm and provides direction for others in crisis.

It is important to realise that these are generic competencies and not just specific to fashion retail buyers. As such there are more specific qualities and skills needed to be an effective fashion buyer. A fashion buyer will typically be expected to 'live and breath' their product, regularly monitoring competitors and thinking about new ideas outside the duration of a normal working day. Those working in the younger fashion market will also be expected to keep abreast of fast-emerging trends in television, computer games, cinema, music culture, sports, nightclubs and trendy shopping locations.

Negotiation skills

One of the most important skills a buyer must master is the ability to *negotiate*. As most high street fashion selling prices are very competitive, the greatest scope for improving profit in a product is the reduction of cost price. There are many factors that influence the final cost price of a product including fabric, garment construction, order volume, lead-time, and delivery terms. These particular issues are discussed in more detail throughout the book.

Negotiation is a process of communication and exchange through which the interested parties make a series of demands and compromises: it involves the trading of benefits between parties. The basic principle is to trade what is of low value to you but of greater value to the other party, thereby reducing the 'cost' of success to you. However the aim of a negotiation should be to ensure that both parties are happy with the final outcome or agreement, otherwise one or the other will not continue to participate.

The old scenario of the retailer always winning and supplier always losing results in both parties effectively losing. Traditionally, the dominant fashion retail groups have seen the availability of large numbers of suppliers as a means of trading one off against another to achieve a cheaper cost price. Consequently many of the suppliers who lost out ceased to do business with those retailers again. Short-term cost–price gains resulted in short-term relationships with many suppliers, with the end result being a large, unwieldy and diverse supplier base not operating as efficiently as it should.

By the same token an inexperienced buyer can be vulnerable to a supplier wanting to secure an unreasonable cost price, resulting in the fashion retailer de-listing them in the future for being uncompetitive. As such it is no better for the supplier to be in a situation where they are winning and the retailer is losing. The common wisdom about negotiation is that both sides should aim to work together to achieve a mutually acceptable result, which is usually referred to as a win–win situation.

The process of negotiation

A successful negotiation outcome does not generally occur through luck, but by following a clear process. The process reflects the different levels of knowledge of the subject of negotiation, various parties and the way they communicate at various stages in the negotiation. The following is an outline of steps essential to effective negotiation.

1 Researching the needs of both parties.

The greater the knowledge a buyer has of their own and the supplier's requirements, the better able they are to construct an acceptable solution. The buyer must be clear about both the department mark-up to be placed on the product cost price and the intended retail selling price so that she can judge the viability of the supplier's products. She should also have sufficient product construction knowledge to understand how changes can be made to achieve better value in the product.

Frequently the supplier will make suggestions to try to bring the cost price closer to the buyer's target. However an experienced buyer can speed up the process by making suggestions which will be acceptable to her. Lead-time is another lever for negotiation with differing operational issues for both parties. If the buyer starts the sourcing process early enough she may have enough time in hand to use extended lead-time as a bargaining tool.

The process of researching needs does not stop once the negotiation is underway as the body language and facial expressions of both parties will signal their reactions to the ongoing discussion. Successful buyers will listen to and watch suppliers carefully, making judgements about how to trade benefits with them. In addition to listening and observation skills, buyers need to be able to use questions effectively. Open questions require a respondent to elaborate, which may provide the buyer with valuable knowledge on how to proceed when meeting a supplier. Closed questions can be used to generate specific responses.

2 Preparation

Effective preparation is also vital to successful communication. The particular preparation required will vary according to the nature of meeting, but some factors are always important. Meetings should begin on time and follow a clear agenda with a realistic amount of time to accommodate the work. Where there is an existing relationship with a supplier, a file containing the relevant notes and documentation relating to the order(s) should be read prior to the meeting and taken in for reference. Supplier meetings are usually held in uncluttered or empty rooms or offices to avoid any distraction from the business of the meeting. It is also usual for there to be two people from buying in the meeting so that the buyer can have an objective view point available while personally involved in the negotiation.

It is essential that the buyer also has identified the maximum and minimum positions that she will accept for a range of factors including:

- Product price
- Order size
- Lead-time.

3 Offer

Having identified where the respective positions lie between them, the buyer and supplier can make specific proposals to set the boundaries of the negotiation. It is unlikely that many of the offers initially made will end up being accepted, so both parties allow for some manoeuvre. This is the opportunity for the buyer to begin trading what is of relatively low value for her but of more value to the supplier.

4 Discussion

The likely framework of a final settlement will emerge in the discussion as each side probes the other and makes suggestions. Answers to suggestions can be revealing, with choice of words and tone signalling interest or reluctance and should be noted as potential bargaining material. There will be areas on which one side can move more than the other and vice versa. It is important for the buyer to make a note of which ones provide the greatest and least opportunities for flexibility, for the trade off later on in the negotiation.

5 Counter and revised offers

This is the real bargaining stage where elements of the order, such as numbers of units, product detail, lead-times and so on, are being decided in the context of an overall cost price. The buyer should make firm proposals and be cautious of offering concessions unless she is getting one in return. The final element that will pull all of the other variables together will be the cost price, which is agreed at the end. Although the bargaining may be tough, the spirit of the communication should remain friendly and not adversarial. Parties are more likely to cooperate if they perceive they are being treated fairly and reasonably.

6 Summarise

It is vital to summarise at key stages throughout the negotiation when significant points are agreed, to avoid losing early gains and to ensure that both parties understand each other. With so many potential variables included in the negotiation, small but significant points can be easily forgotten unless there is a record of agreement throughout. Records will also provide both sides with an explanation of how the deal was constructed should a particular variable become contentious at a later date.

7   Agree and commit

Once the parties have agreed an order, they have to communicate the details to other functions. The supplier may need to book production space, order fabric/trimmings and source labels/tickets. The buyer will need to inform the merchandiser of the retail selling value of the order so that a track can be kept on spending.

Tip

The fashion buyer must be able to:

1 **Manage:**
   - The development of the range
   - Suppliers
   - Their team
   - Themselves

2 **Turn fast-changing fashion trends into commercial products**

The assistant buyer

The role of an assistant buyer varies in both responsibility and scope of activities according to the size of fashion retail business. In a large multiple retailer the role is very structured with a hierarchy of levels (commonly levels 1–3, with level 3 being the highest) through which to progress to become a buyer. Generally in smaller fashion businesses the role is less well defined and structured, resulting in an assistant buyer becoming involved in overlapping functions like merchandising, design and garment technology.

   In a multiple retailer the levels of assistant buyer reflect the training that is required to progress to a buyer and relates to development associated with the buyer competencies previously discussed. This progression is achieved through a combination of 'on-the-job experience' and specific in-house company training programmes which are primarily concerned with management training and skill development in textiles, and IT (usually focused on spreadsheets).

   The experience that the assistant buyer develops on the department is very practical, as they are expected to deputise for the buyer in her absence. This could range from making simple decisions over the telephone to taking full responsibility for a small product area within the garment type.

The buying assistant

This is the very first step on the ladder to becoming a buyer, sometimes called buyer's clerk, and is a stage that everyone new to buying must go through, irrespective of education and academic qualifications. The length of time spent at this level depends on aptitude, motivation and to some extent luck, should an opportunity for promotion arrive at the right time.

Some graduates can accelerate the process through experience gained in a buying office placement with a fashion retailer arranged through their college or university. However this will only enable them to learn and progress more quickly once they have graduated and secured a buying assistant position with a company. Principal tasks include organising and controlling the distribution of samples, both prototype (fit samples) and production (photo samples for marketing promotion), filing fabric and colour swatches and administrative tasks concerned with stock orders and deliveries.

Key qualities that fashion retailers are looking for to recruit at this level are:

- Being organised
- Motivation and initiative
- Ambition
- Commercial awareness
- Fashion awareness
- IT skills
- Numerical ability.

Many of the large retail groups will also require the applicant to be a graduate, although this not always the case, especially with smaller companies.

Garment technology

Definition

'Garment technology' refers to that retail function that supports buying on all stages of the development of products. In most large fashion retailing organisations the buyer and garment technologist work very closely, with the technologist often involved right from the earliest conceptual stages.

The job has many responsibilities but is mainly focused on providing advice on fabric performance and overseeing the various product sampling stages up to delivery into distribution centres. A garment technologist is also referred to as a 'technical services manager' in some fashion retailers.

The work of a garment technologist is primarily concerned with *monitoring and ensuring quality in the final product*. The responsibility for quality may involve a variety of tasks ranging from visiting new suppliers, to ensure that they can meet the company's product standards, to overseeing all stages of sampling. The complex process of checking product samples and testing fabric is explained in Chapter 7. However, the garment technologist is responsible for implementing the retailer's quality control procedures, ensuring that there are no problems with the final production of products. The work of merchandisers is potentially affected by the efficiency of the technologists as stock delivery times can be delayed through late sample approvals.

Main responsibilities

1 Work with Buying and Design to comment on fabric suitability and construction of product designs

In the early stages of transition from 2D images to product specification sheets a garment technologist will work with a buyer and designer to establish what the most appropriate choice of fabrics is to meet the performance requirements of a particular product design. This advice may also extend to identifying make up problems, sourcing issues and size grading, according to the experience of the buyer and designer.

2 Visit new suppliers to ensure that they are able to meet company's product standards

The garment technologist will visit product manufacturers to assess their capability to meet the quality requirements of the brand. As comprehensive supplier manuals are given to all manufacturers, the visits are used to evaluate the suppliers' ability to comply and to provide further explanation where appropriate.
   Things checked:

- Work in progress
- Third-party processing
- Production critical path.

3 Oversee all fabric testing and wearer trial

All products need to have a *fabric test report* to accompany the sealed sample. More details of the kinds of tests are given in Chapter 7, but they can range from colourfastness to pilling. In addition to independent fabric test reports, samples are frequently given a wearer trial to test for common fabric and construction weaknesses. Members of the product teams in the buying office generally carry out these trials.

4 Oversee all fits of first samples

The main stages in the development of a garment through to its delivery into a distribution centre (DC) are discussed in Chapter 7. However, a key feature in the development process is the 'fitting' of initial samples on the regular 'fit model' who represents the ideal/average size 12

5 Oversee sealing of pre-production and production samples

After the initial fit sampling process is complete the buying team keeps a physical record of these pre-production sample garments ('sealed samples') which have been agreed with the supplier following all amendments. Production samples are those garments that are from the production batch and are accurate in all respects but precede the delivery of the rest of the line into the distribution centre (DC). They are checked for everything including swing/barcode tickets and hangers. Although their role appears very technical, garment technologists are still expected to develop their commercial acumen and be just as aware of the seasonal trends as buyers (Figure 1.5).

8.30 a.m. (Arrive in office)

- Check e-mails from DC referring to any production problems (liaise with buying team if so)
- Measure all samples from previous fittings, identifying and recording spec' changes, adding comments and sketching complex alterations
- Check any new deliveries of production samples specifically looking at:
  - Size fit
  - Fabric
  - Stitching
  - Care labels

(sign and pass on to buying team when complete)

- Organise new deliveries of first fit and sealing samples for the afternoon fit session
- **Lunch** – average 30 minutes
- Attend two-hour fit session with buying team member and fit model
- Review fit of all garments tried on by model, noting changes and comments
- Write up and fax all fit comments/sketched amendments to relevant suppliers
- Approve sealed samples after reviewing textile test reports, allowing merchandising to allocate stock
- Ensure all filing is completed by assistants

6.30 p.m. leave

Figure 1.5 A' day in the life' of a garment technologist

The need for integration between buying and technology

The need to improve quality has led most fashion retailers (even those targeting the lower end of the market) to introduce and strengthen their quality control and garment technology. This has similarly required all fashion buyers to become far more proficient in the recognition, control and acquisition of quality product. Many larger retail organisations will provide training for buyers with no technical background, and many smaller fashion retailers buy into external quality control agencies as an outsourced service. Today's buyer has to acquire a wide range of skills in order to deliver well designed, well manufactured quality garments to the consumer.

The technical requirement for many garments are extremely complex – i.e. the bra or the tailored suit. Both these garments have a multitude of components in them; the more components they have the more likely that something can or will go wrong. The tough wear on garments such as swimwear and outdoor performance wear makes it important that the fabric can stand up to extremes in use. Again the buyer will almost certainly turn to the garment technologist for help.

Historically, the concept of fashion quality control came at the end of the production line. By the time the garment reached the final stages of production, it was simply too late to save the delivery should anything have gone wrong during manufacture. A failed delivery usually means lost sales, especially in a fashion environment where customers want the latest fashion now.

The development from quality control

Retailers realised that it was better to stop problems happening earlier rather than later, and have invested and still are investing heavily in garment technology. Pioneers like Marks & Spencer were early advocates of this approach. As more and more garments are generally being purchased from abroad, it has also become more important for technologists to visit and assist these distant manufacturing sources, to ensure that they were able to deliver the quality levels originally demanded. Often manufacturing sources were in developing countries with little technical support or know-how available from the indigenous population. More and more foreign manufacturers are training their own technologists in an attempt to deliver the increasing quality demanded by the developed economies of the world.

As technological advances continue, in both garment and fabric manufacturing, the demands for expert knowledge will undoubtedly increase. Buyers and technologists alike will need continually to train and update their knowledge if they are to keep abreast of technical developments in fabrics and garments.

■ ʀ̌ **2** The role of merchandising

Definitions

Within fashion retailing there is often a misconception about the role of the merchandiser, partly because the term 'merchandising' is used in various ways by different industries and countries. For example, 'football merchandising' refers to the wide range of products sold by football clubs to its supporters. An American store manager when changing the department layout will often refer to having 're-merchandised' the floor. Additionally the term 'merchandising' is further confused, in fashion retailing, with 'visual merchandising', which is the function specifically concerned with the aesthetics of window and store presentation.

The term 'merchandising' in fashion retailing refers to the total process of *stock planning, management and control*. The job requires highly developed numeric skills and an innate ability to spot trends, relationships and co-relationships within regular sales and stock figures. The sales information is captured from price ticket bar codes, detailing style, colour, size, season and price, and read by the Electronic Point Of Sale (EPOS) terminals before being fed into centralised computer systems.

A background to merchandising

The overall responsibility is similar to that of the buyer in that the merchandiser is responsible for maximising the profitability of the department, working within the normally accepted conventions of the business. Quite clearly each buying team must plan and buy ranges that fit in with those of other buying teams, in terms of styling, age targeting, colour palette, pricing and quality level. Without such synergy, any large fashion retailer would soon create disparate and varied ranges, in turn leading to total customer confusion. The merchandiser is generally helped in the process by regular interaction, intervention, advice and control from a more senior buying and merchandising executive. The level of such intervention again depends upon the size, internal structure and culture of the individual fashion retail organisation. In reality, it varies dramatically between organisations, and often varies over time as result of trading conditions and changing management fashions.

The amount of money that a buyer can spend is referred to as the 'open to buy' and is explained in Chapter 6. In essence it is simply a measure of how much more money a buyer can spend at retail value at any period. The merchandiser is very much the guardian of 'open to buy'. Buyers always have many more styles to buy than they have money to spend on them. It is here that the merchandiser helps the buyer to evaluate which course of action will be best for the business to take. Buyers generally claim that there is never enough 'open to buy' for them. In fact, they are simply saying that they have already spent their buying allowance on garments that they like less than the one they now are proposing!

Buying is an imperfect science, merchandising is there to help the difficult decision-making processes. With modern computers and information systems, today's merchandiser has an ever-increasing ability to analyse sales and stock information in more and more innovative and detailed ways. Chapters 6 and 8 fully detail the complexity of information now available to the merchandiser. As computer speeds, capacities and capabilities continue to increase at an exponential rate, the merchandiser's capabilities and their role will undoubtedly expand accordingly.

The changing structures of merchandising

The issues raised in this chapter refer to generic merchandising responsibilities common to all fashion retailers. However, the specific allocation of these general responsibilities may vary by company, according to the merchandising structure they adopt. There is the traditional merchandising role, integrated with buying on a product area, which has the merchandising team responsible for both range planning and stock allocation. This role is shown in Figure 1.2 (p. 12).

However many fashion retailers have revised the responsibilities of merchandising to remove the distribution role, leaving merchandising to focus on analysis and planning. The responsibility for stock distribution is then given to a separately managed stock distribution team. Figure 2.1 illustrates the relationship between the new merchandising role and the separated distribution role.

The new merchandising structure

Many larger fashion retailers with separate and dedicated distribution teams believe that the specialist and highly detailed work of allocating garments effectively at a very low level of detail – i.e. by individual size and colour to an individual shop – is best done as a separate operation. The benefits of centralising this process range from simple cost savings to, more importantly, maintaining a more rigorous and uniform control of the entire process. Businesses that apply erratic parameters to stock management can easily lose control of their stock at both an overall and line level of detail. ('Line' in this context refers to individual product styles.)

The distribution team is clearly focused exclusively on maximising sales and profit, through effective stock allocation to stores, and through utilising more detailed and accurate information about branch needs from product planners. In addition, they can respond more quickly to the changing stock needs of branches, replenishing or substituting lines where appropriate and can feed

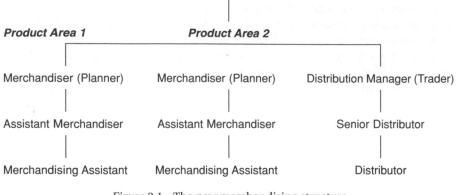

Figure 2.1 The new merchandising structure

back to buyers and merchandisers any need for repeat buying. However, the distribution team always works closely with the merchandiser to ensure that they are working within the parameters of the department buying plan, as well as within the context of the overall business plan. This greater emphasis by a dedicated team on the detailed movement of stock can enable the business to maximise profitability emerging from fast moving sales trends.

Limitations of the traditional merchandising structure

In Figure 1.2 (p. 12) the merchandiser is managing the detailed allocation of stock as well having overall responsibility for the analysis and planning of future ranges. The work load, particularly as a result of increasingly complex management information systems which deliver sophisticated sales and stock analysis, has simply become too great. This is especially the case for merchandisers working in the very-fast moving fashion product areas, such as accessories, underwear and cosmetics.

The benefit of the improved analysis available to merchandisers also enables them to focus on the forward planning of the department. Many fashion businesses are planning as far as two years (or four seasons) in advance, although changes will need to occur as trends become clearer nearer the season. Many would argue that it is more difficult to take such a strategic forward planning role at the same time as having to manage the highly complex stock flow to stores. Total control would appear to be better, although getting bogged down in trivial detail can result in them losing sight of the bigger picture. Figure 2.1 shows the new structure being adopted by the majority of high street fashion retailers. Whereas before, a buying and merchandising team would work on a single product area, the new structure now has the buyer working with the merchandiser in a focus planning role. It is important to understand that the distribution team works across a number of product areas.

The merchandiser's job combines support for the buyer (in terms of providing the buyer with information) with responsibility for effectively managing the flow of stock *into and around the business* after the suppliers have completed the range. The role is one that requires highly developed numeric skills, the holder usually having a natural grasp of figure work. While the role may not seem immediately as exciting as that of the buyer, it is important for the reader to appreciate at this early stage in the book that the job of merchandiser is not simply that of the glorified 'number cruncher'. The creative interpretation and use of numbers is a skill that once developed can fundamentally improve the trading performance of any fashion business.

The merchandiser's response to change

Buying fashion products by guessing quantities, and then sending them out to shops on a whimsical rather than an informed basis is usually a recipe for trading disaster. It is for this reason that so many one-man fashion businesses collapse after a short time. With fashions changing so fast, it is vital to have a detailed knowledge of what is selling, in what quantities and where at all times. The merchandiser ensures that the business 'de-risks' itself by making the best decision at a point in time. 'De-risking' refers to the process of optimising sales performance and minimising stock risk, by making informed decisions. The good fashion merchandiser always views stock as an investment that must always try to generate the best return for the business. Any garment hanging up in a shop has a cash value – would you leave your own money hanging around if it was not going to make a return for you?

Tip

Stock is money – it must always be in the right quantity, in the right place at the right time

Main areas of merchandising management activity

The process of merchandise management reflects the activity of both the merchandise planner and the distribution manager. The way in which merchandising works within the context of a fashion retail business can be split into two main areas of activity.

Planning stock to be delivered into the business

- Analysing historic sales patterns and trends
- Recommending forward fabric buying levels
- Recommending forward garment buying levels
- Monitoring and managing delivery of new stock into the distribution centre

- Ensuring that overall stock levels and buying are in line with the organisation sales plans.

Moving delivered stock around the business

- Initial allocations of new stock to shops – what quantity to each?
- Store replenishment – as garments start to sell – how much more stock and how quickly do we send to individual branches?
- Recommending the level of repeat buys of best selling lines.
- Transfers and recalls of faulty or non-seasonal stock.

This reflects the fact that the division of work load is based upon the need to plan the stock levels well ahead of the trading season and then to ensure that, once bought and delivered, the stock is sent to the right shops.

The merchandiser, like the buyer, is often trying to work on many seasons at once. They will be helping the buyer plan ahead for distant seasons' colour ratios; they will also be helping the buyer to decide on how many garments to buy within each garment category for the coming season. In addition they will be controlling the current seasons' stock flow into the business and advising on whether or not repeat buying will be necessary, whether late deliveries need to be cancelled or whether or not poor selling lines may need to have their price reduced, to ensure that they will sell out.

The role and responsibilities of the merchandiser

Responsibilities

Earlier in the chapter a brief description was given of how the merchandiser is responsible for the moving of stock both into and around the business. A more detailed list of a merchandiser's responsibilities is shown below. Again they may vary from organisation to organisation, but in general they are the key responsibilities found in most merchandising job descriptions. The role of merchandiser is a senior role, usually of the same status as that of buyer.

1 To estimate sales and plan stock levels to achieve the planned sales and margin for a specific garment type

A key function of the merchandiser is to develop the range plan for the product groups/lines which the designer and buyer have conceptualised. The merchandiser must ensure that the specific product range is balanced in terms of style and colour (core[1] and fashion), size and price point, and that there is sufficient stock available to meet the garment type or category sales targets. The process of range planning and development is complex, involving marketing and merchandising issues, which are discussed in detail in Chapters 4 and 6.

A major problem for the merchandiser is timing the deliveries around peaks and troughs in sales demand. As such, they have to strike a balance between stock deliveries to meet sales demand and stock on order to meet future demand. Fashion is probably the most seasonally affected of all retail businesses. Seasonal demand for products such as knitwear in winter and T-shirts in summer needs careful planning, analysis and control. The control of margin – or profit, as it is more commonly known – is also a key element of the merchandiser's role. 'Margin' is simply the difference between the buying and selling price of a garment. Margin and the accurate control of stock through the supply chain are discussed later in Chapter 6.

2 To provide regular analysis and progress reports referring to stock levels, sales performance and stock purchases to senior management

Much of the merchandiser's time is spent in front of a PC monitor, evaluating sales performances in relation to sales 'targets' and 'planned' stock levels. In order for senior management to assess the overall performance of the company, the merchandiser produces weekly reports indicating their product area's performance compared with the targets set. The words 'target' and 'plan' are generally interchangeable, although some businesses set the target higher than the plan for motivational purposes.

A key element of the merchandiser's work is to react effectively to the information as it arrives. Fast sellers will need to be re-purchased quickly; poor sellers may need to be 'marked down' to lower the price and increase consumer demand to clear them before the end of the season. It is rare that the merchandiser takes no action after having received the latest weekly stock and sales figures. As most information flows into the buying office on a Monday morning, the merchandiser is generally very preoccupied with analysis and action planning during the first two days of the week. The merchandiser will automatically be expected each week to analyse and summarise the information received, together with the proposed plan of action, for senior management's review and approval. This generally takes the form of a weekly meeting of the entire buying and merchandising team, together with senior management. During this meeting the best and worst selling lines for all product areas are identified and discussed. The level and formality of such meetings depends upon the prevailing business culture within the organisation.

3 To work with buyer on range planning to maximise commercial opportunities for products

Chapters 4 and 6 of this book examine the issues of range development. In simple terms the range is developed by the buyer and merchandiser working together providing different inputs. The merchandiser is most concerned with balancing the range commercially, ensuring that there is the correct mix of styles, colours, sizes and price points in the range both nationally and regionally.

The quality and accuracy of the range planning process provides the fundamental foundation for the future of the organisation, and its importance must not be underestimated. While perceived as a highly numeric exercise, it requires a great deal of creativity in the analysis and interpretation of historic and predicted future trends. Experienced merchandisers are able to add a great deal to the process through their highly developed intuition into what figures are either significant or insignificant. It is not simply about the straightforward application of a series of mathematical formulae.

4 To manage intake and commitment to accommodate the stock requirements of the business at any given time and the open to buy requirements of the garment type

Inevitably when we start to break down the specific responsibilities of a complex and analytical role like the merchandiser we will come across industry jargon. 'Intake' refers to new stock delivered into the business for distribution to stores, 'commitment' refers to stock on order and 'open to buy' as we know is the amount of money available to spend on new stock. To the uninitiated, it may appear fairly obvious that stock needs to be delivered into a business at the right time and in the right quantities. With the complexities involved in the production and manufacture of clothing, there is a vast array of events that can cause delays in delivery of product to the distribution centre. The merchandiser will keep a wary eye on daily and weekly deliveries, to ensure that the shops are adequately stocked with the right goods at the right time. They will undoubtedly need to take daily decisions to either try and bring forward or delay future deliveries of merchandise, to ensure that current stock provides a balanced offer to customers. In general, late deliveries will lose the business sales, which can very rarely be regained later. If the shop is out of stock, most customers immediately walk along to the nearest competitor who does have the stock they want. Chapters 6 and 8 look in detail at the way in which merchandisers aim to control stock flow into and through the business.

5 To manage stock distributions to stores optimising customer demand, available selling space and seasonal selling opportunities

A key contribution that a merchandiser can make to the profitability of the garment type is to make the best use of the stock available, by trying to meet as much of the demand in branches as possible and by maximising the profitability of the sales. For example, the merchandiser will need to take into account the different stock needs (e.g. styles, colours, sizes and price points) of different stores according to their local customer requirements and available selling space.

Too little stock in a branch can result in lost sales opportunities whereas too much stock can result in other branches, which could have sold more units of the stock, going short. Therefore sales will not be maximised across the business. It is an incredibly difficult balance to get right and a problem which can be made worse by timing, as the opportunity to sell products at full price lasts only a season. Shops vary dramatically in terms of size and the amount of stock they can hold, as well as local customer profile and special local tastes and demands. Every shop in the same chain is fundamentally different from the rest. Before development of sophisticated and powerful computer systems, it was hard for merchandisers to undertake as much detailed sales and stock analysis at individual shop level as they can now. The need to understand each shop's 'micro market' or local trading environment is likely to be the new area of fundamental development in merchandising and merchandise systems planning in the future.

6 To effectively manage and develop the merchandising/distribution team

The merchandiser has the same line management responsibilities as the buyer and the overall success of the garment type is dependent on the effectiveness of his management of the team. It is a misconception to believe that either of the roles is more important than the other. In common with many sectors of European business, buying and merchandising departments have an increasingly high requirement for skilled and developed management. Much training in the fashion industry is carried out 'on-the-job'. Good merchandisers have a key role in the training and development of merchandising and also often the distribution teams. With highly sophisticated merchandise planning software being developed to higher and higher levels of capability, the good merchandiser must also ensure that they keep abreast of what they need to be able to understand and use.

The merchandiser needs to be a good lateral thinker, who can work on several things at once, able to re-prioritise their work all the time. Life-long learning is the mantra for today's progressive merchandiser. The fluctuations of the fashion business ensure that the type and flow of work within merchandising is always changing. Figure 2.2 is a typical day in the life of a merchandiser, although the reader must realise that it can vary dramatically depending upon the time of year, the state of trade and 'events'! The very changing nature of fashion retailing makes a merchandiser's average day very difficult to explain.

Current season is Autumn/Winter

Arrive 7.45 a.m.
- Review sales figures and prepare/print mini report for SMT* weekly sales review
- Review work load and delegate tasks to assistant
- Work on specific sales analyses: best and worst style, colour, size (previous season)
- Update the delivery schedules (stock on way and future commitment)
- Chase up late deliveries (current season)
- Review stock distributions for the week/monitor those for the day
- *Lunch* – 15 minutes: sandwich at desk whilst chatting to colleagues
- Joint interview, with Human Resources, for new merchandising assistant
- Meeting with buyer to finalise deliveries for next spring/summer
- Continue meeting to plan product groups two seasons ahead
- Discuss current branch grading list for department with assistant merchandiser

7.00–7.30 p.m. leave

*SMT: Senior Management Team – normally Heads of Buying and Merchandising and Directors.

Figure 2.2   A 'day in the life' of a fashion retail merchandiser

Figure 2.2 represents a snapshot of a typical Monday for a merchandiser in a similar way to that outlined earlier for a buyer.

The demand for merchandisers

The importance of the merchandising role is often not appreciated by those outside of the fashion industry. It is often poorly understood by new entrants to the industry, who usually only possess a rather vague and confused understanding of the difference between fashion buying and merchandising roles. However, it is not unusual for large fashion retailers to pay good merchandisers anywhere between £30K and £60K, plus various perks and benefits. These salary levels give a good indication as to the importance that fashion organisations place upon this pivotal role. Currently there is a well reported shortage of good fashion merchandisers throughout Europe. Such is the problem that some large retailers have resorted to paying a £1000 bonus to staff who manage to recruit friends or acquaintances who are already merchandisers in competitive businesses.

Often new entrants wrongly believe that merchandising is simply a boring numeric support role to buying that has limited career opportunity. Analysis of many top fashion retail executives will reveal that a large proportion have progressed through a merchandising rather than buying route. The increasing reliance on and involvement with latest IT technologies makes merchandising a very interesting and versatile career route into the fashion business.

The key merchandising competencies

In the same way companies have identified competencies for buyers, the following represent the merchandiser competencies.

Personal characteristics

- Logical, rational
- Multi-tasking flexibility
- IT-oriented
- Numerate
- Analytical
- Detail conscious – but aware of bigger picture
- Assertive
- Retentive memory.

Awareness

Awareness is split into specific data awareness, reflecting the significance of computer-based information to the job, and commercial awareness, highlighting the need to place analysis in a commercial or business context.

1   Data awareness

The merchandiser:

- Balances interpretation of data with commercial common sense
- Looks for ways to improve range, collection and use of data
- Understands the procedures for calculating figures
- Can spot and interpret trends
- Can cope with multiple tasks and remain accurate
- Can produce accurate forecasts based on all available data.

2   Commercial awareness

The merchandiser:

- Remembers garments' sales histories and can judge optimum selling prices
- Builds up knowledge of the style, design and colour characteristics of best and worst sellers
- Makes commercial recommendations about supplier performance to buyer
- Understands how the garment type's budget and performance affects the company
- Monitors and influences the progress of products in the garment type's critical path
- Manages the balance of mark-downs and repeated (full-price stock) to maximise profits.

Planning

Effective planning of the garment type finances, sales, stock levels and critical path timing lies at the heart of successful merchandising. The merchandiser:

- Collects all relevant information to contribute to range planning
- Develops a commercially balanced range plan with the buyer
- Monitors sales performance against stock levels
- Monitors progress of orders against forward commitment and stock needs
- Develops and maintains efficient administrative systems for self and team
- Manages self and team through prioritising work load effectively.

Action

The merchandiser:

- Combines analysis of information with experience in the management of risk
- Adjusts forward stock commitment according to sales performance
- Times new deliveries and repeat orders to optimise sales opportunities and profits
- Negotiates appropriate discounts (from cost price) in response to late or incorrect deliveries.

As with the buying role, the merchandiser is expected to demonstrate other qualities and skills in addition to these competencies. The merchandiser will be required to have an immediate grasp of all numeric detail relating to their department. At any moment senior management may call upon their expertise to give a quick commercial appraisal by any level of detail. Usually this will be required 'yesterday'. The merchandising role is a challenging analytical role that at times can be tough but is always rewarding.

Assistant merchandiser/assistant planner/ senior allocator

In a similar way to the assistant buyer, each of these roles contains responsibility for particular planning or distribution activities. The jobs will also require the assistant merchandiser to deputise for a merchandiser when necessary and to have line management responsibility for junior members of the team. Normally the holder of this position will have already spent time on the distribution team as an allocator or distributor, where they will have gained a good grasp of the product, people and systems. This position is the key springboard towards becoming a fully-fledged merchandiser.

Merchandising assistant/allocator/distributor

As with the buying assistant role these three jobs are the first steps on the ladder towards a merchandising-related career. The different titles reflect the split in the merchandising function adopted by some of the larger multiple retailers. Essentially the merchandising assistant role is related to the planning function whereas the distributor works with the distribution manager in allocating the stock. It is here that a majority of graduates enter fashion retailing. The work can be repetitive and demanding, but is rewarding in terms of enabling the new entrant to fully understand the systems, individuals, culture and product of the fashion organisation in question. Diligence, accuracy and enthusiasm are the key ingredients for success at this level.

In many cases, though, the first position on a merchandising team is still that of an allocator whose primary function is to implement the allocations of stock to the stores. Depending on the size of the retailer, and thus the number of garment types and personnel on the buying teams, the allocator will report either to a senior allocator or an assistant merchandiser.

Key qualities that fashion retailers are looking for at these levels are someone who is:

- Organised
- Willing
- Accurate
- Diligent
- Self-motivated

- Able to show initiative
- Numerate
- Analytical
- IT-oriented
- Commercially aware
- A team player
- Ambitious.

The future for merchandising

The enormous developments in all aspects of IT are undoubtedly impacting upon the role of the merchandiser. From the humble origins of the buyer's clerk in Victorian department stores, we now see the modern merchandiser as needing to be a key strategic player in the buying and merchandising process and across the entire supply chain. The ability to be a multi-skilled and multi-tasked manager is clearly evident from the diversity of job content.

In American businesses, we are now hearing the term 'information jockey' being used to describe that person who has the greatest access to the most information. In many ways, the fashion merchandiser is now the information jockey of fashion retailing. It is the highly skilled and numerate merchandiser who now enables the better businesses to analyse and potentialise fashion trends that competitors may have missed. With so much information available, only the best merchandisers avoid information overload and are able to see 'the wood for the trees'. Too little detailed analysis may mean that trends and relationships are missed, while too much emphasis on number-crunching can often lead to 'analysis paralysis', where there is so much information available that confusion ensues. This frequently causes management to become confused, either taking the wrong decision or no decision at all. Good merchandisers never allow that to happen. In Chapter 10 we examine in more detail the likely future trends relating to fashion merchandising.

Applying for fashion buying and merchandising positions

It is common for fashion students to want to progress into a career in fashion buying or merchandising on completion of their studies. However, there are some important points which those interested in such a fashion retail career should consider. Although design and product knowledge is important for a buyer and useful for merchandisers, IT and numeracy are essential core skills. A part of the interview process for either role will normally include a numeracy test, with or without a calculator. Such a test is concerned with identifying the applicant's ability to solve simple arithmetic problems as quickly an accurately as possible. It is essential therefore, for applicants to be very familiar with:

- Ratios
- Percentages
- Spotting numerical trends
- Long multiplication and division
- Conversion of fractions into percentages.

A word of caution, while appearing relatively simple, many candidates stumble under pressure when relying on their GCSE mathematics from their earlier education. You are advised to practice these skills in advance of any interview. Also candidates may be asked to talk about their fashion interests and their views on specific garments. Whilst it is expected that you will have a knowledge of current trends, they will also appreciate some basic commercial understanding.

Note

1. Core represents safe best sellers whereas fashion reflects the riskier fashion styles in a season.

■ ☑ **3** Fashion design

Definitions

This chapter will look at the role of fashion design as part of the wider process of buying and merchandising within fashion retailers. Although successful sales of fashion products result from the combined efforts of the retailer and its suppliers, involving careful planning, commercial judgement and effective stock management, product design is at the heart of what a customer is buying. If a fashion garment doesn't grab the attention and generate desire in a consumer to want to wear it, clever sourcing and stock management will not be enough to sell it.

For the purpose of this book, the role of a fashion designer will focus on those functional activities commonly undertaken within fashion retailers. These include research and interpretation of fashion trends, and the production of both two- and three-dimensional product designs which provide the basis of what manufactures will make up for the retailer. There is some variation in the roles of designers across the fashion retail sector according to the structure of the retailers' buying and merchandising operations and the quality of the products sold. For example, a fashion retailer selling value-for-money interpretations of high-fashion products will use basic fabrics, whereas fashion businesses selling high-priced fashion products will have to spend time and money ensuring that the fabrics are right for the product.

The role of a fashion designer

The specific role of a designer may vary among fashion retail businesses according to the degree of significance afforded the function. For example, a luxury fashion brand like Hermès will place design at the heart of its business, allowing the designer considerable freedom as the brand depends on originality and creativity for its unique differentiation. Similarly, some retail businesses will have their development of product ranges dominated by a design director while in others the responsibility for product ranges rests with the buying and merchandising director using a team of designers and a trend manager.

Luxury brand

As an exclusive global fashion brand product design must reflect the corporate image of Hermès across the globe, but the mix of product ranges and styles

Figure 3.1   Luxury designers

will vary in its stores according to the local demand of each. Since the managers are also the buyers for their stores, in a similar way to that of a boutique, they are able to use their knowledge of their customers to select from a centrally designed range. However the ranges are not made up in volume, as they are with a mass-market retailer, instead the store manager/buyer places orders for styles in particular fabrics and colours which are then made up to their requirements. The design process outlined in Figure 3.1 facilitates this 'local' form of buying for individual stores.

In this situation, the designer has the dominant say over how the products will look and the buyers select from samples and colour/fabric options according to the particular needs of their stores. Once the orders have been placed Hermès sets about making the products. This *very customised approach* is able to work where a brand is uniquely differentiated in its products and has a loyal customer base willing to buy the distinctive range of life-style products produced.

High street retail designer

In contrast, a mass-market high street retailer like Top Shop will place design within the commercial constraints of buying and merchandising, as it has to operate in a *very competitive value-conscious market*. Consequently the designer's role will be different from that of a luxury brand, being more concerned with spotting and interpreting fast-moving trends, and working with the design teams of suppliers to achieve the latest look at a competitive cost price.

It is becoming more frequent for multiple retailers to substitute full-time designers with freelance specialists to work alongside the design teams of their suppliers. The role of the retail-appointed designer in this case is to ensure that appropriate designs are delivered to buyers and that the designs are in the 'hand writing' of the retail brand. The decision over which products will end up in the range in what colours and quantities is very much in the hands of the buyer and not the designer in this kind of business. For example, a buyer may make a commercial decision to include a product in a range that has caught the imagination of the mass market as with the case of the cargo pant (combat trouser). This garment is now a staple garment replacement for the denim jean in the youth market. Similarly, sustained demand for the 'gilet' over a number of seasons means that buyers for most high street fashion retailers need to represent it in their collections.

Although the design of the products will still be a key factor in sales, much greater attention will be paid to costs as the retail selling price will need to be very competitive. Additionally, a centralised buying and merchandising team as opposed to individual store managers operating as 'local buyers' will make the overall selection of products in the range. Significant differences exist, therefore, in the role and influence of a designer on the range of products sold, depending on the nature of a fashion business.

In Figure 3.2, the 'high street' designer has less personal authority over the final product range, as there are other functions making important contributions to the product. This more democratic approach is common in mass-market retailers, which have to buy in significantly greater volumes than businesses selling luxury fashion products and so need to de-risk their product ranges as much as possible.

Each of these functions has a *distinctive contribution to make to the success of the product*:

- The *buyer* has overall control of the collection, taking direction from the designer but often editing what is produced in line with commercial pressures within the business.
- The *merchandisers'* input is dominantly concerned with ensuring that historical sales relating to best- and worst-selling colours and styles are considered and that there is a balance of risk in terms of newness and traditionally safe (core) designs.
- The *garment technologist* may provide technical advice on garment construction and fabrics, according to need, but will play the greatest part in all stages of sample development. They will work closely with the designer's

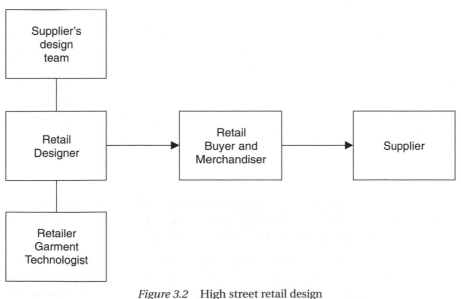

Figure 3.2   High street retail design

initial specification sheets amending them where necessary when fit samples are evaluated before production begins.

The key tasks of a designer

As there is significant diversity in the role of a fashion designer according to the nature of their fashion business, it is important to review the key tasks involved in the process, which are common to all product designers involved in fashion.

To research new trends and product ideas for a season through attending relevant trade and fashion shows, and making shopping trips with the buyer when appropriate

Designers will attend a variety of different events, partly to seek inspiration and partly to confirm the direction of trends in colour, fabric, styling, print and trimmings. In addition, shopping trips are common during which a designer and a senior member of the buying team will target a particular country/city which is believed to reflect a particular 'look' or be ahead in terms of trends. Generally designers will either purchase garments or take photographs of them to inspire new looks in their own product ranges. Although this is common practice with a number of retailers it is not a method used by all fashion designers. Additionally fashion designers will regularly read a variety of specialist fashion magazines and trade press, including the influential *Textile View* and *Collezioni* magazines.

To create the appropriate fashion direction for a season through the correct interpretation of fashion trends for the business

As trends emerge from a variety of sources, some of which are discussed later in this chapter, it is the responsibility of the design team to interpret and reflect them, where relevant, in the products. An important balance that must be struck is that of contemporary fashion trend verses core styles, which the customer has demonstrated they want to buy year after year. Sometimes it is difficult for a retailer to accept that the customer wants to buy 'old fashioned' looking products – e.g. floral pinafore dresses. If this is an issue for a designer, it may be that the market positioning of the retail business is moving away from its traditional customers.

To produce a range of product designs which reflect key looks for a season, maximise sales opportunities for the retailer and represent value for the customers

The designer is responsible for creating the look of the final products, balancing considerations of garment performance and fashion look with cost and delivery. A key issue to any garment design will be the fabric, with the designer frequently seeking to create a distinctive garment through fabric print, handle, finish and colour.

To finalise the product groups with buyers, taking account of constraints to creativity imposed by budgets and historical sales trends

Throughout the design process, the designer will be in close contact with the buyer receiving feedback regarding aspects of the designs. Inevitably a degree of 'editing' occurs as decisions over styling, fabric and colour are changed for a variety of reasons, some of which include cost, sourcing difficulties and changes of fashion direction closer to a season.

To develop mood, customer and product storyboards illustrating the design plans for a season

A key part of the designer's job is to produce a 2D representation of the range accurate in all styling, fabric, colour and print detail. This is usually done on a computer-aided design (CAD) system that provides a superior visual effect. In addition to boards showing the computer-generated designs of the products, the designer will produce boards reflecting the target customer and key directional themes for the season.

To present the various boards to senior management in seasonal range presentations

Before a season's range is signed off, or agreed by the buying director, the designer and buyer show it at a range presentation or product review. As most retailers are not able to have the designs made up in accurate colour, fabric and print detail, products are illustrated on storyboards using CAD technology. It is not possible to have accurate samples until colour and fabric have been confirmed. Customer and mood boards provide a context for the designs accompany storyboards showing individual design options for each product group.

To develop seasonal product styling records

Once the range has been agreed for a particular season an accurate record of each style with a style number needs to be kept by the designer. The buying department generates the style numbers, but the designer develops this vital visual reference document.

To develop specification sheets for all product designs

A specification sheet – or 'spec' as it is most commonly called – is the construction blueprint for the product. All product measurements and other relevant detail are recorded on a sheet, copies of which are kept in the department and sent to manufactures. The specification sheets are used to check the accuracy of the first sample garments produced by the manufacturer. First samples are usually called 'fit samples' as they are tried on by models for comfort and fit, issues explored further in Chapter 7, Sourcing and Supply Chain Management.

Figure 3.3 shows a 'day in the life' of a fashion retail designer. This reflects a relatively light workload for a designer

---

Current season is Autumn/Winter
8.30 a.m. arrive at desk
- Resolve supplier problems over garment trimming issues for S/S *range – e.g. select new button style
- Receive fax from supplier stating *minimums* on planned fabric are too high
- Meet with buyer to tackle this and similar problems on new S/S range
- Continue meeting to confirm next A/W *trips, in particular shopping trips and fabric trade shows
- Review the garment spec of a fit sample with the garment technologist after a fit session
- **Lunch** – 30 minutes
- Start organising ideas for the next A/W season
- Look through important style magazines cutting out images to stimulate new product looks
- Remainder of afternoon developing ideas for the A/W range

6.30 p.m. leave work

Note: S/S = Spring/Summer; A/W = Autumn/Winter.

Figure 3.3 A 'day in the life' of a fashion retail designer

What is successful fashion design?

There are many possible answers to this question, just as there are many points of view over how to define both the terms 'fashion' and 'good design' in general. However, this book is concerned with the buying and merchandising of products in fashion retail and as such, success in terms of aesthetics and 'form, fit and function' (commonly quoted as outputs of design processes) must be expressed through sales. A fashion retailer is in the business of selling fashion products and not art.

Successful fashion design in commercial terms is based on providing what customers want, frequently before they realise it. In fashioning retail, successful design is related directly to sales. If a garment design sells well the basic shape will be 'milked' and re-worked in a variety of fabrics, colours and prints. However, if a trial garment fails or a new style sells badly the garment design is unlikely to be repeated.

An exception lies at the exclusive end of fashion, where success maybe interpreted differently, with many *couture* designers achieving fame and status for their directional designs. These designs are often artistic interpretations of garments rather than practical products and frequently ensure huge publicity at the international Ready-To-Wear (RTW) and *Couture* shows. Although clothing forms part of their business, many such designers often achieve greater financial success through the sales of perfumes and toiletries sold using their high-profile names as brands.

Defining the contribution of fashion design

One view of the general contribution of design to a business is expressed through the following definition: 'the processes and activities that need to be carried out to enable the manufacture of a product that fully meets customer requirements' (Fox, 1993).[1] The difficulty with using this definition to try and define success in fashion design is that it does not differentiate between the specific role and contribution of a fashion designer and the vital contributions of other retailer functions to meeting customers' needs. The contributions of some functions have already been referenced in Figure 3.2 (high street design model), but others include marketing, which provides image benefits through its promotional campaigns and retail management, which delivers customer benefits through the store service environment.

Another view describing design as 'a valuable marketing tool devoted to visual problem solving' (Bruce and Cooper, 1997)[2] introduces the idea of customers experiencing fashion or clothing 'problems'. This idea of solving customer problems is an important concept in marketing and is related to the idea of providing customers with product and service benefits to satisfy their needs.

Benefits for customers

If sales are the ultimate test of good garment design for high street retailers then designers must take account of what their customers are seeking in the products that they are buying. Customers are seeking benefits from the fashion products they buy. These will vary between groups of customers (market segments); but may include

- 'Looking cool'
- 'Feeling special'
- 'Fitting in'.

Marketing theory explains a product in terms of different layers of benefits, that customers are seeking and ultimately buying. Figure 3.4, adapted from a generic marketing model, illustrates how this works for fashion. The model conceptualises the 'package of benefits' that a fashion retail business is selling to customers in its unique selling proposition (USP).

The core product

At the centre is the '*core*' benefit representing the fundamental reason to buy the product, and answering the question 'what is the customer really buying?' Some examples are listed in Table 3.1.

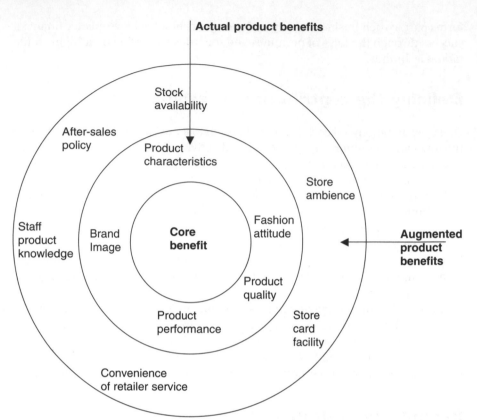

Actual product benefits

Stock availability

After-sales policy

Product characteristics

Store ambience

Staff product knowledge

Brand Image

Core benefit

Fashion attitude

Augmented product benefits

Product quality

Product performance

Store card facility

Convenience of retailer service

Source: Adapted from Kotler, Armstrong, Saunders and Wong (1996).[3]

Figure 3.4   Augmented product model for fashion retailers

Table 3.1   Core benefits

Product	Core benefit
Raincoat	Keeps you dry
Belt	Secures a garment/decoration
Suit	Smart appearance
Bra	Support for breasts
Jumper	Keeps torso warm
Lingerie	Feel special
Make-up	Feel attractive

Although the core benefit of a raincoat is to keep the customer dry, it is likely that other factors will influence their decision to select one product or 'brand' over another. These factors are present in the second and third layers, which represents the 'actual product' and 'augmented product', the attributes of which provide further benefits to the customer.

The actual product

This layer is concerned with the attributes most closely aligned to customers' perception of the physical product. The product as it appears to consumers is made up of a series of tangible characteristics, such as shape, fabric, colour and print, all possessing attributes which combine to provide further benefits. The fashion product also includes a strong attitude or image that is intangible and built into the product through image promotion. Frequently an image or attitude that is associated with a particular brand will be an important factor in the decision to buy a fashion product. However, it is important for designers to appreciate that a design can have 'attitude' ascribed to it only if there has been an effective image developed by marketing promotion in the media.

Actual product attributes and benefits

- Product characteristics (see Table 3.2)
- Product performance (durability/easy care/waterproof/breathable)
- Brand image/fashion attitude.

Table 3.2   Product characteristics of a trouser

Attribute	Benefit
Colour (neutral)	*Flexible*
Silhouette (classic)	*Sophisticated*
Fabric	*Crease-resistant finishing*
Invisible pockets	*Flattering appearance*
Trimming (buttons)	*Decorative*

The augmented product

Augmented benefits

The augmented (literally 'added') layer of benefits of the model represents many of the intangible service benefits that have an impact on customers' decision-making. These are important when fashion brands are easily substituted and the customer is concerned with the benefits of the purchase process as much as the product itself. These include, in no particular order:

- Service process
  - Convenience (payment choice, opening hours, till queueing, changing facilities)
  - After-sales (returns policy)
  - Product advice, fittings
- Stock availability
- Ambience of purchasing environment.

This third layer includes additional benefits, which impact on customers' decision-making but are not the responsibility of product designers – for example, shopping experience, service delivery and brand image are the responsibility of other retail functions.

Although this model helps explain the overall product that the customer maybe buying from a fashion retailer, it doesn't differentiate the particular contribution of the product designer from other functions. As this chapter is concerned with fashion (product) design it is important to analyse the specific contribution that the designer is making to the sale of a fashion product.

Designing benefits into fashion garments

Sir Ralph Halpern, ex-chairman of The Burton Group (now Arcadia), made the point that price alone would no longer make a sale and that a fashion retailer must provide the customer with an *outstanding product*. This does not mean that retailers can necessarily increase the selling price to fund a more expensive product: it means that the product must contain the right mix of benefits at a competitive price, which the customer recognises as value compared with alternatives.

Key elements in the fashion designer's contribution to the overall package of benefits in a fashion product can be categorised as follows:

- Product function
- Fashionability
- Added value.

Product function

Product function satisfies the intrinsic purpose or core benefit of the product. This will normally be defined by customers' product performance requirements and the customer's intended 'user occasion' for the product. For example, I need a:

- Jacket to keep me warm outside
- Trendy outfit to go clubbing
- Suit for work
- Leotard to wear at the gym
- Bikini for the beach.

Traditionally fashion retailers address such needs by structuring their operations into appropriate departments (separates, underwear/nightwear, etc.), with designers and buyers grouping products into stories within a range. Fashion designers can create new user occasions for existing products to reflect changes in consumer life-styles. For example, trainers are increasingly worn with both tailoring and casual garments and no longer just for sport.

User occasions are changing for some product categories, as many garments have become *multi-functional* and the distinctions between product categories based on traditional uses are becoming blurred. There are signs of the deconstruction of barriers between formal wear and casual wear, sports wear and active wear, and underwear and club wear. For example, a pair of hotpants and a bra, which are part of an underwear product range, can be adapted with simple styling features to feature in a club wear product range. Similarly, some night wear styles have found their way into club wear ranges as short dresses. This is more typical of the fast-moving younger women's fashion market.

Designers are responsible for keeping abreast of changes in fibre and fabric technology and functionality that can lead to new product opportunities, such as easy-care or anti-bacterial garments. However, problems arise for some fashion retailers who decide to replace traditional products with more 'fashionable' ranges in an attempt to 're-educate' their customers as part of a re-branding or re-positioning process. This can be very risky if customers' user occasion needs are no longer being satisfied.

Fashionability

A key ingredient of good design in fashion products is the customer perception of how *fashionable* or *stylish* the product is. The level of fashion in the product needs to be appropriate for the customer according to their life style, personality, fashion attitude and the degree of fashion innovation they are comfortable reflecting. These issues are explained in more detail in Chapter 4.

The term 'fashionability' is used to convey the intended level of contemporary style reflecting a particular season's fashion trend. Garment fashion trends within a season are expressed in a variety of ways using the physical elements of fashion garments including colour, fabric, silhouette (shape), styling features, prints, and trimmings.

Customers will interpret the level of fashion in a garment according to these elements and determine whether or not it is appropriate for them. Each element makes an individual contribution to the overall fashion statement, but fabric also has a strong influence on perceived product performance which may be both a fashion issue and a practical consideration. Product designers need to judge the appropriate level of fashionability for their customers, and express it through these elements.

Added value and value-added features

In addition to these fashion elements, a fashion product designer must also consider how to build value for money into a garment, as customers frequently buy from a variety of similar retail brands. The ease with which customers can substitute one fashion retailer's product with another means that product differentiation through a combination of fashionability and value is a key factor in making a sale. Value can be represented by a competitive price and by designing useful additional features into the product.

Such added-value features may be less striking initially than the colour, shape and fabric of the product, especially if they are not obvious until the garment has been handled or tried on. They may also be a secondary consideration in a customer's purchase decision with the additional benefits supporting a decision to buy. However, they still have an impact and remain within the remit of the of the product designer.

The definition of value-added features will vary among consumers according to the importance of the feature and the cost of the garment. However they include such things as:

- Secure internal pockets
- Extra/invisible pockets
- Detachable linings
- Twill taped side seams
- Spare buttons and fabric
- Unusual/quality linings
- Foldaway hoods.

Figure 3.5 represents the three dimensions that a designer of fashion products must consider when designing a product for a fashion retailer. The model indicates no order of importance for each of the elements, as it is likely to vary tremendously among different groups of consumers. However the shaded area, where all three overlap, indicates the potential overall impact of a fashion designer on the consumer' s decision to purchase.

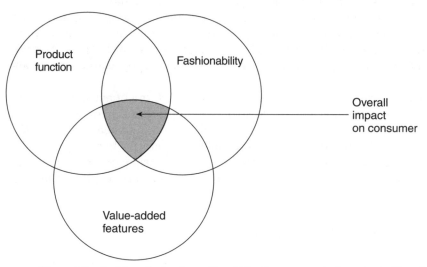

Figure 3.5   Fashion design benefits within the augmented product offer of
a fashion retailer

Tip

Fashion designers should compare the benefits provided by each product option against the target customer's needs.

Fashion trends

As fashion is a fast-moving and fickle phenomenon it is difficult for a designer to predict and accurately interpret the 'fashion look' for a particular season. A major problem facing a fashion designer and buyer is how to decide what fashion garments and products its customers will want to buy each season. The problem is simple to articulate but not easy to resolve, as most customers do not know themselves which particular fashion designs they will want until the products have been promoted in the media and arrived in the stores.

There are many reasons for this, including the impact of the media in picking up on and promoting particular looks throughout a season. Although retailers are involved with the media in terms of both PR and advertising few are sure of the actual customer impact of such promotion prior to the season.

Another factor contributing to the problem is that customers' particular fashion wants for next season cannot easily be expressed prior to the trends being established. It is not always possible to ask customers what style or colour they will want to wear to satisfy their future fashion needs. As such, the fashion designer must interpret the key looks from a whole range of information and then adapt them for their market.

The influences on a fashion designer are many and may vary according to their specific job and the kind of company they work for. For example, a designer working for a traditional men's wear retailer targeting a more mature age group will be less influenced by changing fashion trends and the factors which drive them, than a designer working for a teenage fashion brand. This is because the products require less change from season to season and evolve slowly.

However, what designers can do is to analyse the major social, cultural and technological changes impacting on a season and address the resulting changing needs and behaviour of their company's market.

Tapping into the changing external environment

Although social and cultural changes are important determinants of changing fashions, they are themselves affected by other major drivers of change, which include globalisation of world markets and the accessibility of more sophisticated communications technologies. The latter has provided people with greater access to more ideas and influences from other cultures and societies. For example, satellite television and the Internet provide access to fashion, sports, films and music from any country around the world. Consequently consumers have a broader and more sophisticated appreciation of popular cultures in other countries. This greater awareness affects individuals' tastes and impacts on the demand for particular products and fashions. Long gone are the days of a few large retailers producing predictable looks for recurring Spring/Summer and Autumn/Winter seasons!

The task of summarising the overarching trends for a season and interpreting how the changing world is likely to impact on customers' desire for fashion will be handled differently by retailers. Some will use trend managers with others preferring the direction to come from the head of design. Most fashion retailers will also seek the help of fashion forecasters and send designers to appropriate textile and fashion shows.

The model in Figure 3.6 identifies some of the major drivers of change which influenced fashion trends in the late 1990s. The model is designed to give the reader an idea of the scope of factors impacting on fashion design rather than represent a complete list of all possible factors:

- **Globalisation** – This is a term used to signpost the fact that the world is getting more *accessible*. Greater travel increases consumers' awareness of other fashions, and the increasing presence of global competition provides access to a wider range of products and styles.
- **Greater media communication** – This provides consumers with exposure and access to a wider range of ideas, styles and cultural influences through films, satellite television, magazines, and more recently the Internet. Global 'catwalk trends' can now be interpreted by fashion retailers and sold in their stores within a matter of weeks instead of months.
- **The health and well-being of individuals** – these are increasingly important in today's society, with issues ranging from detoxification to keeping fit. Consumer concern and interest has generated developments in fibres, resulting in fabric benefits ranging from anti-allergenic to UV protection in swimwear. General interest in health has led to breathable fabrics and a whole series of fitness-related products.
- **Technology** – This is influencing design through 'smart' textiles and computer-generated prints. Developments in finishing processes are providing consumers with garments that are easier to care for and softer to feel. Developments in manufacturing technology have increased the speed

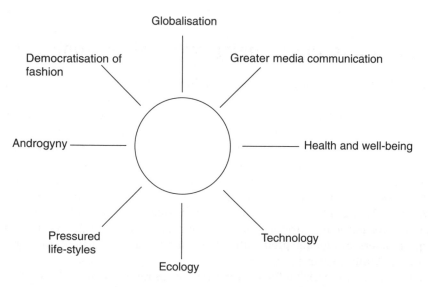

Figure 3.6 Some drivers of fashion change

and quality of production and introduced new methods such as laser fabric cutting and garment welding.

- **Ecology** – Ecological concerns including global warming, pollution and the erosion of natural resources have raised awareness of the need to recycle and use renewable raw materials. Innovative sources of fibre are emerging and include nettle, hemp, pineapple and products such as plastic water bottles that can be recycled to produce sportswear fleece fabrics.
- **Pressured life-styles** – The pressured life-styles of people have created a need for 'easy wear' and 'easy care' garments, leading to wrinkle-free finishing processes and unstructured/less fitted clothing styles. A perceived need to do more things more quickly is being fuelled by products such as mobile phones, which are increasingly able to do more than simply make phone calls. Accompanying this change in life-style is a more informal attitude towards dress. 'Casualisation' of dress – in particular, a move away from fitted tailoring towards unstructured garments with minimalist styling, and relaxation of work dress codes ('Dress Down Friday') – has resulted in less emphasis on formal suits and more emphasis on smart casual garments.
- **Androgyny** – This reflects the convergence of men's and women's status in our society. Cargo pants, or 'combat trousers', have replaced jeans as the key basic for many teenagers – both male and female and there is demand for unisex products and fashion looks – e.g. Calvin Klein's 'CK One' perfume.
- **Democratisation of fashion** – Promostyl, an internationally based trend forecaster, refers to the 'Democratisation of fashion' to explain the growth of previously ultra-exclusive brands like Prada and Gucci into mass-market acceptance. In the past such luxury names were for the few whom could afford them, whereas today owning a Gucci bag is becoming a common and achievable aspiration. Even a conservative luxury brand like Hermès is selling a widely used product like a trainer.

Technological innovations in fibres and fabrics

Sometimes the development of a completely new product is the result of a particular functional need, like a 'trainer sock' or a 'body', but it is often driven by the benefits offered by a new fabric.

Specialist textile consultancies such as 'Line' make the point that technology is changing the range of benefits that designers can build into garment products through the textiles used in construction. As more functions and properties are integrated into their structures, textiles can provide a new range of benefits for garments, including greater protective capabilities, body-enhancing qualities and the benefits associated with 'smart textiles' like Amicor, the anti-bacterial fibre from Courtaulds.

The development of fabrics and cloths from new fibres or blends of fibres has historically provided customers with particular benefits. Earlier developments included blending synthetic and natural fibres like cotton and polyester which reduced the creasing and increased 'launderability'. However, as we enter the twenty-first century, a whole new series of functional fabrics has been

Table 3.3 Fibre development examples

Level	Development
Fibre	Amicor – a modified acrylic with anti-bacterial capabilities that is designed to eliminate odour and skin irritation
Yarn	Improved cotton-spinning processes producing a softer handle
Fabric	Gore-Tex fabric, which uses a hi-tech membrane sandwiched between an outer and inner layer of fabric to allow skin to breath while protecting against wind and rain
Finish	Chemicals added to finished fabric to provide performance benefits – e.g. a Teflon finish to provide a dirt-resistant effect
Colour	Development of non-toxic vegetable dyes/and Fox Fibre – a natural pigmented cotton

developed with benefits – dustmite-proof, rot-resistant, anti-bacterial and insect-proof, for example. Indeed, without the development of elastane (Lycra) a whole series of sports and casual wear-related products might never have appeared.

However, not all improvements are derived simply from the development of new fibres, as innovation can occur across the entire textile development process (Table 3.3).

Fashion forecasting

Fashion forecasters, or 'trend forecasting agencies' as they are also referred to, offer fashion designers objective and early guidance about the changes in colour and fabric and shape, and also some longer-term analysis of social trends that will ultimately affect fashion. Most fashion retailers use forecasting agencies to find out how fashion trends are evolving, to explain the global influences on fashion and to reflect the changing mood of fashion from a colour, fabric and styling perspective. However, some retailers prefer to research and interpret the trends themselves to maintain their originality, or alternatively buy in external forecasting services to support their own research.

The process

These agencies are able to reflect the earliest views on trends some eighteen months ahead of a season. At this stage, colour is the crucial consideration for the yarn mills that need to know what the requirements of fabric weavers and knitters will be. As such, it is also the focus of discussion among others who have with an interest in very early trend decision-making. The sequence of decision-making is tabulated in Table 3.5 (p. 56) and reflects the wide range of different and specialist inputs that contribute to a season's fashion look. Fashion forecasters combine the specific trends emerging about colour and fabric from the early yarn and fabric shows, with their own socio–economic and cultural analysis, to provide their clients with an early interpretation of fashion trends. Major trends in life-style, attitudes and culture – in particular, music, sports, cinema and television – are used to predict changing consumer demand.

Trend forecasting agencies

There are a number of forecasting businesses each offering their own specialist combination of products and services. Some of the better known include Sacha Pacha, Peclers, Line and Promostyl. There are also online forecasting services, available at a cost via the Internet, such as Worth Global Style Network (WGSN).

Promostyl is a good example of a trend forecasting business as it has a global client base and offers both a customised consulting service to clients as well as a range of trend books for each season. Their trend books provide forecasts about colour, fabric and styling for different market sectors, like women's wear, men's wear and children's wear. The books also provide companies with a quick and relatively cheap global overview of major evolving trends.

Table 3.4 includes an indication of the date in the calendar when Promostyl makes a presentation of Spring/Summer trends, for the following year, at the Victoria & Albert Museum in London. However, like other forecasters, it makes a number of other trend presentations over the course of a year, as the trends for a season gradually evolve. Table 3.4 shows the sequence of presentations that it makes in a year. Readers should note that they refer to more than one season as fashion forecasters work ahead of the fabric shows. Thus when Premiere Vision (PV) is showing for Autumn/Winter (A/W) 2000/2001, Promostyl is presenting its views for Spring/Summer (S/S) 2001 at the show and so on.

Table 3.4 Promostyl trend presentations

Event		Promostyl showing
October 1999	PV* (A/W 00/01)	S/S01 – Influences, Colour, Fabric
January 2000	V&A London	S/S01 – Influences, Colour, Fabric and Shapes
March 2000	PV (S/S01)	A/W01/02 – Influences, Colour and Fabric
June 2000	V&A London	A/W 01/02 – Influences, Colour, Fabric and Shapes

Note: *PV: Premierè Vision.

As fashion affects more and more products from cars to paint, Promostyl is just as likely to be advising a plant grower about the consumer life-style trends that will impact on the demand for particular shapes and colours of plants, as it is a fashion retailer. Although there is clearly an evolving process of trend development, which is reflected through the various textile trade shows, it is very hard to define the creative process which companies like Promostyl use to identify major influences on the design of a range of products. Their view is that at the heart of the forecasting process lies an intuitive ability to spot a potentially strong trend, based on many years of experience. Another observation they make is that the forecaster needs to look for what is 'ugly' or undeveloped, but innovative, rather than beautiful and established.

Table 3.5 Key decision-making events for the season Spring/Summer 2001

Date	Event	Textile shows	Garment Shows
May 99	Fashion forecasters plan colour		
June 99	British Textile Colour Group (BTCG) meets Intercolour Group meet – (Paris) BTCG representatives return to review		
October 99		Premiere Vision (AW 00/01) incorporating Indigo S/S01	
November 99		Filo Yarn – (Milan) (mainly weavers)	
December 99		Expofil yarn show – (Paris)	
January 00		Pitti Filati yarn show – (Florence) (mainly for knits)	
January 00	Promostyl conference at The Victoria and Albert Museum		
February 00		Tissu Premier fabric show – (Lille)	
February 00		Moda In Tessuto fabric show – (Milan)	
March 00		Prato Expo fabric show – (Florence)	
March 00		Premiere Vision – (Paris)	
July 00			Pitti Uomo Men's Wear – (Florence)
August 00			40 degrees Casual Wear – (London)
August 00			Herren Moda/Inter Jeans – (Cologne)
Sept/Oct 00			Designer Ready-To-Wear shows
Jan/Feb 01			Designer Couture shows

The importance of shows

Designers are able to predict what is likely to be 'in fashion' through a combination of influences, including wide reviewing of important textile and style magazines, the specialist services of forecasting trend agencies and visits to key textile and garment fashion shows.

Different kinds of shows

The word 'show' is given its widest possible interpretation here to refer to the range of organised textile and fashion garment shows, which operate over the sixteen months preceding a season. It is important to realise that trade shows, whether yarn, fabric or garment, have a basic function which is to *sell products*. The use of these shows for prediction is often a secondary function to add value to the experience and attract visitors, as all shows are selling environments in their own right for the exhibitors.

In very simple terms, yarn mills sell to weavers and knitters who sell to garment manufactures who sell to fashion buyers. These different needs have resulted in a sequence of yarn trade shows, fabric trade shows and garment shows evolving over the years. The sequence reflects the lead-times needed by the various businesses at the various stages.

Who uses the shows?

Visitors vary according to the nature of the show.

- A *yarn show* will attract a range of people including fabric manufacturers and some retail buyers and designers, although the mix will be more weighted to people involved in fabric production than garment design and buying. Fashion trade press will cover the shows to inform those buyers and designers, for whom the shows are too early, of the major trends emerging.
- The *fabric shows* perform a more balanced role, with great emphasis on the sale of fabrics but with more retail designers and buyers attending, as the products on display have more direct relevance to garment design and the shows are that much closer to the season.
- *Garment shows* are much more diverse, ranging from the product trade shows through to the high profile Ready-to-Wear Designer shows, like London Fashion Week and then the exclusive *Couture* shows. The product trade shows are segmented according to broad sector, like men's or women's wear, and by specialist product category, like sportswear or lingerie. Over time product trade shows can be replaced by new versions or even change their names to revitalise interest in an ever changing market.

Lead-times

The term 'lead-time' is used widely to refer to the period of time between significant events. In this case it is used to refer to the period of time prior to a season that a particular show is being held. As a general rule of thumb fabric shows are held approximately twelve months before a season and garment shows approximately five months before a season. It is important to realise that the beginning of the trading season referred to here is January for Spring/Summer and August for Autumn/Winter. However, the transitional Spring ranges are in store late December with the main Spring range in early January. The subject of seasonality is dealt with in more detail in Chapter 4.

The sequence of trade and fashion shows

Table 3.5 illustrates the evolving sequence of trend decision-making for the season Spring/Summer 2001. The same sequence is mirrored for Autumn/Winter at different times. Not all the events or shows are directly relevant to fashion retail designers and buyers as they have particular specialisms and audiences. However, rather like pieces of a jigsaw, they all contribute to the final fashion picture for a season.

National and international colour bodies

In the United Kingdom the process really begins with the British Textile Colour Group (BTCG) meeting, where around 25 representatives of a range of companies from different industry sectors, including, retail, forecasting and automotive, meet to discuss colour and their views on factors likely to affect the season's fashion trends. Two representatives are selected to attend the Intercolour Group meeting, which is traditionally held in Paris, but occasionally moves to other countries. Here, the equivalent representatives from many countries around the world, including Europe, Asia and the Far East, meet to exchange views on the likely development of trends and especially the development of colour. The UK representatives then return to the United Kingdom for a review of the global position with the rest of the BTCG.

The next early sign of trends for the season emerges in the Indigo exhibition held as part of the Autumn/Winter fabric show, 'Premiere Vision', commonly referred to as PV. This particular PV is showing for Autumn/Winter, but incorporates the Indigo show of textile prints for the next season within it.

Premiere Vision (PV)

Traditionally PV has been considered the 'first view' of colour and fabric trends for much of the European fashion industry. It is still arguably one of the most important shows in the calendar. Held in Paris twice a year, March for Spring/Summer and October for Autumn/Winter, the show is considered to be an accurate view of colours and fabric trends for the season. Within the vast exhibition halls (referred to as salons) there are approximately 850 European weaver–exhibitors with their most representative fabric samples for the relevant season, all on display to 45 000 visitors over the four days.

The presentation of key trends on display within the vast exhibition is the result of the combined views of a European Concertation, a body of 65 fashion experts who identify the current trends emerging from around the world, and the Premiere Vision Fashion team. Colour palettes and key theme statements are signed around the exhibition summarising the trends, and there is an audio–visual show, which provides an overview of the season at intervals throughout the day.

How to use Premiere Vision

Premiere Vision not only provides an opportunity for fabric manufacturers to sell their products and the industry to review trends, it is a meeting place for business. Retailers can catch up with suppliers on a face-to-face basis and forecasters like Promostyl can meet many of their global clients and provide them with a special summary of the key trend themes. Those visiting who are not trained designers but are trying to obtain a feel for the particular season's trends should realise that PV is not a garment show and so should expect to gain mainly fabric and colour information:

Advice for visitors:

- Obtain a map of the exhibition identifying the various sections
- Plan a route taking in areas most relevant to your product area (e.g. sports wear fabrics)
- Identify the times of the audio – visual shows and target an appropriate one
- Visit the General Forums area which provides a summary of themes and colours
- Plan meal breaks and rendezvous points/times with colleagues
- Use a dictaphone to make voice recorded notes of trends.

Although Premiere Vision is an important show many designers believe that new, directional shows like Tissu Premier in Lille and Moda In Tessuto in Milan are providing earlier insights into colour and fabric trends. Tissu, in particular, is considered a good earlier source of trend information even though it is not so large and has fewer fabric categories.

The designer shows

The Ready-to-Wear garment shows really provide the last opportunity for fashion retailers to incorporate styling changes or overlooked 'must have' items in their ranges. These shows provide the influential fashion press with an opportunity to review and promote the particular season's trends and provide publicity for the designers. The shows are held in London, Paris, Milan, New York and Tokyo with the sequence changing every year. The final set of shows reflecting the season's trends are the *couture* shows which are held in London, Paris and Milan in late January and February for this particular season. They have little impact on high street fashion retailers as early spring stock is already in the stores with summer already being shipped.

Tip

- Fashion trends continually evolve as the sequence of trade shows progresses
- Trade shows can be categorised into Yarn, Fabric and Product
- It is increasingly common for trend information obtained from fabric shows to be applied by buyers sooner than the season to which the show refers

Notes

1. Fox, J. (1993) *Quality through Design, The Key to Successful Product Delivery*, McGraw-Hill International (UK) Ltd.
2. Bruce, M. and Cooper, R. (1997) *Marketing and Design Management*, International Thomson Business Press.
3. Kotler, P., Armstrong, G., Saunders, J. and Wong, V. (1996) *Principles of Marketing – The European Edition*, Prentice-Hall Europe, p. 546.

4 Market planning for fashion retailing

The importance of marketing

This chapter moves on to cover the key marketing theory underpinning the development of a range of fashion products. It explains some of the preliminary marketing considerations arising before specific design, sourcing and merchandising activities begin. It also explains some basic concepts which lie at the heart of what is meant by a 'range' of products, in preparation for Chapter 6 – Merchandise Planning.

A problem of poor or slow sales is commonly addressed in fashion retail by the use of *mark-down*, which discounts the selling price to customers and, so long as demand is 'elastic', results in increased sales of the product line. However, this is an expensive method of selling products, as it reduces the profit achieved on the products. In fact mark-down is the single largest cost to a fashion retail business after the cost of the products themselves. It is worth remembering at this point that the main – and frequently only – source of income for a fashion retailer is the profit from the sales of its products. Less profit per garment means less income to pay its bills. Furthermore, this tactic is less effective when general trading conditions are poor, as the competition is usually doing the same thing.

It is vital then that the fashion retailer knows what its customers want and are expecting. Problems in defining and then keeping up with changing customer needs and expectations are arguably the most important factor in successful selling. Large retail businesses like Marks & Spencer face a bigger problem keeping up with the changing expectations of their customers than a very focused niche business like The Gap, as their customer base is much broader.

It is essential for students to understand what the term 'marketing' means. As a subject for academic study and a function for a wide range of industries, marketing is the process of identifying and satisfying customer needs through the profitable supply of product and service benefits. As such, it is concerned with *managing the marketing mix* to ensure that the benefits are delivered effectively.

The marketing mix

The marketing mix is a series of elements which have traditionally been referred to as the 4 Ps but which subsequently have grown to 7 Ps with the acknowledgement of the importance of service to the overall package of benefits bought by customers (Table 4.1). As customers are buying a combination of

Table 4.1   The 7 Ps

- **Product**
- **Price**
- **Promotion**
- **Place of distribution**
- *People*
- *Process*
- *Physical evidence*

benefits in the products they purchase, it is essential that fashion retailers manage the integrated contributions of all functions in the business to providing the benefits. For example, a customer may choose to buy a blouse from one retailer because she can always find her size and get served quickly. Thus the reason to buy is influenced by the contribution of the store management.

As competing high street fashion retailers provide very similar products, an increasingly important differential is the level of service offered. More and more frequently mass-market fashion products are being sold because of efficient and effective service.

- **Product** refers to the complete package of benefits offered to the customer but represented in a *tangible fashion product*. The complexity of benefits provided by a product – whether garment, accessory or other fashion-related item – is explained in Chapter 3.
- **Price** refers to the *retail selling price* consumers have to pay. It must represent value, compared with competing alternatives and real choice through offering similar product styles at a range of different price points. Designers, buyers and financial managers need to be aware of the limits a competitive retail selling price places on product cost price and profit per product.
- **Promotion** refers to a wide range of activity from product labels/ tickets/packaging to image-based advertising/PR and in-store visual merchandising. It also refers to incentives designed to increase sales, which include all mark-downs. The term 'promotion' has a very wide application and is the combined responsibility of a number of retailer functions. However, *image promotion* is responsible for influencing the 'fashionability' perception consumers have of products and the attitude or personality benefits they are buying into.
- **Place** refers to the *channels* through which the products are sold. Important issues will include the accessibility, location, available selling space, layout and presentation of the channels. Customers must have access to sufficient choice of styles, colours, sizes and price points, with stock being changed regularly to maintain the perception of fresh fashion looks.
- **People** refers to all individuals, including customers, suppliers and the fashion retailer's staff, who are involved in the buying and selling of the products. For a fashion retailer to succeed in selling its products it must ensure that all involved in the supply chain have a clear understanding of the customers' *fashion product needs and expectations.*

- **Process** refers to the *intended customer experience* of the retail facility, ranging from store/website layout and function to more specialist personal shopping or home-delivery features. These will vary tremendously among small boutiques, multiple retail outlets and department stores.
- **Physical evidence** refers to the *presentation of the store/website*, its fascia, windows, stock and staff. Also included could be promotional material such as in-store posters, point of sale leaflets and brochures, all of which reflect the brand image of the retailer.

These additional three elements are extremely important to fashion retailers as any retail business is dependent upon its service provision for its success (see Chapter 3, p. 46 on 'The Augmented Product Model').

Marketing within fashion retailing

Marketing in fashion retail is handled slightly differently, with responsibility for most of the marketing mix variables managed by functions other than the marketing department. Key variables of product and price are the specific responsibility of design, garment technology, buying and merchandising functions. Although many fashion retailers have marketing departments few, if any, expect the marketing department to be involved with the complete marketing mix, preferring instead to concern it with promotion.

In fact, the primary role of a fashion retail marketing department is to promote the brand and its products, using the promotional mix of advertising, public relations, sales promotion, personal selling, visual merchandising and the Internet (websites).

The remaining elements of the marketing mix are the primary responsibility of other retailer functions: buying and merchandising, design, retail operations, human resources and systems (Table 4.2).

Although the planning and development processes for fashion products are specifically buying and merchandising responsibilities, students should appreciate the significance of 'marketing' in effectively developing and distributing products in markets; in particular, the vital role it has in segmenting markets and monitoring the market positioning of the fashion retailer. Some large retailers have euphemistically referred to their failure to do this as 'taking their eye off the ball'.

Table 4.2	Retailer-functions in the marketing mix
Product	Design, Buying & Merchandising, Technology
Price	Buying, Merchandising
Promotion	Marketing, PR
Place of distribution	Merchandising, Distribution, Retail Operations
People	Human Resources
Process	Systems, Merchandising, Retail Operations, Supply Chain
Physical evidence	Retail Operations (inc. Visual Merchandising), Marketing

Defining customers

Where to start?

It sounds obvious but no business can succeed without *identifying and satisfying its customers' needs*. This process of identifying customer needs is called 'market segmentation' and its purpose is to identify a market 'gap' or opportunity where a group of customers sharing broadly similar needs are not being targeted or catered for by other businesses.

There are many ways of dividing markets into meaningful and homogeneous (similar) segments that include those listed below. It is important to remember that the final target market must be clearly identified, measurable and 'reachable'. A segment that cannot be reached effectively, possibly owing to intense competition, lack of a credible brand image, or inappropriate distribution channels, does not represent a meaningful market.

Methods of segmentation

Geographic

- Region – North, South, South East, Greater London
- City centre/Town high street/Out-of-town shopping centre (Bluewater)
- Variations in weather patterns.

Demographic

- Gender
- Occupation
- Income
- Age
- Family life-stage
- Size / height.

Geo-demographics

There are specialist software packages available to retailers, which combine consumer demographics with geographical location. Basic information on the structure of the population is obtained through the Census and merged with the Postal Address File, which contains all UK postcodes. Profiles of consumers are then matched to specific regions. Although some fashion retailers have developed their own versions, a leading classification system in the UK is **A Classification Of Residential Neighbourhoods** known by its acronym '**ACORN**' (ACORN is a system owned by CACI Ltd).

The six **ACORN** categories are shown in Table 4.3.

		Table 4.3 ACORN categories	
A	Thriving	1	Wealthy achievers, suburban areas
		2	Affluent greys, rural communities
		3	Prosperous pensioners, retirement areas
B	Expanding	4	Affluent executives, family areas
		5	Well-off workers, family areas
C	Rising	6	Affluent urbanites, town and country areas
		7	Prosperous professionals, metropolitan areas
		8	Better-off executives, inner city areas
D	Settling	9	Comfortable middle agers, mature home owners
		10	Skilled workers, home-owning areas
E	Aspiring	11	New home owners, mature communities
		12	White collar workers, better-off multi-ethnic areas
F	Striving	13	Older people, less prosperous areas
		14	Council estate residents, better-off homes
		15	Council estate residents, high unemployment
		16	Council estate residents, great hardship
		17	People in multi-ethnic, low income areas

NRS socio–economic classification

Although this is an old system, originally based on class, companies still use it to make broad judgements about people's needs, based on their occupation. The categories are listed in Table 4.4. It is hard to see how this is relevant to determining fashion needs as many people simply do not adhere to their stereotypes and people from all classes and occupations share the aspiration to be fashionable.

Table 4.4 NRS classification

Social grade		Occupation (chief income earner)
A	Upper class	Senior professional/managerial
B	Middle class	Managerial
C1	Lower middle class	Supervisors, junior management
C2	Skilled working class	(White-collar) skilled manual workers
D	Working class	(Blue-collar) Semi/unskilled manual workers
E	Subsistence level	Low fixed income – pensioners, students, unemployed

Diffusions of innovation – Rogers (1983)

Rogers[1] developed a five-level classification (Table 4.5).

These are often referred to as '*fashion leaders*', '*fashion followers*', '*fashion mainstream*' and '*commodity buyers*' in the fashion industry. Fashion retailers need to reflect the appropriate level of fashionability in their products, or risk alienating customers through being either too forward or 'old-fashioned' in the designs they offer.

Table 4.5 Rogers' classification	
Innovators	Individuals who like to be first to use a product
Early adopters	Individuals who like to buy early in the product life cycle
Early majority	Those who pick up on a trend when it is established
Late majority	Those who pick up on a trend late
Laggards	Those who buy products when the trend is over

Fashion attitude

Customers' interest in and perception of fashion varies widely. Their perception of a fashion brand is influenced by the promotion of an image that the brand portrays. The image is designed to reflect an attitude that is consistent with the *self-image and aspiration of the target customer.* Fashion retailers can segment by targeting certain types of personality through getting them to respond to a specific attitude.

Life-style

Customers sharing the same occupation and culture may have quite different life-styles. Marketing theory explains 'life-style' as an individual's pattern of living, which is expressed through their activities, interests and opinions (AIO).

These elements are critically important to fashion as they can identify user occasions (activities) and the particular level of enthusiasm a customer has for fashion-related issues. For example, a common trend across a range of fashion-related industries, from clothing to cosmetics, is a desire for good health and general well-being. A range of media including magazines, newspapers, radio and TV fuels people's opinions about individual 'well-being' and health. Greater awareness of health issues has driven a whole range of developments in textiles, ranging from UV protection, built into fabrics, to moisturised fibres for use in hosiery to provide a smoother feel.

The Values and Lifestyles (VALs) typology is a common form of customer classification which identifies nine categories according to whether the person is inner-directed, outer-directed or need-driven:

- *Experientials*
- *I-Am-Me*
- *Achievers*
- *Socially conscious*
- *Emulators*
- *Belongers*
- *Integrated*
- *Sustainers*
- *Survivors.*

Historical purchasing behaviour

There are many ways for a fashion business to try and segment its customer base, most of which have already been discussed. In addition to these characteristics of the customer, retailers have access to a range of information about customers' *past purchase behaviour*. This is valuable, as it provides factual data about sales of products and their various skews, as opposed to speculation about future behaviour based on potential needs and wants.

EPOPS and EFTPOS tills provide the data in which skews include: colour, size, fitting, season, price point. Store cards and loyalty or reward cards also provide important information about purchasing behaviour, which can add to the segment profile:

- Product details (style, colour, size, fit, price)
- Frequency of purchase
- Time of purchase
- Linked items
- Value of transaction – leading to average spend per customer
- Store location
- Reaction to sales promotion / new lines.

Pen portrait

With so many important variables to consider, some fashion retail businesses have developed customer profiles or 'pen-portraits' of their target customer. The pen portrait is a written description of the kind of person the fashion retailer is selling to and includes many of the segmentation variables. Typically, 'mood' and 'customer' boards that illustrate key features of the target customer's personality and life-style support the pen portrait. An example of a pen portrait is given below. Fashion retailer brands such as Warehouse and Miss Selfridge, which sell their own label merchandise, commonly use them to direct the designers and buyers. However, pen portraits must be based on accurate research of meaningful customer characteristics. If buyers simply guess at probable life-style activities, degree of fashion innovation and attitudes, they may buy inappropriate products.

EXAMPLE: 'FRAN'

> Fran is a nineteen-year-old fashion student who is living at home with her family while studying fashion design at a leading art college. Working part-time in a trendy fashion boutique, she earns enough money to finance her hectic social life and expensive shopping bills. Conscious of her appearance, she wants to be seen as different from the crowd but also sophisticated when she is out socialising. Her busy social life includes working out at the gym at weekends, clubbing on Friday and Saturday nights and hanging out with her friends at college during the week. Fran spends Sundays with her family recovering from her hectic week.

Tip

Ensure that your customer profile includes the following:

- User occasion
- Life-style (AIO)

- Attitude
- Innovation category
- Income band
- Age band

What is a season?

In the fashion business the term 'season' means a period of time during which fashion products are sold. For example, to a fashion retailer selling swimwear, the season will be March to August, with a peak in sales in May. The term may also refer to a collection of products, which are linked by a common theme, most commonly the weather: Spring, Summer, Autumn/Fall and Winter.

Traditional and contemporary fashion seasons

In the past there have been two clearly defined and traditional fashion seasons and these are still firmly ingrained in our culture, even though they have increasingly less relevance to both consumers and fashion businesses. They are Spring/Summer and Autumn/Winter. Where historically there were just the two main seasons contemporary fashion works on the basis of up to twelve.

Current fashion seasons are less defined by stark contrasts in the weather as the climate is generally milder in the winter, and so the distinction between product ranges is based less on the need for light and heavy garments and more on *relevant user occasions*. Additionally many buyers and merchandisers are of the view that customers are generally buying closer to the season, rather than anticipating and buying in advance.

Factors which have led to a change in the structure of seasons

- Less distinct and predictable weather patterns, as winter is milder and the summers begin later
- Greater travel, as customers require clothing for a variety of climates and occasions out of season (e.g. swimwear in winter, supplied by many airport retailers).

Fashion seasons and user occasions

With a greater emphasis on satisfying the fashion needs of customers' changing life-styles, fashion retailers have to buy more quickly and keep ranges focused on what customers want at particular times of the year, as opposed to buying to satisfy two large periods of demand. In marketing terms it could be said that they are 'buying' to satisfy discreet 'user occasions'.

These user occasions are the situations when customers develop a particular need for a product, either as a result of their attitudes and lifestyle activities or because of the time of year. Some reflect traditional occasions like swim wear in summer and party outfits for Christmas, but increasingly consumer demand is forcing retailers to rethink product ranges around changed customer behaviour. For example swim wear is required in December and January, as more people fly off to sunnier climates on holiday (Table 4.6).

Table 4.6   Some Fashion user occasions for which product benefits need to be created

Occasion	Product
Holidays	Warm/cold climate, sports/active, family, destination (Ibiza)
Calendar events	Christmas, Valentine's day, major sports meetings media events
Active leisure	Health club/gym
Non-active leisure	Football strips
Teen leisure	'Must have' logos/brands
	Club wear/pub wear
Back to school	School wear/Half terms Holiday wear
Weddings	Traditional/package overseas

Modern seasonal trading

A more common fashion retail approach to seasons is set out in Table 4.7.

Table 4.7   Key seasonal segments in the fashion year

Sub-season	Period	Approximate contribution %
Early Spring	Jan/Feb	7
Spring (events – Valentine's Day)	Feb/March	9
Early Summer (Holiday)	April/May	12
Summer SALE	June	11
High summer	July/August	8
Transitional Autumn	August	8
Autumn	September/October	14
Party wear	November	9
Christmas presents/Transitional Spring	December	9
Winter SALE		13
Total		100

The number of weeks of full price trading in a season may vary between fashion retailers, according to when they begin their sale. For clarity, there is a distinction between the bi-annual summer and winter sales, as shown in Table 4.7, and the mid-season or product-specific mark-downs. Most fashion retailers go on winter sale soon after Christmas in the United Kingdom, although some may decide to begin their sale prior to Christmas if trading is poor. A number of exclusive fashion and general retail businesses differentiate themselves by beginning their sales later.

There is greater government regulation over the timing of seasonal sales in France and Germany, which limits retailers' flexibility to start and end bi-annual sales in response to trading conditions. Equally, cultural difference results in timing differences for the same user occasion – for example, in France party wear tends to be bought after Christmas for the New Year.

Despite the changing significance of weather and thus the blurring of boundaries between seasons, it is important to remember that a new fashion season presents a retailer with an opportunity to freshen its stores with new stock. This maintains the perception of 'newness', as well as providing the retailer with an opportunity to see how early deliveries of the range are selling. Fast-selling styles can then be 'repeat ordered', making the rest of the season more profitable.

However, it is not always possible to sell all the new stock at full price and there are periods within a season where the fashion retailer is 'on mark-down', effectively discounting the stock, just like a sales promotion to clear slow-selling lines.

____

Tip

Seasonality

1 Understand customers' life-style activities
2 Satisfy their fashion clothing and related product needs by occasion
3 Plan for linked occasion products

Market positioning

Why is it important?

Market positioning is an important concept in marketing, as it determines how a product or brand will be seen and understood by its customers compared with competitors. As most successful businesses rely on providing customers with benefits which are perceived to be superior when compared with an alternative, it is critical that fashion retailers have a distinctive market position and maintain it. Failure to do so can result in customers failing to understand what the retailer represents and drifting away to similar but more clearly defined competitors. This is especially true of mass-market 'high street' fashion retailers, which struggle to balance distinctive fashion identity with the need to appeal to the 'fashion majority'.

A distinctive market position is communicated to fashion consumers through the marketing mix. As the end result is a perception held in the mind of consumers, so retailers rely on *distinctive branding* to identify themselves. This is achieved through a variety of promotional activities including advertising, PR, corporate identity and visual merchandising. The latter two reinforce the positioning statement every time customers walk past or into the fashion retailers' shops.

Although the image generated by the combined promotional mix creates a context for customer perceptions, other elements like price and product fundamentally influence fashion retailers' market positioning. For example, a high price tends to position a product or brand 'up-market' in the eyes of customers. A very classic or conservative range of products suggests an older customer profile.

Similarly, the range of products that a fashion retailer carries positions them in a market:

- Bennetton is in the knitted garments and casual wear market and although their customers may be happy to buy a range of associated products e.g. casual/sportswear from them, it is unlikely that their customers would want to buy formal suits from them.
- Equally, New Look has a very defined market for young female customers wishing to buy the latest fashion look at value prices. A move to increase prices or target conservative career customers with quality formal wear would confuse customers' perceptions.
- Laura Ashley is an example of a fashion retailer, which in the early 1990s attempted to move away from its core customer base and win new ones, without significant attention to addressing its image before changing its product offer. Such a change in market position was not sufficiently supported by promotion to update its image and position in the fashion retail market.

Implications for buying

Market positioning, therefore, provides the boundaries of what a target market would expect to buy from a business and provides a good starting point for determining the range of products to be included. Fashion retailers need to be careful that any 'me-too' new products provide relevant value and benefits for their customers. New 'me too' products which do not 'sit' with the rest of the range and do not provide value will be unlikely to sell if the customer can get a better alternative elsewhere.

Significant changes to the product range or its pricing structures – in particular, the range of price points – will have an impact on customer perceptions. In order to justify these changes the fashion retailer must then communicate this *repositioned image* to its customers. Equally significant are the implications of product changes for minimum quantities and product quality.

Fashion retailers who make significant changes to product ranges, whether through design, line extensions, or new products, *without* communicating the fact to customers, risk mark-downs and high terminal stocks on such products.

Fashion retailers should:

- Monitor customers' profiles/changing needs and understand what fashion products they expect
- Not make fundamental changes without effective customer marketing communications
- Remember that brand images are not changed over night
- Track what customers are asking for – both
  - a *What is not in the range and should be*
  - b *What is currently out of stock and shouldn't be*

What is a range?

In fashion retail, a 'range' is an assortment of products, most commonly garments and accessories, which is developed under different categories to sell to customers. Products may be organised according to the size and structure of the business, from fashion boutique to department store, historical trading and current or anticipated trading plans. Arcadia's centralised buying and merchandising structures have changed over recent years, as it has absorbed new businesses like Racing Green and some of the ex-Sears brands into its group. New brands bring new product and range opportunities.

Scope of a range

The principles concerned with range development are explained in detail in Chapter 6. However, there is an important link between market positioning and product range. As customers get to know a fashion retailer over time, so they define the boundaries of its activities and products. Expectations, therefore, exist about the range of products and choice available.

A critical issue in developing a range of products is to balance the *width* and *depth* of the range.

Width

'Range width' refers to how wide a choice of products is to be offered to customers. Some fashion retailers – e.g. Miss Selfridge – began selling clothing and accessories but have widened their product ranges to include jewellery, make up and a whole host of other products reflecting the life-style needs of their customers.

Depth

The 'depth' of a range refers to the choice of styles, colours, sizes and price points available to customers in significant numbers of units within product categories. Customers expect to find new styles of fashion clothing in a variety of colours and their size. Where a fashion retail business is very focused on a niche segment, it can stock in depth with customers accepting its specialised range of products.

Price points

Price points are sometimes referred to as price 'architectures', implying a structure of price points from low to high for the same product category. Mass-market fashion retailers have to allow for the normal distribution of customer needs, which will range from basic market entry-level items to more stylish ones where a premium price can be charged.

It is very important that the fashion retailer decides what kind of price points its market will respond to. Psychological price points ending in 50p, 95p or 99p offer perceived value to some markets. A pair of trousers seems better value if it is priced at £19.95 rather than £20. It is also important, with higher-priced garments, to provide breaks or gaps between different product styles. Sometimes £5 and £10 are used by mass-market fashion retailers as distinguishing breaks. This acknowledges that many customers have a particular price point or zone in mind when they go shopping for a particular item.

A worrying development in 'Rip off Britain', as the media have dubbed it, is the emergence of confused pricing, which in the authors' view is a deliberate policy of 'confusion marketing'. Confusion marketing occurs when the customer is bombarded by so many price offers that they become unable to understand what true value the product represents. Unscrupulous retailers will create an artificial price reduction, having originally offered a product at an unrealistically high price for a limited period and in a restricted number of locations. Customers are becoming wise to this as result of seeing structural price shift downwards in other retail sectors. There appears to be scope for a fundamental price lowering of all clothing products in the UK.

Striking a balance

The difficulty fashion retailers face is where to strike the balance between the width of range they offer and the depth of choice available in their range of products. Additionally, they have to balance the provision of real customer choice with the need to achieve the best return on stock investment.

The starting point for many fashion retailers is *sales history*, as it identifies what customers expect to buy from the business, based on their current and past needs. Sales history may refer to last week's sales, and as such also reflects customers' current-season needs. This is especially relevant for repeat orders. A difficulty facing some buyers is deciding whether or not to continue with products which have sold well in the past but which are becoming 'old fashioned' – e.g. Laura Ashley pinafore daisy print dresses. The problem is balancing the need to move on and be seen as fashionable, or at least not unfashionable, with the need to retain best sellers and core customers.

A clear and up-to-date statement of the retailer's market position and target customer, based on continuous research, will give the buyer confidence to be ruthlessly pragmatic over what to include and what not to keep in a range. Many retailers fail to rationalise ranges effectively, seeking instead to blame the vagaries of fashion for poor sales.

Product options

Fashion retailers plan new season ranges around the financial investment allocated across the business. The budget is usually allocated at division (women's wear, men's wear), department (blouses) and product category (short/long sleeve) levels. At product level, designers, buyers and merchandisers make decisions about styles and colours. Styles are represented by variations in silhouette, fabric and print design. Product designs initially begin life as two-dimensional black and white outlines with some distinguishing detail. Some examples are shown in Figure 4.1.

These outline drawings form the basis of the products, which will be organised in groups when decisions about colour and fabric are made. As these individual designs will need to end up as part of a coordinated collection, the range is broken down into easy-to-manage and meaningful groups or stories. These groups will reflect the need for a balance of core and fashion styles and the

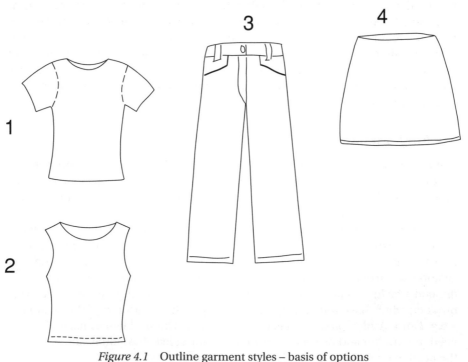

Figure 4.1 Outline garment styles – basis of options

appropriate user occasions planned for the season. Fashion stories can be built around a combination of colour, style, fabric or print themes.

In order to develop a range of products from such basic designs, variations in fabric and colour are used to create design 'options', frequently using the same product shape. A fashion product option therefore is one product style in one fabric or one colour-way.

Typical options

EXAMPLE

Lamb's wool sweater, styles 1a and 1b

Style 1a	V-neck	red	1 option
Style 1a	V-neck	blue, black, cream	3 options
Style 1b	Crew-neck	red, blue, black, cream	4 options

Wool/Acrylic mix sweater, styles 2a and 2b

| Style 2a | V-neck | black, red, cream | 3 options |
| Style 2b | Crewneck | black, red, cream | 3 options |

Options form the basis of merchandise range planning, as they can provide a visual representation of every product line and colour to be included in the range. It is important to stress at this stage that an option is *not a unit of stock*, unless the business is providing one-off exclusive items in a very exclusive luxury market. Numbers of product units are assigned to options according to the expected sales of a particular fabric or colour option and the selling prices. For example, more units will be allocated to a core colour option, like white, in a summer collection than a fashion colour like yellow.

Options are important when planning a range, as they provide a degree of control over the numbers of lines planned by the buyer, and help visualise the coordination of the range when juggling large numbers of potential product designs in different colours and fabrics. A balance needs to be struck between the choice of styles and colours to provide the right fashion offer with the number of units allocated to the various core and riskier fashion styles. It is not uncommon for some fashion retailers to have 50 per cent of sales coming from 10 per cent of their options which are Key Value Items (KVIs) and stocked in depth.

Table 4.8 illustrates the breakdown of colour across the tailoring product area of a leading women's wear retail brand. The table indicates the significant difference in sales achieved by the core colours compared with fashion colours and the higher percentage level of mark-down attracted by fashion colours. To a large extent this reflects the conservative nature of tailoring products, which tend to be dominated by more formal garments.

Coordination

Some products are flexible enough to coordinate both within a specific group and across other product groups. For example, a key value item (KVI) like a basic pedal pusher pant can work well across a number of product groups organised

Table 4.8 Colour performance in the tailoring of a leading fashion retailer

Colour breakdown Women's tailoring	Sales (%)	Mark-down (%)
Black	25	13
Silver	20	32
Neutrals	10	34
White	14	26
Navy	15	23
Core colours	**84**	**(Weighted averages) 24.00**
Indigo	5	51
Khaki	1	20
Sage	2	48
Aqua	1	24
Fashion greens/blues	**9**	**(Weighted averages) 44.00**
Lilac	1	44
Red	1	22
Rose	1	36
Fashion reds/purples	**3**	**(Weighted averages) 34.00**
Gold	1	31
Chocolate	1	79
Orange	1	56
Sunflower	1	30
Other fashion	**4**	**(Weighted averages) 50.50**
Total dept.	**100.0**	**(Weighted averages) 27.16**

by different fabrics and colours. This creates more potential sales, as customers are able to mix and match products, with the same fabrics and colours, but with different shapes or print designs.

A successful skirt style may have a shape which will last for three or four seasons before the garment looks unfashionable, but the fabric and colour-ways will change for each season as the garment is made to look 'new'.

Strategic development

The development of a range of products for a new season raises important strategic issues for fashion retailers about new products and markets. In any season there is always a balance struck between up-dated basics, that will be repeated in some form, and completely new fashion products. In addition there are often stores opening in new locations which sometimes represent new markets (e.g. overseas store openings). The problem of balancing the portfolio of new and existing products with existing and potentially new customers needs buyers and merchandisers to consider some basic strategic options. A useful tool from marketing theory is the Ansoff product–market matrix shown in Figure 4.2. This planning tool helps distinguish the basic alternatives for increasing sales by manipulating product and market opportunities. It works well for the fashion industry, where products are ever-changing and new markets continually developing.

	Current product	**New product**
Current market	Market penetration	Product development
New market	Market development	Diversification

Figure 4.2 Ansoff's product–market matrix

Table 4.9 Strategic alternatives

	Strategic option	Example
1	Market penetration	Selling more of the same garment option
2	Market development	Selling the same products abroad
3	Product development	Widening the range into complementary products
4	Diversification	Moves into new business areas

Buyers and merchandisers should recognise the strategic alternatives indicated by the Ansoff Matrix,[2] and the differing implications of each to developing product ranges in a season (see Table 4.9).

Essentially these alternatives represent different methods of increasing sales. Market penetration is a strategy for increasing sales of the same product to the same market, while market development and product development increase sales through changing markets and products. Diversification is a strategy of increasing sales through entering new markets with new products in a way that could be either related or unrelated to the existing business activities. There is an increased risk of failure with a strategy of diversification than market penetration, as both products and markets are new and not fully tried and tested. However, no business can remain the same for long and it is usual for fashion retailers to be looking at both new markets and products while extending sales of their current offer.

Danger exists where a fashion retailer develops a range within a season which may be a move away from a successful core strength, through following a design philosophy which would appear to be a natural extension of the current offer. However by doing this the retailer may be attracting new competition through trading in new unproven products.

This type of fundamental range repositioning can work if properly planned and implemented using a new marketing mix, although failure to do so is very likely to result in large mark-downs as customers stick with the original better-known competitive products.

Notes

1 Rogers, E.M. (1983), Diffusion of Innovations, The Free Press, 3rd edition.
2 Ansoff, H.I. (1968), *Corporate Strategy*, Penguin.

■ ⊻ **5** Buying and the law

Throughout the European Union (EU) there is still a great way to go with legal harmonisation among member countries. The European fashion industry spans a wide variety of business activities, which come under many different legal and statutory instruments in individual countries. In the United Kingdom, for example, marketing promotional activity, including advertising, sales promotion, public relations and personal selling, are covered by no less than 150 Acts of Parliament and Statutory instruments, quite apart from case law. However, the main Acts that relate to the retailing of fashion garments in the United Kingdom include these listed in Table 5.1.

On a national level, The Office of Fair Trading (OFT) acts as an arm of government as the nation's guardian of the many activities related to buying and selling in the consumer market place. In general, the buyer and merchandiser will not be held directly accountable for the correct and proper implementation of many of these areas.

Table 5.1   Retailing – UK law

Date	Act
1968, 1972	Trade Descriptions Act
1973	Supply of Goods (Implied Terms Act)
1974	Prices Act
1979	Sale of Goods Act (Updated 1893 Act)
1986	Textile Products (Indications of Fibre Contents) Regulations
1987	Consumer Protection Act 1987

Contracts with suppliers

A contract with a supplier is commonly referred to as an 'order'. It is this document which details the terms through which a fashion retailer obtains ownership of goods for sale in exchange for payment of an agreed amount of money. In most circumstances, the order represents the final agreement over the price to be paid for the various goods bought. It is important to remember though, that this may not always be exactly the same as the initial price agreed during earlier negotiations as changes to quantities, trimmings and other variables may have been required which affect the cost price.

Table 5.2   The main elements of the fashion buying order form

- Date order was raised
- Description of garment + supplier's unique reference number or name
- Detailed fabric composition/print + supplier's unique cloth number or name
- Details of all trimmings
- The relevant buying department number
- The retailer's unique order number
- Quantity ordered – in singles, tens, dozen or other normal buying quantity
- Colours and sizes detailed in correct ratios
- Details of sample submission and approval
- Agreed cost price – *less* any negotiated discounts
- Proposed despatch and delivery dates into the distribution centre (DC) + details of DC location and special delivery booking instructions
- Any special packing or delivery instructions – e.g. hangers, covers, boxes, etc.
- Labelling instructions including brand, fibre composition and computer stock control tags – location point on garment is key
- Signature(s) of authorisation to buy
- Any special terms and conditions of trade

The importance of the order form

The *order form* is probably one of the most important documents in the entire buying and merchandising process as it represents a complete record of the various order components. Originally, prior to the wide availability of computers, orders were handwritten, often with many duplicate copies. Even today at the garment and fabric shows smaller fashion retailers still handwrite orders on the exhibition stands. Despite the most sophisticated computer ordering systems, many buyers will also write out draft orders by hand, usually onto a preformatted basic order form.

These draft orders enable the buyer to keep an immediate written note of what has been agreed. When ordering small quantities of samples or other complex parts of a wide range, there is nothing as useful as a written record of what was agreed. Usually the buyer will bring the pro forma or draft order back to the main buying office to be fully completed with any missing information, prior to it being put forward for management agreement and manual input into the computer system. It is usually one of the merchandising assistants who will input the data into the computer system, although this can vary with the organisation.

The order form acts as the main *reference document for a product*, from the time that the order is written, authorised and put into the computer system, until the day that the garment has hopefully sold out. It acts as the contract and is the main source of information about the purchase of products, recording details of the various order components as listed in Table 5.2. It is critical for buyers and suppliers to be absolutely clear about exactly what is to be included in the agreed cost price and as such the order contains a wide range of cost-related information.

Retail selling price and overall percentage profit is shown on all *internal* copies of the order, but these are usually excluded from the supplier's copy. Selling price and thus profit margin details are traditionally kept secret from the supplier to avoid details of future retail price points inadvertently or deliberately being passed to competitive retailers. However, greater openness now exists between many fashion retailers and their core suppliers as the benefits to be gained from supply chain partnerships require the sharing of information. Figure 5.1 is an example of a typical order form.

The order document therefore acts as the fundamental information source for many of the fashion retailer's data bases. As is shown in Table 5.3, each different part of the business will have an interest in the details contained in it.

In many fast-moving fashion businesses, particularly those where buyers are placing high numbers of small and complex orders, good administration is essential at all times. All buyers need to be certain that their orders are 'on the system', thus ensuring that they do not lose track of how much money or 'open to buy' has been spent.

When is an order not an order?

Sometimes buyers are empowered to buy on the spot if a good deal is to be had. While unusual, in this instance the significance of getting the order back to the office and on to the main frame computer is even more pressing. Sometimes buyers are issued with laptop computers that enable them at any point of the day to transmit back to the merchandising team at head office, exactly what and how much they have bought. In turn, they will be fed back quick summary information of total size and colour analysis to guide them with future purchases.

Often a buyer may have to make what is termed as a 'grey' or 'provisional' commitment with a supplier. This very often happens on foreign buying trips when the buyer may be working alone, away from her merchandiser and manager. In essence this can be described as 'gentleman's agreement', although under English law a verbal agreement is as binding as a written one.

The buyer will often need to make such verbal agreements, in order to secure fabric or production that might not be available later, were the buyer to go back home to get agreement. Experienced buyers will be allowed to do this as a matter of course, although more junior buyers may not. It very much depends on the organisation in question. Although the order form is the formal contract for most retailers, it does not mean that other forms of communication are not legally binding: faxed confirmations of telephone orders that are signed and dated by the various authorised parties, for instance, are legally binding.

Where a buyer is putting down provisional orders, it is also important for her and the business to be *tracking the total value* all the time. Again many buyers will have laptops and modems to undertake this task as they travel about.

OFFICIAL ORDER UK

SUPPLIER:	BUYER	DATE	ORDER NO.	10027	6654
HORROCKS FASHION	MERCHANDISER		TOTAL QUANTITY	3000	
1A WISTERIA ROAD	HEAD OF BUYING		ORDER DATE	02/09/00	
LONDON	DIRECTOR		SUPPLIER CODE	600513 VI	
W1N 6AA			DEPARTMENT NO.24		
			TYPE	CASUALS	

									GARMENT SIZES			
IN WARE-HOUSE DELIVERY DATE(S)	CLOTH NO.	SUPPLIER REF/LINE DESCRIPTION	COLOUR	LINE NO.	SEASON	UNIT COST PRICE	LINE QUANTITY	FIT TOTAL	SML	MED	LRG	XLRG
A 30/10/00			BLACK	22500871	51	10.20	1500	1500	195	600	480	225
B 30/10/00			NAVY	22500972	51	10.20	1500	1500	195	600	480	225

GARMENT/MERCHANDISE SPEC
LONG SLEEVE SILK SHIRT
TWIN NEEDLE ALL OVER
2 PATCH POCKETS WITH FLAP

PACKING FLAT PACK
SOLID SIZE
SOLID COLOUR
TO BE PACKED IN ONES

PACKING INSTRUCTIONS
L/12 BOX END LABEL
BG1 CARTON

FIBRE/CLOTH COMPOSITION
A – 100% SILK
B – 100% SILK

GARMENT/MERCHADISE DESCRIPTION
BLACK SANDWASH SILK
NAVY SANDWASH SILK

DESIGNATED MANUFACTURE

BULK DELIVERY TO:
OUR FLAT/HANGING WAREHOUSE CONFORM
ADDRESS:
1A FONTAINE ROAD
PETERBOROUGH
PE8 7QU

LABELLING/PRESENTATION
ALL LABELLING MUST
TO THE BUYER'S
SPECIFICATION AND
INCLUDE: COMPULSORY
LABELS SHOWING:
(A) COMPOSITION
(B) COUNTRY/ORIGIN
(C) CARE
(E) GARMENT CODE
(F) SUPPLIER NO.

COST PRICE INCLUDES:
BUYING COMMISSION
COST OF EXPORT QUOTA.
PACKING AND LABELLING SPECIFIED
AFFIXING COMPUTER TAGS
OTHER (SPECIFY):
DELIVERY INTO UK WAREHOUSE

SAMPLE SUBMISSION/APPROVAL
ORDER SUBJECT TO APPROVAL OF
FINAL SAMPLES

Figure 5.1   A typical order form

Table 5.3 The order form and its significance to other operational functions

• **Distribution centre (DC)**	Needs size of delivery and proposed delivery date to ensure that there are adequate *sorting, picking and transport resources available* at any point to get it speedily into the shops
• **Finance department**	Needs details of cost price and proposed selling price to ensure that *cash flow is there to pay for the stock*. Also needs details of proposed selling price to record *gross or buying margin*. All orders are added together as they are put onto the finance system to enable the business to judge its overall buying in margin or profit. This is sometimes called the 'in margin' or 'rolling margin', and should be distinguished from the net margin which represents the final profit after main-downs.
• **IT department**	Issues *unique order number* as the order is raised and links the unique style or line number with the unique order number. IT department will also produce computer swing tickets or labels, showing line number, colour, size and price. These will be sent separately to the manufacturer just prior to garment production
• **Technology department**	Needs to be certain that *samples have been authorised and have arrived*. Keeps them up to date as to what the buyer has been buying. Enables them to have enough checking and testing resources during the manufacturing period, as well knowing when the bulk delivery will need to be checked
• **Marketing department**	Needs to know what lines are coming in when to ensure that all *promotional materials* are ready for lines that are being specially promoted
• **Buying and merchandising team**	Basic information provided, usually via on-screen interrogation to be used at any time to check, follow through, monitor and make decisions about any specific *line or supplier problem*

Signing orders

Both the buyer and merchandiser sign the orders, ensuring that the company has an accurate record of the cost of the products it is buying. The head of buying and the buying director usually countersign orders. Countersigning is important as it reduces the possibility of fraud: it has been known for unscrupulous buyers to sign an order and declare a favourable cost price to their company while actually paying a higher one to a supplier in exchange for personal gain. Without effective countersigning and order systems in place, inflated invoices based on inaccurate orders could be submitted by suppliers and paid by an unwitting finance department.

Although it is usual for an order to need approval by senior management, as described above, some buyers do have authority to make on-the-spot buys. In general, because of the high values at stake, larger organisations will often require the signature of three people before it is sent to the supplier: usually the buyer, merchandiser and buying manager/director are signatories.

The need for several signatures to provide authorisation ensures that all key players are in agreement as to what is going on at all times in terms of what products are being committed. It also acts as a check and balance against any unusual/illegal buying practice. Most businesses will have regular order signing sessions at which the authorised signatories will be present to discuss the direction and level of the buying.

Copyright

Significant for the fashion business are the laws relating to the *copyright of design*. In today's increasingly international business environment, garment designs and ideas travel around the world at breathtaking speed. Most fashion buyers automatically undertake regular international competitive shopping trips. It is usual practice for them to purchase 'development' samples with the aim of developing the garment in some different way for their own business. Straight 'knocking off' or copying can land a buyer in tremendous legal difficulty, especially if they get involved with large global brand companies, who are prepared to go to international law to protect their garment design or any other unique design aspect of their trading operation.

It is very tempting to buy a garment and have it copied at cheaper price in a low-cost country. It would be impossible for every garment to be completely new and unique, although British law is becoming much more precise as to what can and cannot be copied. There have been several well documented cases in the United Kingdom, where large high street retailers have been taken to court by smaller more exclusive designers and manufacturer who claim that their ideas have been directly copied.

Copyrighting and *patenting* are legal ways of registering a design or an idea or invention. Again the way in which different countries undertake and structure this aspect of commercial life varies dramatically across Europe. To make it easier – and, more importantly, cheaper – to protect a garment design, the *Design Registration Scheme* now makes it possible for even the smallest designers to protect themselves.

A surface design, such as a printed pattern on a garment, can be protected as a *registered design* if it is considered to have some originality or novelty and is of some aesthetic value. However, a basic design of a dress that is defined by its shape rather than its surface detail could not be protected under copyright. A designer could claim infringement if another design had a sufficient number of attributes that were considered to be of objective similarity to their original design. The problem facing many fashion designers, though, is that it is difficult to prove that a design has novelty in the first place. Additionally, as fashion seasons are so short it is frequently not worthwhile protecting a design that will be of interest for only a limited period. Where infringement of copyright is proved then the originator may be able to claim towards the profits lost as a result of sales of the duplicate merchandise. Equally, the merchandise that is considered to be copied could be removed from sale or destroyed.

Pricing

The Consumer Protection Act makes it illegal for businesses to mislead consumers over the price of goods they are selling. This is an especially important issue in today's heavily promotion-driven retail culture, in which many fashion retailers offer regular price reductions in order to tempt consumers into buying. As we have already seen, the frequency with which some fashion retailers undertake price reductions inevitably prompts suspicions about the true value of the products being sold and reflects a growing trend in 'confusion marketing'. However, frequent price reductions in themselves are not illegal no matter how confusing they may appear to consumers.

Price reductions

Where a selling price is reduced the law requires the retailer to indicate the previous, higher price next to it so that the consumer can make a clear judgement about the value of the reduction. The previous price must be the *last price at which the merchandise was available in the previous six months*. In order to combat a 'false' reduction from an artificial selling price – in other words, one that is overinflated for a short period to exaggerate a reduction – the merchandise should have been available at the previous price for twenty-eight consecutive days in the previous six months. In this way, unscrupulous retailers should be deterred from 'inventing' selling prices which were never realistic but which look tremendous value, when marked-down to a competitive selling price. The law stops retailers creating artificial perceptions of value.

Clearly there are situations when retailers need to make a series of reductions to the selling price, typically in the bi-annual sales where 'sale trading' continues for a month, and it is not possible or reasonable for each change in price to have been on display for twenty-eight days. In this case, the highest price, from which the reduction is made, is the one that must be shown for twenty-eight days previously.

Another feature of sale trading is the use of more general references to price reductions like 'up to 50 per cent off' all merchandise in store. This of course does not mean that every item in the store is reduced by up to 50 per cent, but it is a very powerful statement and can be misleading if only a very few items are reduced in price. As such the law requires at *least 10 per cent* of the merchandise on offer to be reduced by this amount.

The price as an 'offer'

When the price of merchandise is on display in a store it is usual for the consumer simply to approach the retailer and pay the amount stated on the price ticket. However, the legal interpretation of this situation is that the customer is *making an offer to the retailer*, guided by the retail price, and not the other way around. This seems strange and has obvious implications for incorrect ticketing. If an expensive item is mistakenly showing a wrong price ticket, which is significantly lower than the intended price, the retailer is not obliged to sell the item.

Labelling

There are many labels which go into an item of clothing, ranging from the brand's own logo through to the care label. However, some have more legal significance than others and in some circumstances, the omission of a label by a supplier can necessitate a new delivery of stock being sent away from a distribution centre to have the labels put in. This is clearly a costly mistake for a buyer to make. The specific labels that the law actually requires a retailer to include will vary from garment to garment according to a variety of factors including country of origin and flammability of the fabric.

Fibre composition

All garments must carry a label indicating the *fibre composition* of the garment. The label must identify the relative percentage weights of each fibre compared with the total weight of the garment, within a 'tolerance' of plus or minus 3 per cent. For example, a garment may be composed of 90 per cent cotton and 10 per cent elastane. Where a garment carries a label stating that it is made up of one fibre – for example, 100 per cent cotton – it is important for the customer to realise that this does not necessarily apply to the stitching. Fibres that are intended for decoration and are visible do not have to be included on the fibre composition label so long as they do not exceed 7 per cent of the weight of the product. Customers may find that dying a 100 per cent cotton garment a different colour does not create the intended effect if the nylon stitching remains unaffected by the dye. However, a main lining of a garment must be 100 per cent accurate.

Labels detailing the fibre content must refer to the *generic fibre name*. Trade marks and brand names are also allowed but they must be accompanied by the generic name and not used alone. Examples of generic names with their more commonly known brand names are listed in Table 5.4.

Woollen products often carry the 'Woolmark' label as an indication of quality. If buyers want their woollen products to carry the 'Woolmark' trademark they must conform to the International Wool Secretariat (IWS) requirements. Garments

Table 5.4	Fibre types

Brand name	Generic name
Lycra	Elastane
Spandex	Elastane
Rayon	Viscose
Tactel	Nylon or polyamide
Tencel	Lyocell

may carry the label only if the manufacturer of the garment holds an IWS licence and has manufactured the whole product. 'Woolmark' labels are neutral in colour and are obtained from named sources. This is an extra consideration for a buyer when organising the different labels needed in a particular garment.

Care labels

It is not a legal requirement to put a textile care label into a garment, although it is clearly in the interest of the retailer to do so as damage incurred by the consumer through incorrect washing could leave the retailer liable for compensation. Where a care label is included in a garment, the Trade Descriptions Act requires the information to be *accurate*. In such cases the care label should give consumers accurate instructions on the most appropriate method of cleaning and caring for the garment. However if the garment requires careful washing, as opposed to machine washing, it is important for the retailer to state the fact clearly.

Country of origin

Most garments have the 'country of origin' printed on a label in the garment. It is important for fashion retailers to be clear about the origin of the garment they are buying on the order form, for quota purposes, as each overseas supplier will have to ensure that they have appropriate quota to export to the United Kingdom. A general principle is that the origin of a garment will be deemed to be that where it underwent its *last 'principal process' or significant stage of production*. The 'principal process' acknowledges the fact that a garment may be formed through a series of processes which could be carried out in different countries. An item of knitwear could have its panels knitted in Taiwan with all other production processes occurring in Hong Kong. As other production processes would be substantial, including linking panels into the shape of a garment, attaching collars cuffs and buttons, washing, pressing and packing the finished garment, then the country of origin would be deemed to be Hong Kong. In other words the Hong Kong quota would apply to that knitted garment.

Country of origin is not solely a business-to-business issue relating to importing merchandise. Under the Trade Descriptions Act the 'Marking Order' requires retailers to identify the country of origin of a product in specific circumstances: it requires the country of origin to be identified if the merchandise is presented in such a way that the customer might believe it was made somewhere other than that where it was actually manufactured. An example of this would be a cap carrying the words 'New York' as a central design feature. If the cap were made anywhere other than the United States it would need a label indicating *where it was actually made*. If the item were made in the United States it would not need a country of origin label. Once again, the intention is to stop consumers from being misled.

Fitness for purpose and satisfactory quality

Under the Sale of Goods Act, when a consumer buys a product there is a legal obligation upon the seller of the product to ensure that it is both 'fit' for its intended purpose and of 'satisfactory quality'. For example, an item of swimwear that develops a colour problem on being exposed to chlorinated water in a swimming pool would not be fit for its intended purpose. It is essential therefore that all garments with advertised performance features do in fact live up to their description. As such, buyers need to be aware of the legal implications of wording on *promotional swing tags* attached to garments. The words 'waterproof' should be used to describe a garment only if it is an accurate description of the garment's ability to keep the person dry. The process of 'proofing' fabric to a level where there will be absolutely no ingress of moisture is a tough technical problem. Some fabrics such as Gore-Tex can do this. However, most garments are not in fact waterproof and so use the term 'shower proof', in the knowledge that the customer may become wet in sustained rainy conditions.

'Satisfactory quality' is an amendment to the original term 'merchantable quality'. It means that merchandise must be of a quality or standard that *any reasonable person would consider satisfactory*, given certain facts such as normal use, description and price. Yet again the interpretation is based on what is reasonable in the circumstances. For example, if a pair of trousers costing £5 showed signs of wear after a six months of regular use, it would be harder to argue that they were not of satisfactory quality than a different pair that cost £50.

Refunds

Where a customer has a legitimate complaint against a retailer because a product is defective, they may be entitled to a complete refund and even additional compensation where the fault causes damage to other items. Where a product is defective and the customer can prove that they bought it, then they are entitled to a *complete refund*; the customer does not have to accept a credit note in place of a full refund. The fact is that many fashion retail brands offer their customers more than their legal rights as a means of fostering goodwill and developing their brand values. It is common for many fashion retailers to provide customers with a refund even when there is nothing unsatisfactory or defective about the goods.

When there are returns which are caused by defective merchandise, the retailer can make a claim against the supplier.

In most large fashion retailing organisations, there is usually an in-house legal advisor, specialising in related consumer law. It is dangerous for the lay person to try and make decisions relating to complex legal issues: if in doubt, consult a legal expert is the advice every time.

■ ⍌ 6 Merchandise planning

The importance of planning

This chapter examines the way in which the flow of fashion merchandise is planned and managed from the supplier to the distribution centre (DC), historically known as the 'central warehouse'. In all types of business, it is usual to measure performance against a set of pre-determined criteria. Fashion retailing is no exception, hence the need to create *numerical plans* against which to measure total business performance.

Unlike many other retail commodities, fashion garments have an extremely varied and changeable sales pattern which varies as a result of fashion fads and weather conditions. The issue of seasonality has already been fully discussed in Chapter 4. Different user occasions also add to the complexity of fashion demand. Added to this are the complex problems of continuously changing colours and styles, so typical of fashion. Other retailers, such as those in the food business, do not experience such highly exaggerated cycles and fads, enjoying much more continuous and stable product sales patterns than are found within fashion. Women's and children's fashion are generally more prone to fashion change than men's wear, thus making the merchandise planning of women's wear one of the most difficult within retailing.

Retail fashion merchandise planning is mainly concerned with the numerical control and management of the range from initial conception to delivery to the shop. Modern retail merchandising is a highly complex activity, requiring highly developed numeric and analytical skills. The advent of modern technology has enabled the merchandiser to undertake far greater levels of detailed analysis than ever before, assisting the merchandiser to 'de-risk' the business. De-risking the business is about ensuring that the business has as much good selling and as little poor selling stock as possible. As with any investment, it is important that fashion stock should be as saleable as possible: the balance between producing a highly risky range against one that is classic and conventional depends entirely upon the market segment being targeted.

Planning and profitability

It is vital to note that one of the most important goals in successful merchandising is to assist the process of achieving the *planned level of buying profitability*. 'Buying profit' can be defined as the difference between the cost price paid for the garment and the retail selling price in the shop. The mark-up or profit made between the two prices can be explained by the following margin and selling price equation:

Margin and selling price equations:

Retail selling price (RSP) – Cost price (CP) = Gross margin (or Gross profit)

EXAMPLE

A style of ladies' coats, £117.50 (RSP) – £30 (CP) = £87.50 (GM)

Gross margin (GM) is usually expressed as a percentage $= \dfrac{\text{Profit}}{\text{Retail selling price}} \times 100$

The percentage gross margin is therefore $= \dfrac{£87.50}{£117.50} \times 100 = 74.5\%$

As is seen in this example, the difference between the cost and selling price is very high. It is often hard for the general public to understand why fashion retailing is not a more profitable business, especially when they see retail prices nearly four times higher than the buying cost price. What is not immediately clear, is that to run a fashion business, there are many other costs that need to be taken from the buying margin to arrive at what is known as the 'net margin'. For example, rents, rates, salaries, heating lighting and stolen stock are just some of many expenses that are necessary to run the modern fashion retail store. In general, it is normal for most European fashion retailers to make final net profit percentages that are only in single figures at the end of each year: usually somewhere between 5 per cent and 9 per cent of total sales. It is also important to realise that complete sell-out of a line in fashion retailing is also unlikely; usually an average of 85 per cent of a line is sold at full price, the remaining quantity generally needing some form of price reduction or mark-down to help sell out the balance. There are, of course, some exceptions to the rule, when every last item sells out.

The management of these other major expenses is outside of the buyer's and merchandiser's direct control, as well as the content of this chapter. Nevertheless, it is important for the reader to be clear on the fundamental difference between buying margin and the overall net profitability of the entire business. Again it is important to remind the reader that the costs of running a fashion business have to be deducted from the 'profit' produced between buying and selling the garments, before we arrive at the final or net profitability of the business.

The problems of planning in detail

Any fashion range is made up of a multitude of styles. Some styles may be part of a coordinated range of garments, which naturally are displayed and sold together, while a majority are sold as individual garments. Planning at individual garment level is called 'line-level planning'. Some retailers call it style-, rather than line-level planning.

However, most retailers tend to group like garments within similar merchandise groups or categories for the purposes of planning. For example, all styles of skirts would be added together to create an overall 'skirt category'. This would enable both the buying team and senior management to examine the weekly and seasonal sales performance of skirts as an overall figure, rather than having to add together, say, several hundred individual lines each week. This allows a high level overview of how skirts as a whole are performing at a glance.

Unfortunately, while individual line-level or style-level sales information is good for reviewing individual line performance, and while a consolidated skirt category sales information is good for examining the overall performance, both sets of information do not allow us to track and examine performance at *skirt sub-category level*. For example, during any one season, we may want to divide skirts into plain and printed fabrics, or possibly into short, midi and long lengths. These would be described as 'sub-categories' of skirts. It would be vital for the buying and merchandising team to be aware of possible changes of demand at sub-category level. Naming and changing the name of sub-categories is a continuous process: in general, if the sub-category name, e.g. mini-skirt, is being used by the customer, then it will certainly be logical to apply it to a new sub-category. Having more detailed sub-category information will help in planning forward buying.

In general fashion retailers plan at the five levels shown in Table 6.1. Fashion retailers plan their categories and departments differently to suit their business, although similar definitions are widely accepted. Departments and categories change over time, as styles and fashions evolve. For example, sports wear is now a category in its own right, as sports wear garments have grown in sales importance and are now standard garments of the modern fashion wardrobe. As fashion trends alter, buyers and merchandisers automatically revisit the categories to ensure that they are able to manage the business as effectively as possible each season. Very often new fashion trends change the usage and definition of historic categories – for example, certain styles and brands of sports wear are now redefined as club wear.

Table 6.1   Fashion retail planning levels

Planning level	Description
Line or style level	By individual garment – all sizes and colour options
Sub-category	A logical grouping – e.g. long skirts
Category	A consolidation of all sub-categories – e.g. skirts
Department	A grouping of related categories – e.g. shorts, trousers, jeans and skirts might simply be described as 'bottoms'
Business	All ladies' departments and all men's departments = TOTAL BUSINESS

The importance of the merchandiser in planning

The merchandiser plays a key role in working with the buyer to achieve the right balance of products within the season's range, by using a balance of previous sales history combined with forward sales/trend predictions. Merchandise planning is a demanding task, requiring logic and intuition to ensure that the business carries the right product range at any point in time. Simply being good at numbers is not enough; the best merchandisers have very developed analytical, estimating and forecasting skills, which enable them to see both large (macro) and small (micro) trends as they occur throughout the trading year. Simply spotting the trends is not enough, the merchandiser must then react, recommend, and make changes, which then have to be clearly and concisely implemented and acted upon.

Starting the planning process for a season

It was explained in Chapter 3 that fashion style trend reviews begin many months in advance of a season. However, the overall merchandise planning process is generally started between six months to one year ahead of the start of the season in question. Starting the planning process too far in advance can be dangerous as it can fail to pick up more recently emerging style trends – for example, certain colours or types of print can change in importance, the closer it gets to the trading season in question. Older, more classic fashion retail businesses, tend to start the planning process further ahead than do younger fashion businesses. Where a business is targeted at the younger more volatile fashion end of the market, it will tend to try and leave decision-making until the last possible minute, which of course has implications upon product sourcing: home-produced merchandise is usually on a shorter lead-time than foreign manufactured garments.

The merchandiser and buyer generally start the sales planning process in conjunction with the Buying Director or Buying Manager at a preliminary seasonal planning meeting well in advance of the season. At this meeting, it is normal for the entire team to examine the historic performance of the previous equivalent season, in order to identify *key trends* that impacted on final profitability. For example, they will look for emerging garment types and or styles that sold strongly in previous seasons, which are likely to sell more strongly in the future. Usually at the end of the previous season, the buying and merchandising team will have undertaken what is known as a 'season's post-mortem'. This is a useful document for planning the future fashion direction of a fashion business and is helpful during the planning of a new season.

Tip

- When starting planning a new season, start by looking back at *what happened last year*, and why
- Always write up a season's *postmortem trading report* at the end of the season: it is very useful to help next year's planning

Authors' special note on fashion meetings

Although somewhat outside of the direct context of this book, the authors thought it important to comment here about the way in which meetings in the fashion industry should be conducted. Much time can be wasted in fashion buying and merchandising meetings unless the following key points are followed:

- Always have a *clear agenda*, with clear aims and objectives – never have a meeting for its own sake
- Always have *the right number of people* at a meeting – usually any more than six–eight people makes it difficult to get through the agenda
- Always have a meeting with a *clear leader or chair person* – some people in the fashion industry like the sound of their own voice, which can exclude others
- Always start meetings *on time and have a clear time limit* – it is simply bad business manners to waste other people's time
- Always have *written minutes with action points* at meetings – without these as an aide memoire, even the best staff often forget what they were supposed to do.

In reality, these tips apply to a majority of business meetings, but in the fast-moving and sometimes apparently chaotic world of fashion, there is a special need to hold only *efficient* and *effective* meetings.

The importance of historic sales patterns

The post mortem meeting will have clearly picked out both the best and worst sellers from a previous season's buying. Usually, the post mortem is written into a report format, in order to ensure that the 'lessons learned' are clearly locked into corporate memory. With large and fast-changing buying teams, it is vital to keep a clear historic record of what happened in the past. A fashion business must not repeat historic buying failures, although a successful history is no guarantee of future success in the fickle world of fashion.

The human mind often blocks out and forgets the bad; with the post mortem, this cannot happen. While it is important to look back for guidance to the future, merchandise planning using 'retrospectoscopy' (basing decisions only upon past known events), often leads to a dull repeat of old formulas. Producing the same range every year can be a dangerous approach to fashion, where change is the life-blood of creativity and excitement. There are many examples of failed and failing fashion retail businesses that have not moved their product ranges on, but simply kept trying to repeat successes of the past. This is a dangerous fashion business strategy and philosophy.

After the 'post mortem' review, the buying and merchandising team will try and fix some of the *key sales ratios* upon which the future planning process will be based. For example, they will start first with an *overall level of sales* that needs to be achieved. This can either be expressed as a simple percentage lift on the previous season's sales, or possibly as an absolute sales number.

In general, the overall level of planned sales is often dictated to the buying team from a higher-level board decision. This in turn is often influenced by the City and/or shareholder's expectations. When proposed sales target figures come downward from a higher level in the organisation, this is referred to as 'top-down planning'. This can be a dangerous way to plan in fashion retailing, in view of the fact that any fashion business is made up of a multitude of changing elements – changing styles, garment types, colours and fabrics, etc. While top-down planning is important, it is vital for the buyer and merchandiser to build the next season's merchandise plan from a 'bottom-up' perspective as well. This has the distinct advantage of ensuring that the overall sales plan can be achieved as a result of the smaller constituent parts of the plan combining. It is common for most fashion retailers to undertake the merchandise planning process using a combination of both top-down and bottom-up planning, trying to arrive at compromise that satisfies the planning objectives of both the buying and merchandising team, as well as those of senior management. In general, merchandise planning is normally a *compromise*.

Creating the initial seasonal sales plan

Once all the teams have been individually consulted, an overall initial sales plan (Table 6.2) will start to emerge.

The importance of growth and Like for Like (LFL) growth

For all flourishing fashion businesses, it is important to assume that growth is an essential ingredient. Without growth no business can go forward and better

Table 6.2 Initial sales plan – Season A/W (£000)

Department	Act. sales LY	Plan sales TY	% +/– VLY	Rationale
Dresses	100	120	+20	Emergence of strong trend in Paris
Blouses	180	60	–67	General long-term decline
Skirts	300	400	+33.3	Strong skirt fashion forecast
Trousers	200	220	+10.0	Better cut this year
Underwear	60	50	–16.7	Deliberate reduction – high markdowns LY
Swimwear	40	45	+12.5	New Fabric improvement
Casual tops	120	155	+29.2	Buyer's new styling gives dual use garments
Grand total	1000	1050	+5	Overall cautious growth – tough trading ahead

Note: LY = Last year; TY = This year; V-variance.

itself and the lot of its employees. Growth is a clear signal of success, although sales growth without profit growth can be a danger signal indicating that the business is chasing sales turnover and losing site of the need for profit. Sales growth is often referred to as Like-for-Like (LFL) growth on buying and merchandising management control documents. LFL is a way of showing *true growth within the business*. For example, adding 10 per cent in the number of branches trading will generally have the effect of increasing turnover of the whole business by roughly a similar percentage. It is important that when trying to judge the true growth of a business that new openings, or new space increases within existing shops, are removed from the equation when comparing this year against last year. This allows the buying and merchandising team to see clearly whether or not they are achieving growth on the existing old part of the business: this is the LFL growth. It is a truer way of looking at the relative success of the business. Total growth can often obscure the true underlying (LFL) performance of the existing business.

In Table 6.2, some departments are clearly being planned as being on sales trend, while other departments are not. In general, strong sales performance during the same season last year encourages optimism for planning high sales during the forthcoming year. It is vital that a great deal of consideration is given to this overall initial sales plan at the start of any season, as fundamental errors in the sales planning process could have profound implications on future buying levels. It is normal for this high-level plan to be reviewed at some length by senior management, before it is 'signed off' or accepted by the business as the final plan.

Tip

- When quoting or using percentage sales growth figures, always be certain that you are clear as to whether they relate to overall growth or to Like for Like (LFL) growth
- Like for Like growth is the best indicator of real growth

Sales planning and the fashion business

It is almost impossible to devise the perfect sales plan that will never need changing at some point in the future. From conception until the end of the season, the plan can be, and usually is, subject to both minor and major changes. However, as the season progresses, it becomes more problematic to make major changes, as it becomes harder to make buying changes once orders, production and delivery have commenced. Some shorter lead-time fashion retailers are more able to make adjustments further into the season, by delaying fabric buying and garment styling decisions until the last minute. On the other hand, more classic and longer lead-time businesses find it more difficult to make such changes. In general, it is the younger fashion retailers that work on the shorter lead-times, while the older more conventional businesses assume that the demands of their customers are less likely to change. Or at least that was the theory until recent fashion trends indicated that the 40 year old + customer is now becoming more and more fashion conscious.

Do the sales plans ever change?

Early on in the planning process it is easier to make larger more fundamental changes to the sales plan. Each version of an early plan is clearly labelled with a suffix number or letter. This enables all involved to be clear which version of the plan is actually being used at any point, and avoids confusion in the future. Sales + stock level re-forecasting occurs throughout the season to accommodate changing trading conditions as the best and worse sellers become apparent. These allow the buying team to increase and decrease intake of key garment categories, styles, colours and sizes in line with sales levels as clear levels of demand emerge. It is during this process that the buyer and merchandiser 'potentialise' the buying. Increasing or decreasing the sales forecast causes the intake demand to go up or down. Buying more best selling lines and fewer slow sellers is the route to successful fashion buying.

The individual departmental forecasts are generally added together, to create a top-level summary, for senior management to assess whether all the buying teams are being either too optimistic or too pessimistic about future sales prospects for the business as a whole. It also ensures that the teams are actually clearly acting upon the sales trends that are emerging from customer demand. The total business summary re-forecast document is generally made available for each buying team for review and amend on a weekly basis. This enables each team to assess their forecast in the light of the forecasts being made by the other buying and mechandising teams. Accurate weekly re-forecasting is a key responsibility of the merchandiser.

It usually emerges each season that some departments are more 'on trend' than others. This means that they are selling certain products that are in high demand by the customer. In the cycles of fashion, we see both the emergence of both long-term and short-term fashion trends. For example, ladies' dresses have been in a general long-term decline, while women's trousers have been on a steady increase over the past decade, as women generally have adopted a more casual approach to dressing. This will clearly impact upon the sales that we should expect from each department. During the season we see new colours emerge that suddenly sell far above the expectations of the original plan. It is vital that the teams react quickly to buy more of a winner, thus maximising sales. Similarly poor selling colours will undoubtedly emerge as well. Where possible, the team will try to reduce their forward buying (or 'forward commitment') on these. This is often harder to achieve than it is to buy more of a best seller. Long- and short-term fashion trends are an inevitable part of the fashion business.

The variable and changing sales patterns of fashion products, makes regular re-forecasting essential, if the business is to be stocked accurately and efficiently to meet ever-changing consumer demand. We now examine why getting the initial sales plans and regular forecast figures are so important, and also how forward sales plans have a direct impact upon when stock needs to be delivered or phased into a business.

━━━━━━

Tip

- If you change any plan, always ensure that you give the new version a new number or code letter – this stops all involved from getting confused as to which plan is supposed to be being used.
- Sales and stock re-forecasting must be done regularly to ensure that the business is stocked adequately in readiness for future sales patterns. This is usually done on a weekly basis.

Planning sales phasing

The hourly, daily, weekly and annual sales performance of a fashion business can be affected by several external and internal influences (see Table 6.3).

As shown in Table 6.3, there are many factors that impact upon a fashion business. The majority of factors are outside of the control of an individual business – for example, the dates of the bi-annual Sales periods are based upon historic precedent (June/July and December/January).

Table 6.3 also shows that there are both planned and unplanned factors that can influence the sales phasings within fashion retailing. More importantly, it shows that there are some factors that are both within and without the control of the buying and merchandising team. Good merchandise management should

Table 6.3   Key factors influencing fashion sales phasings

External factors	Reason
Unplanned	
Hot or cold unseasonable weather	Customers generally buy for immediate use
Heavy rain or snow	Customer flow reduced
Unplanned local or national events	Diverts customer interest
Sudden increase in competition	Other businesses take sales away
National or local strikes	Possible disruption of transportation or services
Competitors regular sales + events	May have better/worse offers
Competitors' ranges	May launch earlier, better ranges
Planned	
Holiday periods	Diverts customers away from shops
Natural seasonal demand for key garments	E.g. Swimwear in May + June
Time of day	Most sales taken between 11 and 4
Days of week	40 per cent of all fashion sales taken on Fri/Sat
Annual Summer + Winter Sales	High spending by consumers on bargains

Internal factors	Reason
Planned	
Increased use of sales promotion tools	Various promotional methods can stimulate short-term sales
Staffing levels	Correct level of sales staff needed at key times
Better ranges, prices and products	Depends upon skill of buying and merchandising team

always be able to cope with the obvious peaks and troughs of trade but there are, of course, many uncontrollable external factors that can dramatically reduce or increase sales over the short term. The funeral of Diana, Princess of Wales, in 1997, had a profound short-term effect upon fashion sales as customers stayed at home on that Saturday to watch the funeral on television.

The significance of a good phasing plan

The effective merchandiser will analyse previous sales history to help plan the basic sales framework for daily, weekly, monthly and seasonal sales patterns. However, it requires quick thinking, reaction and experience to cope with all those sudden unplanned factors that tend to occur when they are least expecting them.

As with preliminary departmental planning, the senior management will request initial weekly sales phasings back from each of the buying teams, which are consolidated into a summary level to ensure that the overall business sales phasing is logical. Some very large fashion retailers pay great attention to phasing, going as far as planning sales phasings by department, by shop on a day-by-day basis. The rationale of such detailed daily phasings ensures that during key periods such as Christmas, Easter, and the twice-yearly Sales, there are enough stock and staff available to achieve and take the sales. For example, Christmas can fall on any day of the week, which in turn can fundamentally change the way people spend their money by day over the two-week Christmas shopping period. Table 6.4 shows typical sales phasing over a twelve-month period, showing the likely percentage participation of the main garment types.

Three key facts and ratios emerge from sales phasings.

Table 6.4   Monthly financial sales phasings of a typical fashion retail business – women's wear (per cent)

J	F	M	A	M	J	J	A	S	O	N	D
10.4	6.6	7.8	7.2	7.9	8.9	8.5	8.2	6.9	7.5	7.8	12.3 = 100

1 **Seasonal sales variation** – Autumn/Winter sales usually represent 51 per cent of annual sales against 49 per cent for Spring/Summer. This is mainly owing to heavier, higher-price garments being worn and sold during the winter season, as well as Christmas trading and the higher importance of the winter rather than the Summer Sale.
2 **Departments with seasonal sales peaks** – Certain garment categories have a very concentrated sales pattern (e.g. night wear and underwear during November and December, swim wear during May and June, T-shirts during the Summer). Few garment types have level demand throughout the entire year. The inference is that buyers and merchandisers must be aware and plan weekly intake accurately to meet these normal peaks and troughs of trade.

3 **Fundamental sales ratios** – e.g. The sales ratio of top garments to bottom garments is approximately 2:1 (i.e. blouses, knitwear, T-shirts and tops have sales value of approximately twice that of trousers, jeans, shorts and skirts). This is due to the fact that many bottom garments are of a basic nature and therefore customers buy a higher proportion of tops to create contrast and change. There are many other fundamental ratios throughout the entire fashion business (e.g. ratio of bras to knickers).

The impact of sales phasings on all aspects of the work of the fashion buyer and merchandiser should not be underestimated. For some buying teams such as ladies' night wear, the highly concentrated sales period of November and December represents nearly 60 per cent of the annual turnover. During the final peak weeks their stock holding will represent only around two weeks' forward sales cover, as this will be needed to meet the trading peak. At other quieter times of the year, the value of stock held may easily equal more than fourteen weeks' forward sales. Forward stock cover therefore varies dramatically in the case of nightwear. Any business selling fashion nightwear cannot afford to enter the critical six-week trading period without being fully stocked with the right quantity category and type of stock.

Having explained the overall sales plan and the phasings required, it is important to now examine how sales phasing impacts upon the way in which stock needs to be delivered into a retail fashion business.

Stock turn and stock intake planning

Before examining the overall flow of stock into any fashion business, it is important to gain a fundamental understanding of the concept of mechandising efficiency in retailing known as 'Stock Turn'. Stock turn is simply a way of measuring *how many times a business changes the stock that it has on offer to the customer during the course of a trading year*. In the fashion industry, where customers automatically expect to find new and exciting garments every time they visit a shop, it is clearly very important for a retailer to 'turn' or change their stock as many times as possible throughout the season and year.

Without regular change and update of stock, a fashion retailer becomes stale and boring. This in turn leads to low sales and ultimately to excess residue stocks at the end of a season. High residue stocks in turn create major problems, in terms of the markdown required to move or liquidate them. To measure annual stock turn there is a simple formula that can be applied by the merchandiser:

$$\text{Stock turn} = \frac{\text{Annual sales value}}{\text{Average monthly stock value}}$$

Table 6.5 Shows a typical stock turn calculation.

Table 6.5 Example stock turn calculation, all values at retail pricing (£000)

Month	Monthly sales (£)	Average value of stock at start of month (£)
J	20,800	34,000
F	13,200	28,800
M	15,600	30,000
A	14,400	30,200
M	15,800	33,600
J	17,800	68,400
J	17,000	33,400
A	16,400	30,200
S	13,800	28,800
O	15,000	30,600
N	15,600	40,200
D	24,600	45,400
Total	**200,000**	**433,600**

$$\text{Therefore average monthly stock holding} = \frac{£433,600}{12} = £36,133$$

$$\text{Therefore Stock turn} = \frac{£200,000 \, (\text{total sales})}{£36,133} = 5.5 \text{ times a year Stock turn}$$

Sometimes, rather than simply quote a stock turn number, fashion retailers refer to stock turn in 'weeks' stock cover'. This is a more meaningful way to express the concept of stock turn. To convert stock turn to weeks' cover, a simple formula is used:

$$\text{Weeks' cover} = \frac{\text{Number of weeks in the year}}{\text{Stock turn}} = \frac{52}{5.5} = 9.4 \, (\text{rounded to 9)weeks' cover}$$

Note that, in general, weeks' cover is rounded up to the nearest whole number – therefore our example above would round down to 9 weeks' cover. The relationship between stock turn and weeks' cover is a simple relationship that is fundamental to measuring the basic stock movement efficiency of a fashion retailer. Weeks' cover is a widely utilised performance criterion in all types of fashion retailing, and is a simple way of expressing how long current stock holding will last into the future based upon current rates of sale.

For example, in Table 6.5 we can see that by applying the stock turn formula, the business used for illustration achieves a 5.5 times' stock turn a year. It is important to realise that stock turn is simply a ratio number. Different types of fashion retailer achieve fundamentally different levels of stock turn. Some typical stock turn expectations are shown in Table 6.6.

From Table 6.6 it is evident that fashion retailers with lower average prices usually have higher stock turns (lower weeks' cover) than those with higher prices. The basic economic law of supply and demand states that more units are sold at low rather than high prices. However, weeks' cover is only one criterion of

Table 6.6 Usual expected weeks' stock cover by type of fashion retailer

Type of fashion business	Approx. annual stock turn	Weeks' cover
Haute couture	2.0	26
Exclusive designer	2.5	20
Up-market branded store	2.7	18
Independent retailer	3.0	17
Department store	4.0	12
Fashion multiple	6.0	8
Value discount shop	8.0	6
Charity shop	16.0	3

Table 6.7 Failing to achieve planned stock turn

• **The danger of seasonal stock carryover**	Residue stocks at the end of a season may be almost impossible to sell, especially if their fabni weight is unsuitable for the following season. Reducing the price during a season is the best way to clear unwanted stock, but reducing summer-weight stock in early autumn would simply not be logical. Customers generally buy garments to wear for the immediate season. Leaving price reductions too late on during any season usually causes the business to enter the next season with too much un-saleable or 'dead' stock.
• **The problem of displaying last year's styles**	Some fashion retailers do try to hold off marking down to the very end of a season. This can be a dangerous strategy, if it does not clear in time. Fashion stock displayed again a year later can do great damage to the customer's perception of a fashion business, causing customer confusion when they are unable to differentiate between good and bad stock. Slow-moving stock must generally be cleared out of the business as soon as practically possible.
• **The problem of range fatigue**	If a retailer fails to 'turn' or sell their stock fast enough, there is the risk that the range will start to look tired and fragmented. Broken and fragmented ranges create a poor visual impression to customers.
• **The problem of blocked buying**	If stock is not being sold quickly enough and therefore does not generate the planned sales level, the business may not be able to re-invest in repeat buys of best sellers or on increasing buying on suddenly emerging new trends. Slow stock turn can give a fashion retailer 'stock indigestion.'

measuring success in fashion retailing. Alone it is meaningless, unless viewed in conjunction with other key success criteria including percentage profit and levels of price mark-down. These are explained later in the chapter.

If a fashion retailer fails to achieve their planned stock cover, the implications on overall profitability can be profound. Table 6.7 shows examples of the knock-on effects of failing to achieve the planned stock turn.

The impact of these effects upon final profitability can be profound. It is therefore extremely important for merchandisers to plan their weeks' cover (stock turn) very carefully. An understanding of the concept of stock turn is probably one of the most important skills needed for successfully planning, managing and controlling fashion merchandise.

Controlling fashion stock – the Weekly Sales, Stock and Intake plan

To assist the overall merchandise planning process, the Weekly Sales and Stock Intake planning document has been adopted in some form by a majority of the large fashion chains. Known affectionately as the **WSSI** or '**Wizzy**', its benefits were soon recognised. Initially developed in the early 1970s by Burton Menswear, it has become a trade standard with most of Europe's successful fashion retailers. Interestingly, the WSSI has migrated into many other areas of retailing other than fashion, a true testament to its usefulness and versatility; even the retail jewellery trade has adopted it as a key planning tool.

With the introduction of desktop computing throughout fashion retailing in the 1980s, the early paper-based WSSI has largely been replaced by spreadsheet formats. Generally individual companies customise it to meet their own in-house requirements. While simple to use, readers are advised to study this most fundamental of document and to work through it using a calculator, to ensure that they understand the basic arithmetic. Whilst appearing complicated, once understood it is an extremely comprehensive document, fundamental to merchandising management.

Each week works on a simple basic stock calculation described on page 106. The figures are always expressed as retailing selling price (RSP), rather than at the cost price (CP) that the buyer buys his/her stock at from their supply sources.

The key information contained on this computer-based WSSI document shown in Figure 6.1 is:

1 Sales clearly phased by week – actual to week 8 and forecast 9–13
2 Stock Intake by value clearly phased by week – actual to week 8 and forecast 9–13
3 The total Start or Opening stock value at the beginning of each week
4 The total End or Closing stock value at the end of each week
5 A valuation of both weekly price reductions and price increases – mark-ups and mark-downs
6 A clear indication of the forward planned weeks Opening stock, Closing stock and Stock cover for the business.

Week No.	Act./For. opening stock	Act./For. weekly intake (+)	Act./For. mark-ups (+)	Act./For. mark-downs (−)	Act./For. weekly sales (−)	Act./For. closing stock (−)	Plan weekly sales	Plan closing stock	Planned forward stock cover	Comments
1	1200*	67*	nil	nil	135*	1132*	140	1127	7	
2	1132*	175	nil	nil	140*	1167*	146	1156	7	
3	1167*	28*	16* A	nil	140*	1071*	144	1012	6	A brand RSP mark-up
4	1071*	104	nil	nil	150*	1025*	155	1022	6	
Sub-period 1	N/A	374*	16*	nil	565*	N/A	585	N/A	N/A	
5	1025*	232*	nil	50* B	212*	995*	218	949	6	B Blue Cross day reductions
6	995*	117*	nil	nil	157*	955*	162	927	6	
7	955*	101*	nil	nil	143*	913*	146	913	6	
8	913*	144*	nil	nil	150*	907*	156	907	6	
Sub-period 2	N/A	594*	16*	50*	662*	N/A	682	N/A	N/A	
Cum.	N/A	968*	16*	50*	1227*	N/A	1267	N/A		
9	907	234	nil	nil	175	955	175	955	6	Forecast Stock, Sales and Intake
10	955	175	nil	nil	165	966	165	965	6	ditto
11	966	157	nil	nil	145	988	145	987	6	ditto
12	988	148	nil	nil	140	996	140	995	6	ditto
13	996	187	nil	nil	132	1051	132	1051	6	ditto
Sub-period 3	N/A	901	nil	nil	757	N/A	757	N/A	N/A	
1st quarter	N/A	1869	16	50	1984	N/A	2024	N/A	N/A	

Notes: Act. = Actual, For. = Forecast. * = Real sales as opposed to forecast.

Figure 6.1 The basic Weekly Stock Sales and Intake document – the 'WSSI' (£000s): ladies' tops – actual for Weeks 1–8, forecasts for 9–13 and plan Weeks 1–13

In the example shown in Figure 6.1, the sales relate to the first quarter of the year for ladies' tops. The business is forecast to not achieve the total quarter's sales plan of £2024K, missing it by £40K. The forecast sales made at the end of Week 8 show that the business is therefore expected to only achieve £1984K. However, by controlling the intake between Weeks 9 and 13, the merchandiser ensures that the closing stock at the end of Week 13 comes in exactly at £1051K, as originally planned. This is a simplistic WSSI, although the format will vary from company to company. Very often it will also show last year's sales and stock levels as a separate column for comparison purposes. It is normal that all merchandisers within the same organisation will use the same house-format WSSI.

The WSSI is usually updated either automatically via computer, or manually on a weekly basis. It is updated to show the actual sales achieved, the stock received that week from suppliers into the business, the value of mark-down/mark-up spent during the previous weeks, the opening stock available for the next week, as well as an updated view of the forward delivery programme. Out of these we can see what forward stock cover is available for the department to trade with, as well as assessing the current sales performance against plan, in order to review the forward forecast sales and make any required changes to the forward stock delivery programme. Increasing the sales forecast over future weeks will generally require the buyer to buy more stock, or bring forward stock delivery on best-selling lines and categories, which in turn is likely to increase stock levels. Getting more of better-selling stock and less of poor-selling stock into the business is the essence of the buying and merchandising process.

Normally each department will update their WSSI on a Monday, in order that all departmental WSSIs can be consolidated to produce an overall WSSI for the entire business. This enables senior management to take a regular and detailed overview of historic and forward sales and stock forecasts for the whole business at the same time. For each buying team the WSSI acts as a clear and concise barometer of past, current and likely future levels of achievement. It also acts as a clear support for decision-making, in terms of speeding up or slowing down delivery and spending more or less mark-down on slow-selling lines. It indicates clearly to the buying and merchandising team and senior management alike how well the department is performing cumulatively against the original sales plan. In today's confused and fast-changing world, there are few planning and control documents that have weathered the test of time as well as the WSSI.

WSSIs are generally kept at major category level and then consolidated to make up a total department WSSI – e.g. all WSSI categories of skirt would be consolidated. In some circumstances, where a fast-moving style, fabric or colour fad emerges during the course of a season, the lines involved are often separated out and consolidated to form a special WSSI to ensure that the business is able to easily monitor the major emerging trends. With many hundreds of lines selling through a fashion business each week, it helps focus management attention onto key product areas/types.

The basic arithmetic of the WSSI is as follows – after working through the example below with a calculator, the reader is urged to apply the same formula to the WSSI in Figure 6.1. As has already been mentioned earlier, different companies customise the WSSI format to fit in with their own information system design and senior management requirements.

EXAMPLE: THE ARITHMETIC OF THE WSSI (USUALLY EXPRESSED IN £000s OR £K)

	£K	
Opening stock (Retail value of stock on Monday morning)	5120	
		+
Intake (Retail value of stock received into business during week)	535	
		−
Sales (Sales achieved during week)	501	
Mark-downs/Mark-ups (Value of price changes during week)	−50 (+ or −(mark-down)	
		=
Closing stock (Retail value of stock at end of week's trade)	5104	

In this example, the business has taken in more stock than it has sold, £535K intake against sales of £501K. This may be a deliberate plan to build stock in anticipation of higher sales in the future. The example also shows that a £50K mark-down has been taken. Possibly a slow selling line has had its price cut, to make it move out of the business faster. This will have the effect of speeding up the line's rate of sale. Sometimes a business may mark up stock (increase the price) to slowdown the rate of sale and make a fast line sell more slowly (as well as increasing profitability). Mark down action is usually taken during the main sale periods, although some fashion retailers have a trading philosophy of regular planned weekly mark-down activity. In general the more up-market a business is, the less likely it is to engage in regular mark-down activity. At the end of the trading week shown in the example, the business closes with a lower stock value than it opened with at the beginning – i.e. £5104K against £5120K. From the example it is possible to see that closing stock can be either higher and lower, depending upon a combination of the level of sales forecast in the future, the value of stock delivered in and the level of mark-up/mark-down that is taken. At low trading periods in the fashion year such as February and August, it is usual for businesses to keep their stock levels fairly low, increasing them quickly as it moves towards the busier trading months ahead. Forward weeks' stock cover tends to be higher during quiet selling periods and lower during peak selling periods. Weekly stock sales and intakes are planned at the start of each season.

Merchandise planning and the WSSI

Throughout the year, it is vital for the merchandiser and buyer to build stock levels in anticipation of trading peak periods such as Christmas and high summer. The WSSI is very good at helping the buyer and merchandiser plan forward stock intake into the DC. Quite clearly it would be unwise to take in all of a season's stock on the first day of the season. Apart from blocking up the warehouse, store stockrooms and the shop floor, the business would have no further new lines to excite regular visiting customers. Buying all of a season's planned intake at once also loses any flexibility to re-buy best-selling lines that may be selling faster than anticipated. Most fashion businesses try to leave a proportion of their seasonal buying plan (sometimes known as 'Open to Buy' or 'OTB') to enable them to go back into the market place to buy/repeat more best-sellers. Most fashion businesses opt for leaving somewhere between 30 per cent–40 per cent of their season's buying unspent at the start, thus allowing themselves spending flexibility once trends start to emerge. Buying everything up-front is a dangerous strategy in the changing world of fashion.

In every buying office, Monday sales figures are eagerly awaited in order that buyers and merchandisers can identify fast-selling lines that need repeat buys on them, to ensure that they are kept in stock. On the other side of the coin, it is the Monday figures that also reveal the worst sellers that eventually will require to have their price reduced (marked down). Buyers and merchandisers will, wherever possible, try to cancel or re-style outstanding orders of poor sellers that are still due to be delivered into the business. This is always a much more difficult process than buying more of best sellers!

The WSSI's role in underpinning forward intake planning is pivotal. The merchandiser, working with the buyer, ensures that the right lines are delivered at the right point in the season. Things that need to be carefully considered are

- Is the line the right *weight of fabric* for the time of year?
- Does the line form part of a *coordinated package* that needs to be delivered together?
- Is the line required as part of *planned promotional activity* – e.g. in an advert?
- Is there too much or too little stock of other *similar lines* in that category?

The new lines that the merchandiser plans to bring into the business each week are very important, in terms of keeping the shops refreshed. This in turn creates continuous interest for customers who visit regularly. New lines are the lifeblood of most successful fashion businesses.

The delivery schedule and its relationship to the WSSI

Buyers and merchandisers need to keep an overall and detailed control of planned intake. The WSSI acts as an *overall control mechanism* to ensure that the flow of stock and money in the business is happening efficiently – but, more importantly, so is the detailed line-by-line delivery schedule, listing the week and day when the suppliers have been requested to deliver the garments to the DC or warehouse. An example of a delivery schedule of a fashion retailer is shown in chapter 8 (Figure 8.2).

As shown in Figure 8.2, the delivery schedule is a highly complex document, clearly listing all lines and their expected delivery date. It is a working document usually kept on computer, but may still be paper, pencil and rubber-based in smaller businesses. Being aware exactly of what is going to be delivered is also of key interest to shop and promotional management functions of the organisation. It is also of key significance to the management of the DC in helping them plan both human and physical resources at different times of the season.

Marking prices up and down using the WSSI

One of the key merchandising activities controlled by using the WSSI is the aspect of line level price alteration that regularly occurs within all fashion businesses. Ideally at the start of the season, the buyer and merchandiser aim to create a price structure that relates to the type of customers to whom they are selling. The prices must also be competitive in terms of ensuring that they are also in line with the major competition.

To be cheaper than the competition all the time is often the way certain 'value fashion retailers' aim to promote their business. Low prices often drive up the number of units sold, but usually mean that the profit margin is lower as a result. Sometimes it is logical for the merchandiser to recommend marking up (increasing) prices, usually as result of a line selling too fast. If a line sells too fast, there is the suggestion that it may possibly be underpriced. Also there is the definite likelihood that the business will sell out of the line before more deliveries can be received back into the business. Putting the prices up or marking up is generally more unusual than marking down.

In all types of retailing, especially fashion retailing, we have to be aware of the 'elasticity of demand'. This is where the change in demand is proportionally higher or lower than the change in price. Products like cigarettes, that have an addictive quality, still continue to be purchased at high price levels, no matter how much taxes are increased. They have what is called an *inelastic demand*. Popular, highly sought-after and prized fashion brands can command high prices because of the fact that they also have inelastic demand. More basic items such as socks, tights and underwear can generate huge sales volumes with small price reductions. These products are said to have a very *elastic demand*.

Price elasticity of fashion products is sometimes hard to measure as a result of the changeable demands of the fashion business. With more stable products, such as basic foods, the measurement of demand elasticity is easier to assess. It is often easy in the fashion industry to reduce prices, generate what appears to be a huge volume increase, only to discover that in fact that the exercise has produced less total cash profit than if the prices had been left as they were. Taking a 10 per cent selling price reduction generally requires around a +15 per cent unit sales increase to compensate for the overall profit lost on each garment as a result of the price reduction. Reducing merchandise to half the original price will usually need the average fashion retailer to sell over three times as many as before (+200 per cent), if the overall profit is to be maintained! Many inexperienced merchandisers often forget that there is no direct corelation between the percentage level of mark-down taken, and the required level of unit sales increase to deliver the same level of overall profitability. Understanding demand levels and demand elasticity is a matter of experience, usually supported by historic sales information: there is no one formula that can be used by the buyer and merchandiser to make all pricing decisions.

It is fair to say that no matter how successful a buyer is at buying fashion merchandise, he or she will undoubtedly buy some lines that do not sell well. These lines will at some time or another require a price reduction to help them sell faster. For this reason all fashion retailers always have to plan a seasonal mark-down budget on the WSSI. This is simply a fact of life within the fashion industry – there will always be goods needing to be marked down, even in a good season, even in a department with a good buyer.

The level or value of mark-down that is planned is very much based upon history, as well as the type of fashion retailer involved. A dress department that has taken a 10 per cent mark-down regularly over the past four seasons, while probably preferring not to spend such a high level of mark-down, will probably plan to marginally improve the situation by planning a 9 per cent seasonal mark-down. A 10 per cent mark-down plan on £1 million seasonal sales plan effectively means that a business will need to reduce prices at some stage during the season by £100 000 thus enabling the business to take only £900 000 of sales as a result. Taking mark-down means also means that the business makes less overall profit. There is no perfect or normal level of mark-down percentage in the fashion industry, it is really dependent upon which end of the market is being traded, and indeed the general success level of the business. Mark-downs for the season or year can represent anywhere from 7 per cent to over 30 per cent of total sales, depending upon the type of fashion business. In general, high percentage mark-downs are symptomatic of poor sales performance, although many of the 'new-value' retailers plan high mark-down levels as both a tactical and strategic weapon. They therefore plan initially high selling prices and high mark-down levels to enable them to offer what appear to be continually discounted offers. This new aggressive trading stance can create a great deal of consumer price confusion, as well destabilising the price structures and businesses of some of the more conventional retailers. Fashion businesses with low mark-down percentages are generally the most profitable.

The WSSI also has the role of helping the buying team plan their mark-down for the season ahead, in terms of how much they plan to spend, as well as when they plan to spend it. Some fashion businesses aim to reduce or mark down poor-selling stocks as they occur, while other businesses prefer to move problem stock only during the two major Sale periods. It is therefore important for the merchandiser to use the WSSI to schedule when the planned mark-down allowance is to be spent. Mark-up is rarely planned, and is simply taken as a bonus as and when it occurs.

On the WSSI shown in Figure 6.1 it is clearly evident that the business is heavily weighted towards a traditional Sale pattern, although it does engage in some minor mark-down activity throughout all months of the year. It is important for the reader to note that the overall effect of a mark-down is to *reduce the value of the stock held*. This in turn means that there is theoretically more buying required to get the stock level back to the planned level. Usually this is achieved by bringing in existing orders earlier than planned, rather than going into the market and buying more stock.

The terminal stock monitor or report

This separate report is used to control the level of old season's stock that will be left at the end of a season. It is simply impossible for any fashion business to sell out completely of the previous season's stock, and even after the very best trading seasons, there will be fragmented lines and ranges left around the business. The best fashion businesses plan a level of terminal stock that will be acceptable to be left with at the end of a season. It goes without saying that the lower the percentage value of terminal stock left the better. Terminal stock-level plans are normally expressed as a percentage of the final closing stock value. It is usually set at anywhere from 5 per cent to 10 per cent by value. However, as this stock may have already been reduced by value in the seasonal sale, it is likely that it will represent as much as 10 per cent to 12 per cent of the end stock in unit terms.

As the season progresses, the terminal stock monitor is completed on a weekly basis. In many ways it acts as an early warning indicator of what will happen at the end of the season. Figure 6.2, clearly shows the sell-out of the old season's stock while at the same time monitoring the intake of the new season's stock and how well that it is selling.

Bringing in too much new season's stock too early can be as dangerous for a fashion business as not bringing in enough. It is very much a balancing act. While in many respects the terminal stock monitor shows much of the same information as the WSSI, it does so in a clear old- and new-season format. As such, this clearly alerts all involved as to what old-season stock is going to remain and how much new-season stock will be required to be brought into the business ahead of the season, in order that the business not only clears old stock, but also achieves its sales plan and forecast. This process is a fine balancing act for the merchandiser to achieve and is subject to many debates within both the team and senior management at the weekly team meeting. As the end of the season approaches, it becomes an increasingly important document.

The WSSI – the answer to planning?

In this chapter, we have looked carefully at the WSSI and its functions. It is important to understand that while it acts as the central merchandising management document within fashion retailing, it is only part of a wider range of planning documents. It is unashamedly an *internal financial control document*, which is a summary of all the trading activity within the department and ultimately the entire business. It is important not to lose sight of the fact that all the real trading activity takes place at line or style level. It is line performance that really drives the buying team's day-to-day decision-making processes.

Taken out of context, the WSSI can be a meaningless page of figures. It requires careful interpretation, using experience to manipulate both it and the buying, if the department is to succeed. Some merchandisers try to use it in a formulaic way, producing it without understanding. Fashion is never formulaic and therefore this can be a dangerous approach. Using a WSSI over many seasons soon trains both buyers and merchandisers not to react too quickly to sudden good and bad sales patterns: reaction to the WSSI must be both considered and careful.

Undoubtedly the weekly line or style sales performance report is the most eagerly sought document each Monday morning. It is from these line-level sales performances that the total department-level and business-level sales performance is built up. The sales performance is, as already, explained the key driving factor for forward decision-making on the WSSI.

Figure 6.2   Example Section of a Simplified Terminal Stock Monitor – Ladies' skirts £000s

	WEEK NO	NOV 1	NOV 2	NOV 3	NOV 4	DEC 1	DEC 2	DEC 3	DEC 4	DEC 5	JAN 1	JAN 2	JAN 3	JAN 4	FEB 1	FEB 2	FEB 3	FEB 4
OLD SEASON SKIRTS (A/W)	SALES ①	50	45	43	41	35	32	25	20	45	20	10	9	8	7	2	3	1
	INTAKE	30	20	NIL	NIL	NIL	NIL	NIL	NIL	NIL	NIL	NIL	NIL	NIL	NIL	NIL	NIL	NIL
	MARK DOWN	NIL	NIL	NIL	NIL	NIL	NIL	NIL	NIL	NIL	25	NIL	20	NIL	NIL	NIL	NIL	NIL
	CLOSING STOCK	450	425	382	341	306	274	249	229	134	89	79	50	42	35	33	31	30
	No. of WEEKS COVER	9	9.4	8.9	8.3	8.7	8.6	10.0	11.4	3.0	4.4	7.9	5.5	5.2	5	16.5	15.5	30.0
NEW SEASON SKIRTS (S/S)	SALES ②	NIL	NIL	1	4	10	20	25	35	25	35	50	36	32	25	33	37	37
	INTAKE	NIL	10	15	35	75	95	110	60	90	50	35	16	24	23	48	57	62
	MARK DOWN	NIL	NIL	NIL	NIL	NIL	NIL	NIL	NIL	NIL	NIL	NIL	NIL	NIL	NIL	NIL	NIL	NIL
	CLOSING STOCK	NIL	NIL	24	55	120	195	280	305	370	385	370	350	342	340	355	375	400
	No. of WEEKS COVER	NIL	2	24	13.7	12	9.7	11.2	9.7	14.8	11.0	7.4	9.7	10.7	13.6	10.8	10.1	10.8
GRAND TOTAL ALL SEASONS SKIRTS	SALES	50	45	44	45	45	52	50	55	70	55	60	45	40	32	35	39	38
	INTAKE	30	30	15	35	75	95	110	60	90	50	35	16	24	23	48	57	62
	MARK DOWN	NIL	NIL	NIL	NIL	NIL	NIL	NIL	NIL	NIL	25	NIL	20	NIL	NIL	NIL	NIL	NIL
	CLOSING STOCK	450	435	406	396	426	469	529	534	504	474	449	400	384	375	388	406	430
	No. of WEEKS COVER	9.0	9.7	9.2	8.8	9.4	9.0	10.5	9.7	7.2	8.6	7.5	8.9	9.6	11.7	11.1	10.4	11.3
% OLD STOCK A/W. V. NEW STOCK S.S ③		100	97	94	86	72	58	47	43	26	19	17	12.5	11	9	8	8	7*

Notes: 1   Sales decreasing on old A/W stock until Jan sale make down applied.
Notes: 2   Now start of new S/S intake of skirts-mainly transitional weight fabrics.
Notes: 3   Note decreasing % of old season A/W stock until at end only 7% of total stock is old.
Notes: * 7% = Final Terminal Stock Percentage.

For the past twenty-five years since its conception, the WSSI has had a profound impact on the effectiveness of fashion merchandise planning. The WSSI, in conjunction with the widespread introduction and development of PC computing within fashion retailing, is giving the merchandiser an ever more effective control over stock level and content.

Some final thoughts on the WSSI

The importance of understanding the workings of the WSSI should not be underestimated. Using this control document the merchandiser is able to keep a weekly update of past present and likely future performance of the department in terms of sales, stock, intake and mark-down. It enables both the buying team and management to regularly check their performance against the original plan. More importantly it acts as a decision-making tool to help the business decide what action to take on an ongoing regular basis. The key decisions that need to be considered each week are shown in Table 6.1.

These fundamental decisions are made by the buying teams, in conjunction with management during weekly progress meetings, which are usually held early on during the week, as soon as the main computer has updated the sales, stock and delivery situation. No computer can really make the intelligent decisions related to the WSSI, as it is the buyer and merchandiser's trading experience that tells them whether or not one good or bad week of sales is indicative of a trend that has set in, or is simply a one-off week caused by an unusual weather pattern or some other local event. For example, a very

---

Table 6.10 The decisions required that are driven out from the WSSI

1 Have we achieved our *weekly sales* – if we are above plan should we forecast increased sales performance forward into future weeks and possibly months? Similarly if we have failed to achieve the sales plan, should we forecast forward sales downwards?

2 If *forward sales forecasts* are either increased or decreased, then there will be an impact on forward stock holding levels, either upwards or downwards to the equivalent level. A reduced sales forecast means that unless the merchandiser takes action to cancel or push back future stock deliveries then the stock level will build above plan. Conversely if sales are higher than anticipated, future stock levels will decrease against plan unless more stock is bought or the delivery of existing orders is brought forward.

3 If sales are *above plan*, what better-selling merchandise can be brought forward or be delivered into the business earlier than originally planned, in order to capitalise on this high-sales situation? Also if sales are above plan, then which best-selling lines should have repeat buys made against them?

4 If sales are *below plan*, should mark-down (price reduction) be applied to slow selling lines in order to stimulate sale volumes? Is there enough mark-down available and planned at any point? It may also be necessary to slow down future production and delivery of slow-selling lines or possibly put the fabric into a new and hopefully better-selling style.

---

unseasonably hot week in May can increase T-shirt sales by as much as three times. Were an inexperienced buying team to read this sales trend wrongly, they might mistakenly believe that forecast sales for the rest of that season should be trebled to meet future demand!

Undoubtedly such a poor interpretation would cause the buying team to increase future buying, with the risk of being left with massive overstocks of unseasonable T-shirts at the end of the season. T-shirts do not improve with age like fine wines! While it might be possible for the business to repack them at the end of the season with the view of bringing them out next year, the likelihood is that the styles and colours next year will be different. Old stock brought out a year later usually looks tired and poor value.

Having explained how the merchandiser plans the intake and control of stock 'into the business', Chapter 8 examines how stock is controlled out of the DC and 'around the business'. Getting the right styles by size and colour to the right branches is probably the most important part of the stock flow process throughout any fashion retail business.

■ ☑ 7 Sourcing and supply chain management

This chapter will explain sourcing and explain how supply chain management has emerged as a crucial function in improving the effectiveness of the suppliers used by buyers in fashion retailing. 'Effectiveness' in this context is judged by a number of criteria, which are discussed in detail later in the chapter, but which ultimately must result in increased overall profitability. In their efforts to improve stock usage, fashion retailers have recognised that suppliers' performance can have a big impact on profits.

Sourcing defined

The term 'sourcing' is used in a very specific way throughout this book to mean, 'the selection of a supplier of either a product or the raw material components and services used in the make up and delivery of the products'. Suppliers have to be reliable, efficient and effective to retain the business of their retail customers, as much of a retailer's success depends on the finished products that suppliers are producing and delivering.

Approaches to sourcing and exactly what has to be sourced will vary among fashion retailers. For example, a fashion business such as Jaeger, which sells to wealthier, quality-conscious consumers, will source fabric for some of its products from Italy as the country has many suppliers able to produce very high-quality fabric. The suppliers can produce the kind of 'fancy' fabric designs that differentiate Jaeger's products in the market place. However, Jaeger can manufacture the garments in its UK factories, using the Italian fabric, and so reduce the lead-time of garment manufacture to delivery. This 'sourcing' scenario will be different for many mass-market high street fashion retailers, which need to source large volumes from other lower-priced countries, to achieve a balance of quality and low-cost price. It is important for readers to note that Europe and other developed countries are not the only source of higher-priced quality products: the quality from many Far Eastern countries has improved dramatically over the past ten or so years, and is now deemed to be world-class.

What needs to be sourced?

Everything that contributes to the finished garment sold to consumers, needs to be sourced (see Table 7.1).

Table 7.1   What needs to be sourced

Fabric	Grey stock – finished fabric
	Manufacturer's range – retailer's own fabric design
Trimmings	Buttons, zips, interlinings, etc.
Labels	'Back-neck' logos, country of origin, care labels, fibre content labels
Tickets	Marketing swing tags – barcode price tags
Hangers	Unbranded – retailer's own brand
Bags	Protective covers for individual or groups of garments
Boxes	Flat packed garments such as T-shirts and knitwear

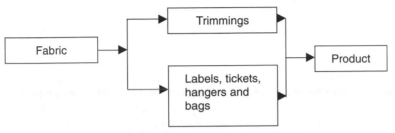

Figure 7.1   A simple supply chain

Figure 7.1 identifies the different components that buyers must potentially source. It is true to say that one supplier could be responsible for sourcing all the components, however it maybe more appropriate for some fashion buyers to source everything separately.

As buyers are looking towards newer, cheaper and more exciting sources of supply, in order to try and maintain a competitive advantage over their competitors, they tend to investigate newer and more innovative supply sources, whilst maintaining their core of proven suppliers. The younger and more fashionable fashion retailers tend to change their suppliers more frequently, as result of a continual need for new creative design and product development.

Changes in sales patterns have resulted in fashion retailers buying smaller initial quantities than they once did. This has happened as result of more competition and the increasing numbers of brands growing faster than the market place. The need for smaller buying quantities has focused retailers' interest on obtaining shorter and more flexible lead-times from suppliers.

There are different issues in sourcing core products that are repeated every season from the same supplier and riskier fashion products that frequently come from new suppliers. In general, sourcing for larger retailers is more complex, as they will source a wider range of product categories, and therefore need to balance the benefits of overseas sourcing against quicker local suppliers.

Different ways of buying a garment

Retailers source products differently according to the nature of the product. Typically, products fall into one of the three categories described in Table 7.2.

Table 7.2	Products to be sourced	

Factored	Where the retailer buys ready-designed garments from a supplier's range and inserts their own labels into the garment, or where the supplier designs and manufactures garments according to the 'handwriting' of the fashion retailer.
Cut make and Trim (CMT)	Where the supplier manufactures (cuts the fabric, makes and trims the garment) using fabric bought, checked and delivered by the retailer.
Brands	Unique ranges, designed either by a retailer or a manufacturer with a clear 'handwriting' and essential extra value in terms of brand attributes created by strong promotion. In general, retailers are unable to alter or change manufacturer-based brands

Some fashion retailers buy all three types of garment. For example a department store would carry mainstream brands as well creating their own house-brand label purchasing a mixture of factored and/or CMT garments. The small specialist boutique, without large buying power, would tend to buy more exclusive branded products, as a way of differentiating itself from the competition.

Historically, fashion retailers preferred CMT, as it enabled them to be fully aware of the true component costs of each garment. The key variable was then the quality and cost of the making up. Supplying a retail business with CMT garments, while appearing to be cost effective, did in its own right create more internal costs for the retailer. CMT buying operations also require the skills of a cloth buying manager, specialist quality control staff for the cloth buying department, as well as often a larger and more sophisticated design department, together with a sample production unit. The CMT approach to garments tended to be more prevalent in those fashion businesses with a high percentage of tailored garments and outerwear in their ranges. This is because tailoring is a complex and highly specialised form of garment making, that needs specialist buying and making up knowledge if prices are to be kept to an economic level.

Despite the apparent advantages provided by CMT, many fashion retailers in the middle market rely upon their supplier's design teams to create appropriate factored garments. The use of CMT by fashion retailers seems to experience cyclical periods of growth and retraction. Running a CMT operation requires a great number of specialist skills, not always freely available in the average buying office.

An historical perspective

Historically, fashion retail buyers have selected suppliers with little input from other functions within their business, with the possible exception of the merchandiser, who prefer suppliers to be reliable with deliveries and flexible with production.

The older buyers were mainly interested in cost, delivery and quality as their key criteria for supplier selection. However, as sourcing has become more systematic and scientific, greater emphasis has been placed upon the role of suppliers, and the criteria for selection have become keener. With fewer systems and controls in place, the buyer of ten years ago was much freer to buy more on a whim than today's buyer.

European and American retailers seem to have a decreasing loyalty to their own home-produced fashion merchandise, as foreign manufacturers have developed and greatly improved their quality and skills base. After the Second World War and into the early 1970s, many British retailers such as Marks & Spencer pursued very active 'Buy British' initiatives. French consumers, similarly, are still very supportive of home-produced goods. However, as home produced versus imported price differentials widened in favour of imports, combined with improving quality and design from abroad, there was no logical reason for British and European retailers to carry on fighting the inevitable. The recent decision by Marks & Spencer to source more products abroad underlines the cost savings to be made from a foreign sourcing policy.

A migration of European fashion buying to the Far East, originally centred upon Hong Kong and Taiwan. This occurred mainly as a result of the need for cost savings. Early Far Eastern deliveries often lacked quality and design, this is no longer the case, as improvements in technology now mean that Far Eastern products are well known for new and innovative design and high quality. The reality is that sourcing from China now means that the products are likely to be made in a factory which may well be an American joint venture, with German equipment and a British production manager. In today's global fashion industry, international business cooperation has become the norm.

As living standards continue to rise in the new manufacturing nations, improving living standards are leading to increased consumer demand. Manufacturing has now moved away from Hong Kong and Taiwan towards newer and cheaper sources in places such as Indonesia and Vietnam. This 'production migration' is a normal phenomenon for all economies, and we now see Hong Kong and Taiwan acting as management and design centres for the new manufacturing countries. Each year, newer and less developed countries, such as Tibet and Laos, are turning to garment manufacture as part of their economic development.

Over time, individual countries have developed expertise and skills in certain types of products, processes and/or fabrics. Often these start as a result of an abundance of locally available natural materials, skills or local technologies. Britain still retains a very high expertise in the production of fine woven woollen fabrics, ideal for both male and female tailoring. Italy has always enjoyed a strong design base and has similarly developed a world-beating reputation for silk printing and design. Sometimes, these local specialisms and centres of expertise are based in distant history, as with the United Kingdom and wool, whilst others have developed over a matter of a few years. For example, the Israeli expertise in women's swimwear has developed over the past twenty years, mainly as a result of a rapidly developing tourist market and plenty of good beaches and sunshine. Table 7.3 shows a list of some more obvious

Table 7.3 Fashion specialisation by country

Garment/Fabric/Process	Country	Rationale for development
Silk garments	China	Long history of silk wearing and production
Silk printing	Italy	Long history of painting and design
Fine cotton yarns/ fabrics	United States	Historic 'cotton-belt' in Southern States
Wool and worsted fabrics	United Kingdom	Grown from medieval origins + water
Swimwear	Israel	Good local design + climate + beaches
Tailoring	Eastern Europe	Plentiful supply of skilled workers
Summer cottons	India	Cheap labour + improving technology and design
Finishing processes	Switzerland	Quality, value-added approach

centres of fashion excellence, together with a brief rationale as to why they have come about.

The list of countries and specialisms continually develops over time, as a result of the ease of technology transference to any part of the globe. Designs can now be quickly transmitted electronically to any part of the planet, making centres of design expertise almost a thing of the past. A designer working in the remotest parts, can instantly transmit a two-dimensional design to anywhere, almost at the speed of light. As picture transmission and quality improves, together with the development of three-dimensional and stereoscopic televisions and computers, the remote design revolution will gather pace. It will be made easy for either a buyer or supplier to see a garment clearly while being many thousands of miles apart. 3D television pictures will improve and speed up buying decisions and processes.

The buyer/supplier relationship

It is quite usual for the buyer to spend more time with a supplier than they do with their own friends, partners and families. The relationship is often close as a result of the need to travel abroad together to foreign supply sources, and to continuously develop new ranges. However, familiarity can breed contempt between both parties involved in such a close business relationships. Getting on with a supplier, and getting the best from them, is imperative for the long-term benefit of both businesses.

Retaining a 'businesslike' relationship is often difficult, and there are many examples of relationships becoming distorted as result of the emergence of personal differences developing between the two parties. There is a saying that 'business and friends do not mix', and this is never truer than in terms of the buyer/supplier relationship. Buying and selling decisions can become blurred and irrational when personal relationships start to cloud business judgements. While there is no accounting for human nature, many large retailers will not allow personal relationships of any sort to exist, preferring instead to move the buyer to another product area away from the relationship.

Another temptation that has been evident in the world of fashion buying is that of bribery. As one individual is often responsible for the possible purchasing of many thousands of garments, it has not been unknown for either the unscrupulous supplier or buyer to offer or demand a bribe in return for an order. While the vast majority of buyers and suppliers do not support this behaviour, it is important for fashion buyers working abroad to appreciate that in some countries, it is a cultural norm to both give and receive 'favours' as part of the normal business process. The sums involved in such activities vary dramatically from the giving of a simple gift to the 'giving' of a percentage or, '*per garment charge*'. Most large fashion retailers at some time or another have experienced such corrupt action.

On a final note relating to corruption, the wider introduction of auto-mated supplier performance analysis will ultimately make it even harder for buyers and suppliers to retain any form of long-term business relation-ship that is not backed up by sound commercial sense and outcome. Clear illogical support for poorly performing suppliers shows up easily with these easy-to-read reports. Supplier performance indicators are dealt with later in this chapter.

A move towards international sourcing

The advent of mass tourism, combined with the growth of affluence and mass international media, now mean that few places on earth are more than 12–14 hours' flying time away. International business travel is becoming cheaper all the time, enabling both buyers and suppliers in the fashion industry to work easily and conveniently in any country. This, combined with the increasing speed and ease of telecommunication, is enabling international fashion business to work effectively anywhere. Higher-quality teleconferencing systems have been successfully employed by UK retailers to deal directly with Far Eastern buying offices and manufacturers.

Governments in developed countries have tried over time to protect their home garment and textile industries against low-cost imports from developing countries. This is usually achieved by using a combination of trade protection measures, a mixture of quotas, tariffs, special import taxes and duties. Other more devious trade protection techniques have included overbearing bureaucracy, burdensome paperwork and stringent labelling requirements for imported garments.

A truly global economy requires the complete abolition of trading barriers, but in reality the political will has not yet emerged to solve the problem. Complete world free trade has obvious benefits, but uncontrolled trade could lead to garment-industry disruption and collapse in developed countries. This debate is discussed in Chapter 10. Several major international trading initiatives have taken place involving virtually all manufactured goods including textiles and garments. These are discussed later in this chapter.

General Agreement on Tariffs and Trade (GATT)/Multi-Fibre Arrangement (MFA)

The two major international agreements covering world textile trading were the GATT and the MFA. The MFA was agreed in 1974 between Western 'developed countries' and 'developing countries', which included many Asian nations. The MFA was a special arrangement, outside GATT (which covered all products and services globally traded), as it specifically related to clothing and textiles.

The MFA explained

The MFA was originally established to provide Western economies with an opportunity to change and restructure their clothing and textile industries, in response to the great volume of imports of cheaper clothing and textiles from developing economies in Asia and the Far East. Manufacturers in these regions had huge cost advantages through the significantly lower labour costs of their workforces. The MFA was effectively an 'umbrella agreement' that was a departure from the principles of free trade nurtured under GATT

Key issues

- The intention was to avoid 'market disruption' to western economies through the decline of clothing and textiles industries in the face of floods of cheap clothing imports from low labour-cost countries
- Four separate MFAs were agreed, during 1974, 1978, 1982 and 1986
- The MFA mainly involves man-made fibres and wool.

The effects on trade

- There is an upper limit beyond which imports will not be allowed
- The upper limit is broken down for each product category
- The limits are calculated by volume rather than value – generally by number of pieces in the cases of apparel, by weight in the case of yarns and by metres in the case of fabrics
- Quotas are set annually
- Quotas are administered by the exporting country which issues export licences.

It was during the 1994 'Uruguay Round' of GATT talks that it was agreed that all quotas, restricting imports of clothing and textiles, would be completely phased out by 2005. Many European manufacturers are unhappy with these proposals as they believe it will further reduce demand for their production from domestic fashion retailers, as more sourcing will go overseas. The increasing penetration of cheaper garment and textile imports into Europe and the United States from developing countries seems inevitable.

General sourcing issues

Overseas sourcing

The principal benefit to fashion retailers of overseas sourcing is generally to obtain a cheaper cost price. However, although overseas buying appears cheaper, mainly as result of lower labour and infrastructural costs, which have obvious attractions to European buyers, this is not always the case. For example, the initial product cost quoted may not always include the complete cost of delivery to the distribution centre.

In addition to delivery costs there are many other hidden costs, which must be evaluated to understand the real cost of importing fashion products. Many inexperienced buyers fail to grasp this important fact. Table 7.4 lists examples of potential hidden costs.

The concept of the hidden costs involved in buying what appear to be cheaper imported goods continues to be of great interest to both the academic and business sectors of the fashion industry. The 'Iceberg Theory of Cost Comparison' and its implications for the UK clothing industry was first proposed by Tony Hines in 1998.[1] The theory suggests that many UK buyers are buying from abroad on the simple justification that prices are cheaper as result of fundamentally lower labour costs. With skilled labour in the United Kingdom at around £6 per hour compared with £1 per hour in India (1998), there would appear to be no argument against the logic of buying Indian manufactured merchandise in preference to that from the United Kingdom. However, the Iceberg Theory shows clearly that the importation of foreign fashion merchandise usually has many hidden costs – as with a real iceberg, a majority of the cost mass is hidden below the surface! The idea of such hidden costs is clearly shown in Figure 7.2.

Figure 7.2 shows the range of hidden costs that would not be easily revealed in a normal presentation of management accounts. Of all the costs listed, probably the most damaging to overall net profitability is the cost of *lost sales* as a result of late delivery. Once a delivery date is missed, the hidden cost of lost sales is very hard to accurately calculate, although it is real and generally very expensive. Lost sales caused by late delivery are rarely recovered later on in the season. The customer will simply walk down to the competitor's outlet rather than wait for your next delivery, a simple and logical action on the customer's part. Most retail DCs have a cost-recovery mechanism in place to fine suppliers for late deliveries.

Good supply chain management techniques are now realising the hidden costs of imported merchandise more clearly, and the once simple cost rationale for buying from foreign cheaper foreign suppliers is being challenged. Many new management information systems are now being developed to assist specialist supply chain managers on how to understand and measure the costs hidden below the 'iceberg'.

Large parts of the UK textile industry have closed as a result of direct price competition from abroad, although these cost savings may well be illusory rather than real. Some of the more enlightened UK retailers are now

Table 7.4	Hidden costs

• **Currency fluctuations**	Make interpreting the true cost price of a product difficult, although most retailers buy currency in advance to try and limit the impact of this on the cost and selling price of the product
• **Quota**	Exporting companies often buy and sell quota from their own government's agencies, the price of quota often rising towards the end of a quota period because as quota becomes scarcer it is thus more valuable: without quota, overseas suppliers can at present not sell to European retailers
• **Delayed delivery**	With distances, transport complexities and the generally large size of import orders, delays in delivery always lead to lost sales in shops
• **Inability to repeat quickly**	Unlike domestic suppliers, shipping lead-times make the possibility of repeat orders within a season less likely from Far Eastern suppliers
• **Methods of transportation**	Most fashion products are carried by ship over long distances owing to cost effectiveness; using airfreight, while much faster than ship, can be prohibitively expensive increasing garment costs by as much as 30%, which will automatically decrease final profitability
• **Increased management costs**	Foreign trips to suppliers, increased communication costs (including sampling), increased management time and involvement all add to the real cost of a garment
• **Dedicated foreign sourcing offices**	Some retailers have opened foreign sourcing or buying offices to manage overseas production, quality standards and delivery. These can be notoriously expensive to run and maintain. Often these offices will take a commission from the cost price negotiated. In some instances, retailers will retain foreign buying agencies, which are run indirectly on their behalf, rather than directly using a dedicated foreign sourcing office.
• **Increased inventory costs**	As a result of the inability to make quick and frequent repeat buys, imported merchandise often needs to be delivered in bulk and held for a long period of time in the distribution centre (DC), holding stock in a warehouse has both investment and storage cost
• **Returns and refunds**	It is usually not financially viable to return small quantities of faulty product back to foreign suppliers, and it is sometimes difficult to get refunds on faulty merchandise

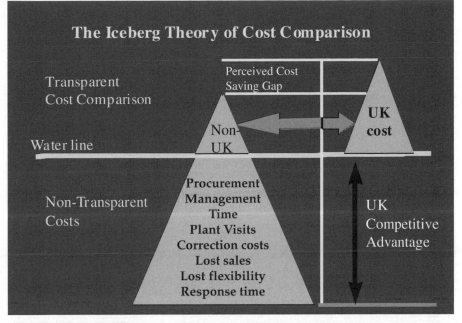

The Iceberg Theory of Cost Comparison

Source: T. Hines (2000), *Supply Chain Management – Strategies, Structure and Relationships* (London: Checkmate Business Books).

Figure 7.2   The iceberg theory of cost comparison

realising the hidden advantages of buying from home suppliers, and some are developing very fast lead-time relationships in order to gain the benefit of quick-response deliveries, once a new fashion look has hit the market. Speed, commitment and mutual understanding are the key ingredients for these new UK retailer/supplier relationships, and they are now being replicated throughout many European countries. The advantages to both parties are immense.

Foreign buying

Stock transportation

When stock is purchased from foreign sources, there are four different ways in which the order price can be constructed in relation to the transportation method used, as listed and explained in Table 7.5.

Owing to the complex nature of international freight forwarding, many retailers employ either an in-house expert to control all aspects of shipping and forwarding, or outsource the responsibility to a specialist freight-forwarding agency. Some shipping agencies have also diversified into the provision of specialist technical services, such a quality control and checking. Buyers need to be fully aware of the implications of transport on-costs when negotiating with

Table 7.5   Shipping terms defined

• **Free on Board (FOB)**	Price of products includes transport cost from supplier's factory gate to the ship or aeroplane, but excludes international transport and insurance costs.
• **Carriage, Insurance and Freight (CIF)**	Price of products includes transport and insurance from supplier's factory gate right through to the home port of the fashion retailer. The retailer will be charged for delivery from their home port to their distribution centre
• **Free House (or DDP – Delivery Duty Paid)**	Price includes all international and local transport and insurance costs directly from the supplier's factory gate until delivery to the fashion retailer's European distribution centre
• **Ex-factory**	Price of products does not include the insurance and transport costs. The fashion retailer is responsible for paying all onward transport costs from the supplier's factory gate, directly to their own distribution centre.

overseas suppliers. A free house cost price is generally far more expensive than an ex-factory price.

Foreign payment terms

One of the most difficult aspects of foreign buying is the transfer of money from the fashion retailer to the manufacturer or agent. This can be particularly problematic with unknown or untried new suppliers, as fashion retailers can be vulnerable to international fraud. There are basically two fundamental ways to pay for foreign goods – letters of credit or cash against documents.

Letters of credit

Usually, a letter of credit is an irrevocable agreement to pay for products ordered once the documentation of the proven loading of the goods has been presented to the relevant international banks. The documentation indicates that the goods *exist and are ready for transportation*. This acts as some security for both parties, but a letter of credit can be very inflexible and is a costly and inflexible instrument.

Cash against documents

This is a faster, more flexible and informal way of paying foreign suppliers. Usually used mainly with those suppliers that have long-standing relationship with the fashion retailer, the system is based upon *proven and mutual trust* and is more conducive to the fast-moving modern fashion retailer.

Table 7.6   Typical international shipping lead times – supplier's gates to UK DC

Area	Time
• Far East (weeks)	4/6 by sea, 1/2 by air
• Europe (weeks)	1/2 by road
• United Kingdom (days)	1/3 by road

Transport lead-times

The term 'lead-time' has many interpretations. In this context, 'lead-time' is defined as the *transport delivery period from the supplier's factory gate to the designated retailer's distribution centre or store.*

It is difficult in the context of this book to give accurate delivery times to Europe from all over the world. There are many factors that can affect the speed of delivery, such as availability of transport, national holidays and customs problems, etc. However, some very average time scales are shown in Table 7.6. Much depends upon the location of the supplier in relation to the fashion retailer.

Transport should not be confused with *order lead-time*, which refers to the time taken from the point that the order is placed, until delivery into the retail distribution centre. It therefore includes the whole production process, as well as the transport lead-time.

The order lead-time can be very variable, depending upon:

- Supplier's geographic location
- Fabric availability/lead-time
- Component availability/lead-time
- Manufacturing capacity and availability of spare production
- Advanced booking of manufacturing
- Transportation availability/lead-time

There are examples of very fast younger market fashion retailers with dedicated local manufacturing sources and available fabric stocks, that have a five-day order lead time. At the other end of the spectrum more up-market fashion, using a combination of foreign fabrics and UK manufacture, may take much longer. An example of a typical critical path for an up-market UK fashion retailer buying tailoring from the United Kingdom using Italian fabric is shown in Figure 7.3.

The changing supplier base

The need for rationalisation

With buyers for many different product categories across different divisions of the same large multiple retailer, the selection of suppliers resulted in some of the larger retail groups having many hundreds of suppliers. A large and unwieldy supplier base can create problems for retailers, in terms of maintaining regular

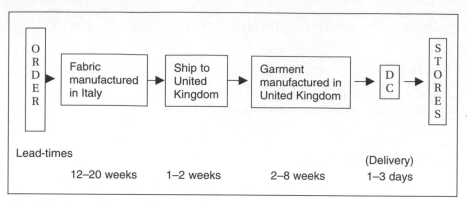

Note: DC = Distribution Centre.

Figure 7.3   A supply chain model for a fashion retail brand – woven product

management communication with so many other businesses. Additional problems included the lack of standardisation of administrative procedures, quality control, sampling processes, packaging of goods, etc. as well as increased costs.

It has been common in the past for large fashion groups not to be aware how many suppliers they were actually buying from. Individual buyers, who may have been unaware of the detrimental implications of the buying policy, were encouraging many problematic, small and incompatible suppliers. Senior management has increasingly become more able to understand the variability of supplier performance, as a result of faster, more analytical and smarter information systems that are now able to focus on all issues relating to individual supplier performance and profitability.

The benefits of having a more focused supplier base, with fewer larger suppliers include:

- *Economies of scale* on all buying, leading to cheaper cost prices and higher margins
- Improved *reliability* in terms of quality and delivery
- More effective *management communication* between both parties
- Greater understanding of *shared business* risks
- Greater *mutual interdependence*
- More sophisticated *supplier service and professionalism*
- Increased *competitive advantage* as a result of faster response to demand.

While supplier rationalisation has many benefits, there are dangers of being too dependent, too focused and involved with a few suppliers. Problems of overfocus on too few suppliers include:

- Failure to see and potentialise *new and creative innovations*
- Failure to trade with businesses supplying competitors
- *Over-reliance on a few suppliers and lack of product development* caused by complacent existing suppliers

- *Sameness of designs and products* from existing suppliers
- Too few suppliers may be risky, if no alternative sources of supply are quickly available in the event of *delivery failure*.

The benefits of supplier rationalisation outweigh the potential difficulties and downside of a wider supplier base. Historically it was not unknown for a few large fashion retailers to have over 2000 suppliers. Currently, most multiple retailers are only dealing with a few hundred, with an inner core of twenty key suppliers providing up to 40 per cent of the total stock intake.

New suppliers will always be added to the rationalised list each season, and of course poor-performing suppliers risk elimination if they fail to make adequate profit for the retailer. New factories need to be carefully vetted, and initial factory visits would be required prior to consideration for their inclusion. Initial factory visits need to evaluate:

- Quality and consistency of production
- Maximum production levels
- How far local employment practices meet reasonable European ethical standards
- Evidence that local health and safety criteria are being achieved
- Quality levels of factory staff, management and technologists.

Buyers should realise that many foreign manufacturers produce garments for several different suppliers or brands and as such it is important that, during the initial visit, the level or involvement of that factory with other suppliers and brands is evaluated, to ensure that it has sufficient capacity to produce their order. Often new factories have future potential for more than one fashion buyer within the same organisation; therefore factory visit reports must be widely circulated to all buyers in the organisation. Information about de-listed factories needs to be similarly circulated to all buyers and buying management.

Regular *supplier performance reviews* are now standard practice among most fashion retailers; often these reviews will invite suppliers along to discuss issues and problems directly with the buyer, in the presence of senior management.

Supply chain management

Definition

A supply chain is the integrated 'chain' of businesses responsible for the manufacture, delivery and sale of a product to a consumer. However, some see the fashion supply chain as the series of manufacturers, agents and wholesalers which supply the product, fabric and trimmings. This chapter will explore the fast-moving and complex issues of supply chain management from the perspective of a large/multiple fashion retailer, which issues orders to suppliers. However, strictly speaking, a fashion supply chain could be any group of sequentially integrated businesses working to supply a product, depending on who the 'customer' is in any particular business scenario.

The model shown in Figure 7.3 is simplistic for the purposes of this book and illustrates a supply chain for a fashion retailer sourcing fabric in Europe and manufacturing the garments in the United Kingdom. Although it identifies lead-times relating to the various stages, the model does not represent other very detailed activities concerned with sampling at the fabric and garment stages. Clearly supply chains vary dramatically between yarns and fabrics (knitted and woven). The fashion retail supply chain model can often be very complex and convoluted; this is another reason why supplier rationalisation makes good sense. Anything that can 'de-confuse' fashion retailing is of automatic benefit to all parties involved.

Although 'supply chains' have always existed, the emergence of a dedicated *supply chain management function* within fashion retailing has become more prominent over the past ten years. Key benefits for retailers arising from this logistical focus are greater efficiencies and consequential cost savings. Savings and efficiency improvements are now a regular feature of fashion companies' annual trading statements.

Traditionally, retailers have bought for two main seasons a year, Spring/Summer and Autumn/Winter, with two seasonal sales to clear surplus merchandise. New stock would be bought for the beginning of a season and placed into warehouses to be supplied to stores as and when demand required it. Greater overseas sourcing meant longer lead-times, thus requiring greater quantities of stock to be bought in advance, as lead times prevented repeat orders within the same season. Retailers faced many problems with this kind of approach – in particular, large inventories occupying space in warehouses, stock rooms and the shop floor, for longer than was necessary. They are now looking for shorter lead-times, often achieved by quick response manufacture, requiring mills to hold stocks of fabric for immediate call off.

Retailers have a stronger position of power in their business relationships than their suppliers. This can result in the use of aggressive buying management and trading practices by some larger fashion multiples. Harsh cost–price negotiations, cancelled orders and tough penalty discounts are all hazards faced by suppliers when trading with the larger fashion groups. Many good suppliers are now refusing to deal with some of the larger more aggressive fashion retailing groups, as a direct result of unfair treatment. Equally, some suppliers have been slack with deliveries, poor on quality and made exaggerated claims on production deadlines and deliveries. To some extent these problems have emerged from differences between manufacturers and retailers' corporate cultures. Such past cultural differences can be summarised in Table 7.7.

Buyers' views of suppliers

Originally many 'old school' buyers believed that they alone had power in the market place. Suppliers were plentiful and could be acquired and lost at will, simply because there were easy replacements available. This was particularly the case as overseas sourcing became more acceptable to consumers: many

Table 7.7 Manufacturers and retailer's corporate cultures

- **Suppliers' viewpoint**
  - No need to innovate, wait for retailers to give us ideas and designs
  - We are interested only in manufacturing – not in design
  - What profit we make is our business – not the retailers'
  - All retailers are untrustworthy and give away our ideas
  - We know the market better than the retailers – we are more experienced
  - We have inflexible production methods – take it or leave it
  - We never change our production methods – we know best

- **Retailers' viewpoint**
  - We are more important than the manufacturer – we have the buying power
  - We are not interested in a long-term relationship – there is no need for it
  - The supplier must do what we say
  - Suppliers work well only when under pressure
  - Our aim is to get the lowest cost price possible – we do not care about the long-term survival of the supplier
  - There are plenty more suppliers out there

suppliers were seen simply as providing a replaceable service rather than being an integrated part of the supply chain. In some instances, where a retailer was over stocked or wanted to get out of imminent deliveries, an order would be cancelled for the most minor reason. This can only be described as totally unacceptable and unethical business behaviour. Unsurprisingly therefore, research into how buyers perceive suppliers is tainted by some of these old stereotypes (Table 7.8).

Table 7.8 Buyer/supplier perceptions of each other

Suppliers	Buyers
• Generally older more experienced	• Young and inexperienced
• Always full of excuses	• Use threats and buying power
• Promise the world	• Make unrealistic demands
• Doing the same job for years	• Change departments regularly
• Too relaxed with plenty of time	• Too busy all the time

The buyer/supplier relationship is now developing from being adversarial, to being one based upon joint cooperation. Simply negotiating price downwards was the old way; now more of an 'open book approach' to pricing has emerged, where the supplier ensures that the buyer is aware of all costs and profits involved in the manufacturing process. Similarly the supplier is also aware of the buyers' required buying margin, as well as being fully acquainted with the buyers' price points and price architecture. Both parties fully understand each other's business demands, and work jointly toward achieving them: the long-term survival of both is critical to the long-term survival of each company. The modern fashion buyer now realises that the supplier is a very important part of the buying equation. Adversarial buying approaches by large European buying groups have lead to the direct closure of many large indigenous manufacturing units. In any business dealings, it is essential for both parties to make a profit, if both are to survive.

The need for efficiency

One of the most crucial areas for fashion retailers is the movement of products through the supply chain, from supplier to retail outlet. If this is not managed efficiently and effectively, retailers can face reduced profit margins, as poor stock control results in the expense of housing too much stock or of lost sales arising through too little stock. Getting garments from sample conception to sample stage, into the DC and then finally delivered to the shop floor is a very complex procedure. The next section examines the stages of this process in detail.

Sample development in the supply chain

A key factor in achieving agreed delivery dates is the smooth process of developing garment samples, which begins once the two-dimensional (2D) shapes have been confirmed and specification sheets drawn up. Suppliers produce samples at different stages in the buying process with various approvals required before manufacture can begin.

All elements of a garment are sampled and approved by the relevant buying departments (buyer or assistant buyer, depending on the significance of what is being approved) before a supplier can proceed with production. Exceptions may exist where the same fabric or trimmings are being used again.

Figure 7.5 identifies both the typical sequences of events in the process of developing garments and the functional area of responsibility associated with each, although sampling procedures may vary from business to business. There is a clear shift in the shared responsibility of garment technology and buying with design throughout the process, as issues become more commercially oriented.

Sample requirements

Once the designer and buyer have agreed the product designs, the buying team will make official requests for samples of all products to be purchased. These need to be clearly identified to the supplier, as they are a cost that will need to be quantified. Samples can range from prototypes, called 'fit samples', to photo samples that are production garments couriered early for press, brochure and other promotional photography.

Base and bulk fabric tests and approval

Fabric approval usually occurs at two different stages, the first being 'base fabric' approval, which is required for all new fabrics that the buyers have not used before, and the second being approval of the bulk fabric. The base fabric tests ensure that the fabric is suitable for its intended purpose in terms of performance and represents minimum standards required. These may include the following:

Activity	Responsibility
Design 2D product options/groups Design specification sheet for each product	Design/Buying/ Merchandising
↓	
Specify sample requirements	Design/Buying
↓	
Base fabric tests	Buying/GT
↓	
Product review/Range presentation	Buying and Merchandising
↓	
Initial/First fit sample	Buying/GT
↓	
Lab-dips/strike-offs[a]	Buying/GT
↓	
Garment pre-production/grading	GT/Buying
↓	
Pre-production sealing	GT/Buying
↓	
Trim approval	Buying
↓	
Bulk fabric approval	Buying/GT
↓	
Production sealing	GT/Buying
↓	
Distribution Centre inspection	DC team

Notes: GT = Garment Technologist.
[a] See p. 134.

Figure 7.5   Key stages in the development of a fashion garment

- Stability of the fabric to various cleaning methods (machine wash – dry clean)
- Pilling/Abrasion
- Tensile strength
- Extension and recovery
- Wrinkle recovery.

The particular combination of tests will vary according to product type. For example, extension and recovery of the fabric used in knitted swimwear is an important test, whereas fabric used for woven tailoring would not test for this, but would test for wrinkle recovery.

The bulk fabric, which is the completed fabric, is tested to check both the agreed standards set at the previous base fabric stage and the performance requirements of the developed fabric after further changes to its colour, print and finishing have been made. At the base fabric stage, the supplier would have submitted a fabric specification sheet detailing a range of information including the correct fibre content. It is a legal requirement at the *bulk fabric* testing stage for an independent testing laboratory to verify the fibre content in the fabric, so that product labelling is accurate.

Bulk fabric approval must be given before the fabric can be cut for manufacture. As the fabric is completed at this stage, with all colours and prints designs approved, further fabric tests would be mainly concerned with colour fastness. Colour fastness tests include reaction to:

- Washing
- Dry rubbing
- Light
- Water
- Perspiration
- Chlorine (swimwear)
- Dry cleaning.

Other fabric tests conducted at this stage would include stability to washing or dry cleaning. Once again, the particular combination of tests will vary according to the product and its design. For example, colour fastness for swimwear would include a chlorine test whereas for wovens it would be a dry cleaning test. It is important to note that the base and bulk fabric tests occur sometime apart from each other, the latter only being possible once the range has been confirmed and the colours and print strike-offs to be used in the final fabric have received separate approvals. However, for this chapter it has been convenient to explain the two fabric tests together to clarify their sequence.

The product review, or range presentation as it is also known, is the forum for confirming the season's range of product designs intended for production. Very little can happen to fabric colour and print design until the senior management has given the buyers authority to proceed. Once the range has been given the go-ahead then the next stage of sample development can occur.

Categories of samples

It is common for fashion retailers to colour code their samples, along the lines of black for the first sample, red for the final correct version needed for manufacture

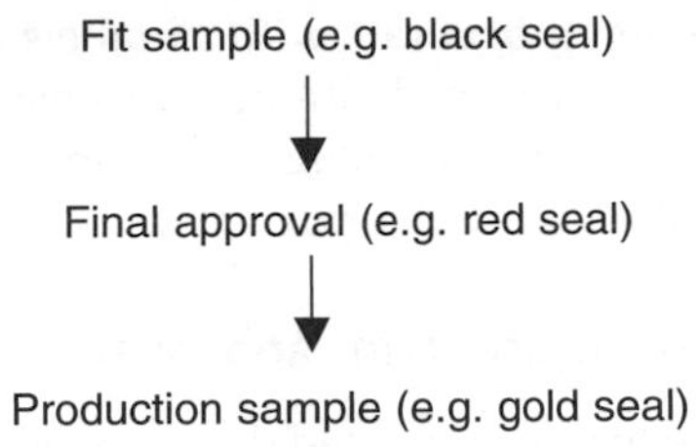

Fit sample (e.g. black seal)

↓

Final approval (e.g. red seal)

↓

Production sample (e.g. gold seal)

Figure 7.6   Sample specification process

and gold for the first garments off the production line. However, readers should be aware that the particular colour code used to identify a stage of sealing approval will vary from company to company, there is no industry norm for this. Fit samples are produced early on in the process as they are used to check how the sample specification works in reality (see Figure 7.6).

Fit samples

This initial sample is in the correct fabric, not necessarily by colour, and its fit is checked on models that are the 'base size' (a medium or a size 12 in women's wear). These are not necessarily catwalk models but individuals who are the right size and are patient and reliable, as fit sessions can be quite time-consuming and frequent. Comments from the buying and technology teams are sent to suppliers along with adjustments to measurements, a process that sometimes needs several attempts. Most fashion retailers have a limit to the number of fit sample amendments they will accept, the common being up to three. After this, the style is at risk of being cancelled.

Final approval pre-production sample

This is the final garment with correct colour and trims but without all the care labels and tickets on it. A full set of garments per style which represent all the sizes are sent by the supplier to the buying department for final approval before the start of production. The samples are checked against the approved first fit sample and garments are measured to check that grading increments are correct across the sizes. Although the final labels will not necessarily be in place, the supplier will indicate where they understand the labels should go. The supplier uses this sample as a sealed record to be referenced when manufacturing. However, nothing can be sealed until the fabric test reports are received and approved by the independent laboratories.

Production sample

As soon as the supplier is under way with production of a style, two garments (in the base size) are sent to the fashion retailer to be checked against what was approved at the final approval stage. Production samples will be the first garments that are completely accurate with all labels and tickets in place. These samples will be tried for size on fit models to ensure no deviation from the approval. If there is a problem at this stage, the sample will not be sealed and the rest of the production not accepted for delivery.

Print strike-offs, lab-dips and trim approvals

Those garments that are to have a printed design need to have the print approved for design and colour on the appropriate fabric. The size of the print strike-off needs to be large enough to show a repeat of the print design. The colour of the fabric also needs to be checked for accuracy, as the wrong tone can create colour clashes or problems in co-ordination with other products. Colour is usually approved by the use of 'lab-dips' although some retailers find that a 'Pantone' colour reference helps manufacturers achieve the correct match. Problems can obviously occur in the coordination of the same shade of colour on products produced by different manufacturers.

'Lab-dips' are swatches of fabric dyed in tonal variations of the specified colour and sent to the fashion retailer for approval. Typically there will be a two or three choices reflecting variations in colour tone, and the retailer will have to make a visual assessment which matches their original colour standard most closely. The purpose of lab-dips is to provide the manufacturer with the best dye recipe to achieve the intended colour. In order for the buyer to make an effective assessment, the swatch of fabric must be big enough and resemble the intended bulk fabric very closely. The buyer or designer, using 'light boxes', examines lab-dips, where differing light bulbs are used to reproduce daylight, store light and ultra-violet conditions. Trimmings, which include zips, buttons, interlinings, shoulder pads, embroideries and many others, also need approval before garment production. Buyers need to take account of the lead-times involved in sourcing from different suppliers.

There are many other details that could be considered here including care labelling, but the important point is that as so much needs to be sampled it is crucial to have a *critical path* indicating progress, in order for the whole supply chain to run effectively. It is increasingly common for fashion retailers to have an on-line order management system that can track progress of the product from sampling through to delivery. Internal systems are integrated with the Internet enabling direct and fast communication with suppliers around the world. This process of sample development allows fashion retailers to reduce the chance of poor-quality stock arriving in their stores. However, the complexity and large number of steps involved require the process to be efficiently managed for the supply chain to be effective. It also requires suppliers to be fully aware of their obligations, and in this respect very thorough supplier manuals are provided by the fashion retailer detailing their requirements.

Changes resulting from supply chain management

Five of the main changes to arise from this new focus on supply chains have been:

1 *Change in business culture* between retailer and supplier, as the traditionally adversarial and dominant approach of the retailer toward its suppliers has been replaced with clearer and standardised communications set in partnerships.
2 The ability of retailers to react quickly, to sales and place repeat orders with short lead-time suppliers, has significantly been improved through the huge advances in *information gathering, transmission and analysis*. Point of sale IT combined with more sophisticated computer-based merchandising systems enable retailers to spot and react quickly to sales trends. Wide-area networks allow retailers to pass on key sales information to selected key suppliers who can repeat produce winning styles very quickly, enabling the retailer to potentialise fickle fashion trends.
3 *Distribution centres* (DCs) instead of warehouses. There has been a move away from a business philosophy of filling up warehouses to hold stock until, or if it is required by the stores, to one where a DC receives, quality controls and distributes new stock to stores within twenty-four hours.
4 *Reduced numbers of suppliers* – smaller supplier base focusing on improving relationships/developing partnerships with a small number of key suppliers, who consistently achieve good performance in terms of profitability, returns, and delivery reliability. A number of multiples are in a position where their top twenty suppliers are producing 70–80 per cent of their products.
5 The development of thorough *standardised supplier manuals* for all suppliers setting out clear procedures and directions for all products areas across all divisions.

The advent of supply chain management in fashion retailers has resulted in a number of changes to buying and merchandising procedures, including supplier selection and all forms of communication to suppliers from the first order through to the delivery of good to the DC.

IT and the supply chain

Many retailers are now using IT to gain a better control of the overall product development and supply chain processes. Product development information systems are now able to track the progress of a line at all stages of the product from conception through till delivery. Such systems include video records of designs, colour and fabric samples and other key deadline dates along the critical path. This vital information ensures that all functions within the organisation are able to undertake immediate on-line interrogation about any aspect of the product.

Supplier selection

Originally, the buyer was the only person within the fashion-buying organisation who was likely to meet regularly with the supplier. Very often, more emphasis would be placed upon the personalities of the supplier and buyer than upon the long-term joint success of both parties' business. The professionalism needed in good supply chain management now requires the supplier to come into contact with many other support functions within fashion retailing. The buying manager or buying director is able to keep a much better grasp on supplier performance, as a direct result of computerised management information systems.

The selection, and retention, of suppliers is now no longer simply a matter of concern for the buyer alone. The whole management team is now involved in the development and improvement of the trading relationship. The need for an objective, rather than subjective, approach to a fashion business's day-to-day dealings with a supplier is essential if both parties truly want to improve the product, supply the customer with what they want – and, more importantly, sustain profitability over time.

It is true to say that many of today's fashion buyers are now very young, often without the experience of the 'old battle-axe'-type buyer, so often portrayed as the archetypal department store buyer in films and TV. While younger buyers undoubtedly have drive and enthusiasm, by virtue of their age, they usually lack the experience of time: one wag once remarked that they believed that the ideal buyer for Top Shop would be aged about fifteen with at least ten years' buying experience!

Issues for retail buyers

Supply chain management and its associated techniques are undoubtedly having a major impact upon the work of the fashion buyer. The increasingly competitive world of fashion buying in the new millennium is making the buyer's job tougher and more demanding than ever: the need for improving skills and understanding has never been more important. Many larger retailers are now realising that simply having an eye for fashion is no longer good enough to meet the rigours of the new fashion order. Training and the need for personal self-development have never been greater. More and more, fashion buyers will need to create opportunities to ensure that they are up to date with the latest technology and management techniques. Often self-improvement will be the only way to advance personal understanding, often as result of the company itself being too busy to help the individual, something that is unfortunately also a fact of life in many businesses outside of the world of fashion.

Issues for manufacturers

European fashion manufacturers have been and are still being subjected to increasing international competition from developing countries all around the globe. Support for home-produced goods is decreasing every day, as consumers vote more with their wallets than with their hearts. Today's international consumer is less and less bothered by where a garment is made: if the price, quality and looks meet expectations, then generally that is all that is needed.

In the past, older customers tended to be very loyal to home producers, but this is becoming less so. Occasionally, one country or another will have its goods internationally boycotted, usually on some political ground: there have been historic examples of fashion boycott of South Africa, and in the future no one knows which country will be next.

As such, suppliers now have to be more and more competitive than ever – not just on price but on design, quality, delivery and value for money. As fashion buyers travel more and more, as international markets widen and barriers to trade drop, there is no room for second-rate suppliers. The forces of the market will eventually take their toll on the weak. It is for this reason that many European garment manufacturers have moved their manufacturing to cheap labour-cost countries. This movement is continuing and seems an inevitable outcome for many non-specialist manufacturers. Only those higher-quality manufacturers with either unique selling propositions or successful brands (that can command higher prices) seem to have a future in high cost Europe.

Measuring performance

The increasing use of technology in the control and measurement of fashion retailing was stressed throughout Chapter 6. This is turn has meant that more and more information and data can be collected and analysed than ever before, and this ability has given a new impetus to supply chain management. The continual monitoring and measurement of supplier performance, on both an individual and a comparative basis is now clearly revealing true levels of supplier performance, in more and more detailed formats. There is simply no hiding place for poor suppliers, or for buyers who continue to deal with suppliers with a poor performance record.

The better more efficient supplier welcomes comparative details of performance, as this can act as an enabling yardstick to future improvement. In some fields of non-fashion retailing, particularly amongst branded foods, the retailer makes weekly sales' data available for the supplier, but at a cost. Having spent so much money capturing sales and stock data, more enterprising retailers have realised that this information is a powerful competitive weapon for branded manufacturers, who are usually quite prepared to pay for it. It is likely that this will also happen on a wider scale in fashion retailing, as competition becomes more intense.

While some retailers are already transmitting sales and stock data directly to suppliers on a regular basis, this is not yet widespread within the fashion industry. This data is transmitted in a similar way to Internet signals down telephone wires. This is commonly known as Electronic Data Interchange or EDI. Receiving sales information almost immediately will enable the more enterprising clothing manufacturers to ensure that the production line is set up adequately to meet the sales demands of better-selling styles, poorer-selling styles being cancelled or delayed. Often the supplier has more time to consider such decisions than the hard-pushed buyer and/or merchandiser. Data and information will increasingly become a valuable commodity throughout the entire fashion industry.

The benefits of supply chain management

There are a number of key benefits for the fashion retailer from supply chain management:

1 The retailer is able get products *from the manufacturer to the customer* more profitably
2 *Stock inventories* are kept to their lowest and most efficient level at all stages of the year. This keep shops looking refreshed and minimises poor-selling lines in favour of best-selling lines by more frequent and smaller deliveries
3 Sales, stock, delivery and other *key performance indicator (KPI) information* is generally more easily gathered, distributed, analysed and effectively acted upon by both retailer and supplier
4 A firmer and longer-lasting relationship is created between both retailer and supplier by the development of *longer-term production commitments*
5 Response to *consumer demand* is more timely and accurately focused
6 *Terminal stocks of unseasonal stock* at the end of the season are minimised as result of better overall control methodologies

Supply chain management is an important function within the world of fashion buying and merchandising. As suppliers become more global in their approach to production, it is becoming more and more important for the buyer and merchandiser to understand clearly the implications of dealing with home suppliers versus foreign imports. As explained earlier in the chapter, there are often hidden costs involved with foreign buying. Submerged under the small peak of ice (perceived costs) showing above the water is huge and dangerous mass below (real costs). Colliding with icebergs is not to be recommended!

Note

1. Hines, T. (2000), *Supply Chain Management – Strategies, Structure and Relationships*, Checkmate Business Books.

■ ☑ 8 Stock management and distribution

Definitions

As explained in Chapter 2, the merchandising role has responsibility for, first, getting stock 'into the business' and then, secondly, for getting it 'around the business', in as effective and efficient way as possible. This chapter examines both stock management and distribution. In Chapter 6, we examined the stock flow into the business, mainly at an overall and category level. In many respects overall stock management can be viewed on two levels. First, the *macro level* looks at the value of stock in total to ensure that the department and/or business is not buying too much or too little stock that it has the potential to sell in its shops. Secondly, there is the need to control stock at the *micro level*, which looks at the number of units in stock by line, colour and size level by individual branch. This chapter deals mainly in a micro-detail level.

Once the business receives stock into the distribution centre (DC), there is the problem of dealing with stock as individual items, each with a colour and size – and, more importantly, each option has to be sent to the right shop or store where it is needed. This low level of stock control is called either *distribution* or *allocation*. Adding up all branch or micro stock levels by value gives a simple macro stock level by total value. With a large business consisting of a wide range of lines and possibly having many hundreds of stores; control at the micro level is extremely complex and time-consuming. IT systems and application developments have made it possible for even the most complex fashion businesses to continuously monitor sales performance at line level detail, as well as providing easily accessible details of current shop and distribution centre stock holding on a near-immediate basis. The power and usefulness of such merchandise information systems is awesome.

Fitting the number of lines to the business

Once the business has decided to buy into a category, there is the need to ensure that the number of lines bought actually creates an effective offering to the customer, as well as fitting accurately into the space available. Very few European fashion retailers have any two shops that are identical in terms of floor space and fixtures available upon which to hang or display the stock; this is mainly as a result of the random way in which shopping centres have developed through time. Many large-scale retailers have been more fortunate and have been able to create much more standardised store layouts as result of being able to build them to a formula from scratch, usually on new sites away from the congestion of the old high streets and city centres.

The merchandisers will automatically take into account the problem of variable shop size as they start to plan which styles or ranges go to each shop. In general, smaller-sized shops have to carry a smaller range by width and depth of stock, to ensure that they are able to display as much stock as they can on the shop floor without it being too congested. Most modern fashion retailers try to have no stock rooms at all, preferring to force stock onto the shop floor where it has an immediate chance of selling to the customer. Keeping stock in stock rooms away from the shop floor is no use at all. The costs involved are enormous, as high street and city centre rentals make the stock room one of the most expensive warehouses possible. Good fashion retailers use every spare square metre to trade from to ensure that they are optimising sales densities.

The difference between the size of the smallest and the largest shop or store in a fashion chain can be immense. Chains having large shops with nearly ten times as much space as the smallest are not unusual. Quite clearly this does not necessarily mean that the large shops need ten times as many ranges as the smallest, but probably five–six times as many is a good approximation. Very often a fashion chain may need to undertake a special buying and ranging process if they do have a small number of extremely large stores.

Tip

Retail space

Always ensure that you know the physical size of every retail outlet to ensure that you do not send in too many or too few lines

The range plan and initial allocations

The *range plan* is the key document in the range planning process, as well being the main source document for planning what lines and how many of them will go to each individual branch (Table 8.1). This document places shops into logical size groupings, which ensures that each group carries the right number of lines at any point during the season. It also forms the guideline document for initial

Table 8.1   Typical range plan – also showing initial allocation quantities of a line, by units

Turnover of store	Line					Total
	A	**B**	**C**	**D**	**E**	
Very large	24	24	18	18	12	96
Large	18	18	12	12	9	69
Medium	12	12	9	9		42
Small	6	6				12

allocations, and will be used by the distribution or allocation team as their planning base. An initial allocation defines how many of each size and colour of a style will be sent to each retail outlet after initial delivery of a new line into the DC. Most fashion retailers will send out to shops between 60 per cent and 70 per cent of the overall imtral quantity bought; the remaining 30 per cent–40 per cent being retained for replenishment allocations on a weekly basis thereafter, to those branches that are selling the line freely.

As is shown in Table 8.1, the number of lines held in the very large group of branches is over twice that held in the small branches. The actual level of initial allocation by line also reduces as the turnover of the store decreases. Wherever possible, fashion businesses generally phase delivery of all-store lines into the DC at the start of the season to ensure that the small shops start with a full range of new products. In reality, deliveries do not always run to plan, and often initial allocations of new lines may be delayed over a period of time, as fragmented deliveries arrive at the DC in dribs and drabs. The merchandiser, in conjunction with the distribution team manager, may decide to wait until a more balanced selection of sizes and colours is available before sending out initial allocations: sending out broken or disjointed runs of sizes and colours to stores can cause a great deal of customer dissatisfaction.

Tip

Sending out stock

Never send all the stock of a line out at once. Keep a reasonable percentage back for later replenishment to those shops that are selling it well

How allocations are planned

When, for example, the buyer and merchandiser have planned to buy a line for either all or for a limited number or group of stores, they will be faced with the decision as to how many of each size and colour to buy. The *size ratio* that needs to be bought will most likely be based upon historically gathered data from previous season(s). Sizing throughout any population generally follows the standard distribution curve, as shown in Figure 8.1.

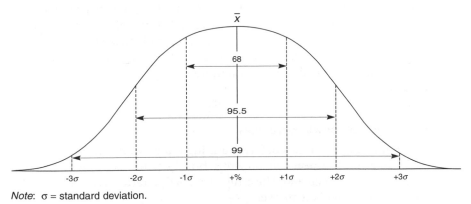

Note: σ = standard deviation.

Figure 8.1 Standard distribution curve

Table 8.2   Typical size buying ratio calculation, ladies' dresses

Sizes	8	10	12	14	16	18	20	22
% of total population	2.8	11.8	23.1	23	17.4	11	5.7	5.2
% historic sales of business	2.2	9.9	27.8	26.7	20.0	10.0	2.2	1.2
% proposed buy	2.8	11.8	23.1	23	17.4	11	5.7	5.2
Unit buy based on 10 000	280	1180	2310	2300	1740	1100	570	520
Proposed initial allocation 70%	200	820	1620	1620	1220	770	400	360
Best distribution ratio	1	4	8	8	6	4	2	2

In Figure 8.1 the extreme left-hand part of the curve could relate to the number of smaller women (say, sizes 8 and below) and the right-hand part could relate to the number of larger women (say, sizes 16 and above). Clearly the overall level of demand for these extremes of sizes is much lower than for the average sizes 12–16. However, if a business is aiming solely at outsize or petite women, then the size distribution curve of that particular business will need to represent the sizes of the targeted customer profile. It will need to be skewed towards them rather than at the standard distribution curve of the whole population (see Table 8.2).

From Table 8.2, it becomes evident that it is actually very difficult to send out the initial allocation in exact proportion to either the historic sales pattern – or, indeed, to that of the total population. The unit ratio finally sent out can never exactly match the percentages of the historic sales. The ratio is as close as it is possible to get when a business is initially allocating such small quantities to an individual shop or store; at best, it is always a compromise.

However, any variations from the true level of sizes demanded by the consumer, will automatically be picked up as stock is replenished by regular weekly repeat allocations sent out from the DC to individual shops. Each week, as result of the individual size/colour unit sales, there is generally an automated allocation system that makes recommendations at individual shop level as to what needs to be sent out. Originally, before computers were available to read this mass of low-level data, the merchandising and/or distribution team would have to manually examine and read the hand-prepared stock counts and then make line/size/colour allocation decisions. This slow laborious task was both time-consuming and generally quite inaccurate.

Tip

Correct size ratios win extra sales

Check national size ratios before planning a buy; your own business size ratios may be the result of previous buying patterns, rather than real customer/market demand. These historic sales patterns may not reflect the true requirement of the market.

The merchandiser's involvement with stock management and distribution

The degree to which a merchandiser gets involved with the day-to-day management of stock into shops can vary. This is dependant upon whether or not the organisation in question has either an integrated distribution function within individual buying and merchandising teams, or whether or not it is run as a separate distribution team, usually managed by a dedicated distribution manager. Whichever way the management of distribution has been set up, the merchandiser must at all times have a near complete grasp of what lines have been allocated or distributed to which shops, and in what quantity. With larger, fast-moving businesses it would be impractical for the merchandiser to know everything that is happening in their department, although with the intelligent use of IT interrogation routines, it is usually a simple matter of knowing the right question to ask and where to look for the answer. In all fashion organisations, it is essential that the merchandiser has an immediate grasp of what value of stock the business is holding, as well as the value of stock commitments in the future. The combination of these two is usually referred to as the *potential stock* or sometimes the *total level of commitment.*

For more classic or older targeted age group businesses, there is generally less risk in investing further forward into the fashion season. Basic garments for older more stable customer groups do not suffer from swings in demand, as do the more fashionable garments that are aimed at younger more fickle customers. However, even classic fashion businesses like to be flexible enough to ensure that they have enough 'open to buy' to undertake trials of newly emerging fashion trends.

The automated distribution system

The automatic replenishment or distribution system is now a standard part of the management information system of most large fashion retailers. These systems, whilst generally described as 'automatic', in reality need a great deal of regular human intervention to ensure that the system replenishes logically and sends out just the right amount of stock. The system basically works by deducting the individual size/colour sales each week from the stock that the shop started with at the beginning of the week, usually referred to as the opening stock. Table 8.3 overleaf shows an example of the calculation.

Replenishment to pattern

As shown in the calculation in Table 8.3, the shop has received an initial allocation of 34 units that has been sent in as close as possible to the historic selling ratio of V-neck cotton jumpers. The replenishment system has, in this case, simply been programmed to recommend that the stock sold is replenished back exactly to the pattern of the initial allocation. This type of replenishment is known simply as 'replenishment to pattern'. A pattern is held on the computer for each different size/group of shops; for bigger shops the

Table 8.3 Automatic replenishment calculation for small size/low turnover store: Description – Men's white cotton jumper, Long Sleeve, V-neck, £29.99, Line no. 123456

Sizes	32	34	36	38	40	42	44	46	Total
Initial opening stock at start of week	2	4	5	6	6	5	4	2	34
Sales for one week	1	2	2	3	2	2	2	1	15
Closing stock at end of week	1	2	3	3	4	3	2	1	19
Recommended replenishment	1	2	2	3	2	2	2	1	15
Opening stock the following week	2	4	5	6	6	5	4	2	34*

Note: *Based upon selling 15 units a week, the recommended replenishment system sends back only 15 more units, thus giving the shop in question only a total of 34 units stock to sell. From the 15 units sold that week, the opening stock of 34 is therefore likely to last only just over two weeks more should no more replenishments are made – i.e. 34/15 = 2.3 weeks forward stock cover.

pattern is usually a simple multiple of the initial allocation quantities of a small shop. The patterns are usually reviewed each week and if sales are better than anticipated, the merchandiser or distributor (depending upon the way the distribution team is structured) may increase the overall quantity of a pattern, or change the size stocking ratio according to actual size sales on that individual line. It is important to note that not all garments sell in exactly the same size ratio, as some garments are looser fitting and able to fit larger customers than other lines.

Replenishment to pattern is the most basic type of automatic replenishment, but is probably at the heart of most large fashion replenishment systems. It gives the business the best chance of keeping all sizes and colours on show to the customer. It is often the case that large businesses moving big volumes of stock will have two replenishment runs a week for their bigger branches, especially if those bigger branches do not have very large shops floors or stock room space. Usually most fashion businesses will have two replenishment runs a week. The DC will have stock picking notes generated on site; the stock pickers pick the stock to make up the delivery and it is generally delivered to shops the next day.

In extreme cases, physically small shops with high sales and stock turnover may even require to have five deliveries a week, in order to keep the shop full of stock. In this instance, you can be certain that the retail operations team will already be looking for a larger shop in the vicinity, as the existing one is undoubtedly too small for the demand of the local market.

Sales reactive replenishment

This type of system builds upon the replenishment to pattern technique, but this time it tries not only to ensure that each shop gets back into all sizes and colours quickly, but also ensures that the stock is built to meet likely forward demand. In the replenishment to pattern example shown in Table 8.3 the replenishment

Table 8.4 Sales reactive replenishment calculation for small size/low turnover store: Description – Men's white cotton jumper, Long Sleeve, V-neck, £29.99, Line no. 123456

Sizes	32	34	36	38	40	42	44	46	Total
Initial opening stock at start of week	2	4	5	6	6	5	4	2	34
Sales for one week	1	2	2	3	2	2	2	1	15*
Closing stock at end of week	1	2	3	3	4	3	2	1	19
Recommended replenishment	5	10	13	16	15	12	10	5	86
Opening stock the following week	6	12	16	19	19	15	12	6	105

Note: *Based upon selling 15 units a week, the recommended replenishment system sends back only 86 more units, thus giving the shop in question a total of 105 units stock to sell. From the 15 units sold that week, the opening stock of 105 is therefore likely to last for seven weeks forward based on sales of 15 units a week – i.e. 105/15 = 7 weeks forward stock cover.

method still only leaves the shop with little more than 2.3 weeks' forward stock cover. Considering the average fashion retailer generally works on between 6–9 weeks' forward stock cover, then the replenishment is not really taking into account the rate of sale being achieved and therefore the forward stock requirement of the business. A sales reactive replenishment calculation is shown in Table 8.4, where the parameters set in the computer are (1) to keep the stock in initial allocation ratio and (2) to ensure that the shop also has seven weeks' forward stock cover based on the rate of sale.

In the calculation in Table 8.4, the computer has been pre-programmed to look at the overall weekly rate of sale, then multiply it by seven weeks' forward requirement of stock. It has then balanced that requirement to ensure that the total stock gets back as closely as possible to the original size ratios of the initial allocation. By using overall sales and stock levels upon which to base the calculation, it will ignore individual colour size occurrences – possibly the three size 38s sold that week were sold to a family of triplets! Had we used this example of size performance upon which to base replenishment, then we might have been tempted to build the stock on this size option to $3 \times 7 = 21$ units. This would have more than likely overstocked it by 5 units.

Smoothing factors

Whilst 'replenishing to rate of sale' is probably a better and more statistically accurate way of getting shops restocked, there is often the ability for the merchandiser to 'smooth' or even ignore the significance of one week's sale. For example, during the T-shirt season, bright summer weather during early May can easily accelerate the weekly rate of sale on a key line by up to three times more than normal. If the replenishment system is not smoothed or altered, there is a risk that the automatic nature of the parameters set into the system will overreact or underreact to this abnormal trading situation. In heavy snow, when customers are unable to get into town, the sales for such a week would be under-representative of the norm. Other peak trading garment areas such as women's underwear on St Valentine's Day can also create unusually high sales peaks. The smoothing factors are applied at the weekly distribution meeting and are simply safeguards in the system to ensure that the previous week's performance is statistically accurate and significant, against historic trading trends, for that time of year on any particular garment type. More basic and seasonally unaffected garments, such as men's underwear, usually have less need for smoothing to be applied because of the more stable nature of their sales pattern.

It is also important to realise that local markets can have a big impact upon what actually sells in any branch. For example, in towns with high immigrant populations, there can be fundamentally different demands for different types and even sizes of garments. In general, the Asian population is generally smaller than indigenous white Caucasians. Similarly, in Afro-Caribbean populations, there is generally a demand for larger, long fit garments. Good sales reactive replenishment will automatically pick up these size trends and will automatically skew and balance size runs, making regular recommendations as to sizes needed.

Dummy branch numbers

Most fashion chains either open new branches or temporarily close down an existing branch for modernisation. Essential modernisation programmes usually take place on a rolling basis every three to four years. Large sales increases of anywhere between 30 per cent and 70 per cent can occur as a result of any shop being modernised or refurbished. Modern customers are greatly attracted to visit and spend in new and exciting retail environments. When a new or existing branch opens after re-modernisation (often referred to as a 'mod'), most automatic allocation systems allow a dummy branch number to be created. The merchandiser can then plan ahead to build up a new and exciting package several weeks ahead of the re-opening.

The stock is then built and held in a special location at the DC, and is internally transferred on the computer and then sent to the opening store. Building effective opening packages is a major part of merchandise management for large fashion chains.

The dangers of automatic allocation systems

The word 'automatic' is a dangerous word, in that there is often a human failing that assumes automatic systems will do things as planned. Good merchandisers and distribution managers will always spot check and sometimes undertake a dummy allocation run, ahead of the real run, to ensure that the system is allocating accurately and logically. Dummy allocation runs are a good way to check that the overall reactivity of the system is working.

It is also possible to link line or style numbers, so that if one particular line number or style number sells out, an exact or very closely matching line with a different style number can be allocated against the original line number. This is known as 'line linking' and is a way of ensuring that stock in the distribution centre is used effectively as possible.

In conclusion, automatic allocation or distribution systems are now the norm within most large fashion organisations. Every year they become more and more sophisticated, more able over time to re-align local branch stock levels to take into account special local market conditions and other trading nuances.

In view of the very variable design and unique nature of any automatic replenishment system, all merchandisers require an in-depth understanding of how their individual system works, if they are to ensure that individual shops are provisioned effectively and efficiently. It is for this reason that a majority of merchandisers spend the early part of their career as a distributor or allocator. The distributor has been likened to the bricklayer and the merchandiser to the architect. If the architect fundamentally creates a bad initial design, and if the bricklayer puts the bricks down wrongly, then the entire building will fall down and never get built. This is a very good analogy of the relationship between merchandise and allocator.

Rigid control versus flexibility – the dilemma of overall stock management

All fashion businesses need to control stock in such a way that they leave themselves as much flexibility as possible. In the fast-changing environment of fashion, not even the best buyer can be certain what colour, shape or garment type will dominate at any point of a season. Sometimes one photograph of a garment in a popular magazine can light the fuse of the latest fashion trend. As soon as the merchandiser spots a sales trend, the buyer will be under pressure to buy more deeply into the line. If all spare 'open to buy' has been spent, then buying the line will immediately cause the buying department or business to be 'overspent'. All businesses have a financial limit as to what they can afford to spend, and a fashion retail business is no exception. The senior management and the buying team will have to make a choice between being 'overspent' or taking action to generate room for the repeat buy. Every business has a finite amount of stock that it will be able to sell at any point.

Good buying and merchandising teams always try to leave flexibility in terms of having spare 'open to buy' – to ensure that when new trends emerge they have open to buy available with which to take positive buying action. Even the best buying and merchandising teams will undoubtedly make mistakes, and from time to time will buy slow-selling garments, often referred to as 'dogs'. As well as poor individual lines, the team can also misjudge the demand for a particular colour, silhouette or even type of fabric. There is no such thing as certainty in fashion buying and merchandising. Poor or slow selling lines simply stay in shops, disappoint customers – and, more importantly, take up valuable space and money that would be better invested in faster-selling merchandise. Once a business fails to clear slow-selling stock, it can suffer from what is known as the 'snowball effect'. As the business rolls on and on, the snowball of old slow-selling stock gradually gets larger and larger, to a point where the whole snowball fails to move. This creates a chain reaction of inertia, leading to rapidly failing sales and ultimately to financial disaster.

During the last few years of the millennium there were many examples where poor stock management lead to the ultimate closure of once-famous fashion businesses. Poor slow-selling stock is like a deadly disease and needs to be dealt with immediately. Bad fashion stock does not get better over time! Price reductions required to clear stock out, generally cost more the longer the decision is delayed. The old saying that 'your first loss is always your least' was never better applied than to fashion retailing. Moving slow stock quickly has been used a marketing tool by several of what are now described as the 'new-value' retailers such as Matalan and New Look. These businesses take swift and deep action if lines start to stick and fail to sell quickly. Releasing cash from these slow-selling lines enables their buyers to move quickly back into the market, hopefully to replace the slow-selling lines with new fast-selling ones.

The delivery schedule

At the heart of any good fashion merchandise management systems is the *delivery or commitment schedule*. This is generally kept in computer format, although it is not unknown for smaller less complex businesses to keep it in a simple paper ledger. The delivery schedule is a regularly updated document that enables senior management and the buying and merchandising team to see clearly what is to be delivered into the DC or warehouse on a monthly, weekly and daily basis.

This document ensures that the business is receiving stock when needed – and, more particularly, in line with both anticipated forward and actual current demand. Most fashion buying and merchandising teams are dealing with many hundreds of garments and scores of suppliers. A well ordered computer based delivery schedule can easily be interrogated to see whether or not there is too much or too little stock of any particular fashion product coming into the business at any point. With intelligent IT, supplier delivery performance can also easily be checked.

Late deliveries always have a hidden cost by virtue of the fact that if your shop is not carrying the fashion that the customer wants, then they will simply walk down the road and purchase a similar item from a competitor. Once lost, sales can rarely be picked up in the future. Deliveries of stock, late on during the course of the season, have a knack of failing to sell, simply sitting there until the end of the season when they will probably need to be cleared by a price mark-down during the Sale. The delivery schedule helps the merchandiser avoid late deliveries before they happen. Figure 8.2 is a typical

Figure 8.2 The delivery schedule: 1st quarter, ladies tops

Each period cell shows £000 (upper) / 000 units (lower).

SUPPLIER NAME	LINE NUMBER + DESCRIPTION	NO	RSP	000 UNITS	P1 (JAN) 1	2	3	4	Pd ①	P2 (FEB) 5	6	7	8	Pd ②	P3 (MAR) 9	10	11	12	13	Pd ③	TOTAL £000	000 UNITS	GENERAL COMMENTS
NEWBERY	Blue Jersey V. Neck SS	1 2 3 4	£10	34.7									4/40		8/80	6.5/65	4.7/47	3.8/38	7.7/77		34.7	347	POSSIBLE YARN PROBLEM
SOMMERVILLE	White Tank Top. SS	3 6 7	£10	26.4											6.4/64	5/50	5/50	5/50	5/50		26.4	264	
SOMMERVILLE	White Vest Short/Sleeve	4 7 8	£15	22.0											6/90	4/60	4/60	4/60	4/60		22	330	
SUB TOTAL S/S				83.1					NIL				4/40	4/40	20.4/234	15.5/175	13.7/157	12.8/148	16.7/187	79.1/901	83.1	941	
HORROX	Blue Jersey V. Neck LS	2 6 4 6	£10	10.1	2.1/21	3/30		3/30		2/20											10.1	101	AIR FREIGHT
HUGHES	White Polo Shirt LS	5 8 9 5	£15	7.0		3/45		2/30		2/30											7	105	
EASTWOOD	White Turtle Neck LS	1 8 2 4	£15	4.0		4/60															4	60	
WALLACE	White Crew Neck LS	5 9 8 5	£20	4.8	2.3/46			0.8/16		1.7/34											4.8	96	
SUB TOTAL L/S				25.9	4.4/67	10/135	NIL	5.8/76	20.4/278	5.7/84	NIL	NIL	NIL	5.7/84	NIL	NIL	NIL	NIL	NIL	NIL	25.9	362	
FELDMAR	Blue Turtle Neck 3/4 SL	2 9 9 3	£10	12.5	NIL					6/60	4/40	1.1/11	1.4/14								12.5	125	CHECK SHIPPING DATE
VALENTINE	Blue Crew Neck 3/4 SL	2 8 9 1	£15	12						4/60	4/60	2/30	2/30								12	180	
MCNAMEE	White Polo Neck 3/4 SL	6 6 6 6	£20	13.05		2/40	1.4/28	1.4/28	4.8/96	1.4/28	0.85/17	3/60	3/60								13.05	261.0	
SUB 3/4 TOTAL				37.55	NIL	2/40	1.4/28	1.4/28	4.8/96	11.4/148	8.85/117	6.1/101	6.4/104	32.75/470	NIL	NIL	NIL	NIL	NIL	NIL	37.55	566	
GRAND TOTAL				146.55	4.4/67	12/175	1.4/28	7.2/104	25.2/374	17.1/232	8.85/117	6.1/101	10.4/144	42.45/594	20.4/234	15.5/175	13.7/157	12.8/148	16.7/187	79.1/901	146.55	1869	

delivery schedule, normally available as an immediate screen interrogation on an online basis.

Key information can be easily disseminated from Figure 8.2:

- What line is being delivered and when
- What quantity by line is being delivered
- Full details of the line + prices and description
- Which day it is due into the distribution centre
- Special delivery instructions – box or hanger types, etc.
- Total retail value of the delivery by week

The buyer – and, more importantly, the merchandiser – keep in regular contact with all the suppliers, to ensure that the garments are going to be delivered on the originally agreed date. However, the delivery schedule is always subject to a continuous flow of minor changes. Sometimes the buying team put suppliers under pressure to bring forward delivery of best-selling lines, while on the other hand they will ask suppliers to push back deliveries of slow-selling lines. Preferably there may be an opportunity to cancel the outstanding balance of a slow-selling line, although once a supplier has accepted delivery of the fabric and trimmings, it becomes very problematic. Sometimes a buyer will be able to change the style of a garment or possibly have the fabric made up into a completely different garment type.

The importance of maintaining accurate delivery schedules

Maintaining an accurate delivery schedule is a complex and detailed task, and it is vital that the team updates it as changes occur. Today's merchandiser has the facility of easily manipulated databases, although a decade ago the merchandiser would have had to rely on paper, pencil and rubber techniques to keep the delivery schedule updated and accurate. Table 8.5 shows that there are many things that can cause delay to garment delivery, although within the fashion trade it is well known that suppliers are able to dream up ever-more creative excuses for late delivery as the years go by! It is important not to underestimate the impact of poor deliveries.

Table 8.5   Reasons for late garment deliveries

- Supplier fails to put garments into production on time
- Late approvals of samples
- Late delivery of fabric and/or trimmings to supplier
- Production problems once started
- Technical problems with fabric, trimming or finished garment
- Slow transportation from supplier; often a problem with foreign suppliers, where ship and air freight can cause delay
- Goods held up clearing customs
- Strikes and bad weather
- Wars and civil unrest

Tip

Keeping delivery schedules up to date

Never allow the administration of delivery scheduling to fall behind: knowing exactly what will be delivered and when is vital to ensure that your forward buying is accurate and timely

The importance of suppliers delivering orders on time

Failure to have the right garments delivered into the business at the right time usually has one major impact – loss of sales. If the product is not available in store when the customer is buying, then quite clearly they will simply go elsewhere and buy from the competition. In hot weather, the customer may need a T-shirt for immediate use; they will not delay the purchasing of it and come back later. Once lost, that business will not miraculously come back at a later date: it is lost forever.

Therefore if a supplier delivers late, they are effectively causing the retailer to lose turnover and ultimately profit. As the fashion business has become so competitive over the past decade, fashion retailers have developed a *late delivery penalty clause*, which effectively 'fines' suppliers who do not deliver on time. Generally the fine increases in severity as the delivery date gets later, the theory being that the later a line is delivered into the business the greater the potential loss.

In turn, garment manufacturers are increasingly developing similar penalty clauses with fabric and trimming suppliers, who for so long were the main cause of general late deliveries. The penalty clauses are included in the normal terms of trade to which suppliers expect their own suppliers to conform. The terms of trade are a legal instrument often printed on the reverse of the retailer's official order form. Written in legal jargon, they are often hard for the lay person to understand. More detail on the legal issues associated with terms of trade is contained in Chapter 5.

The imposition of penalties for late delivery within the fashion trade has not been welcomed by many smaller and inefficient suppliers, who basically were directly causing their fashion retail customers to lose money through their own internal inefficiencies. Late-delivery penalties are now an accepted way of life in the fashion trade, even though they are widely disliked by garment suppliers. With modern information technology, larger fashion retailers have late-delivery information produced on a regular basis. Suppliers with a poor delivery record are ranked each week and both the buying teams and senior management are able to see clearly who are the best and worse deliverers. Buyers very rarely keep suppliers with a consistent poor delivery record, no matter how well the merchandise sells once it has finally been delivered. Late deliveries always mean lost profit.

Sometimes a retailer will accept a late delivery, especially if it is the late delivery of a line that is already selling well. If the buying team and senior management agree upon a late acceptance, this is generally on the basis that if it does not sell out by the end of a season, then the supplier will be required to take all remaining stock back and refund the cost to the retailer. Often a retailer will accept delivery of a proportion of the original order, reducing it by the amount of sales already lost as a result of the late delivery. We must stress again that once lost, sales are *never* regained later.

Tip

Late delivering suppliers

Late delivering suppliers cause lost profit: eliminate consistent late-delivering, unreliable suppliers at all costs

The problems of planning imported merchandise

Very often it is not possible for the buying team to accelerate the delivery of imported merchandise. If the supplier is based in Halifax, it is often easier to speed up a shipment of garments from there, than it is from a supplier in China. A shipment by sea from Hong Kong can take six weeks to arrive, especially if it is delayed in customs or with the shipping agent at either end. On the other hand, a delivery from Halifax to an UK-based warehouse (more commonly called a distribution centre or DC) can often be achieved in a matter of hours. Sometimes it is possible to speed up the delivery from more distant countries by the use of air freight rather than sea freight. However, it is important to note that air freight is as much as 30 per cent more expensive than sea freight. Air freight therefore increases the cost price of a garment and therefore may ultimately increase its retail price, or reduce the margin of the product.

The impact of air freight costs on small-volume, high-value items such as jewellery is therefore very low. With larger-volume, less expensive products, such as a basic T-shirt, the cost of air freight has a larger percentage impact on the cost price. It is more common to use air freight for repeat orders on higher-priced, best-selling garments. For first deliveries planned well ahead of the season, it is usual to use sea freight for cost advantage reasons.

As more foreign merchandise is being imported into Europe, there is an increasing necessity for the buying and merchandising team to be aware of the problems associated with importation. They must plan as much as they can ahead of shipment to ensure that deliveries arrive on time, in an acceptable condition and in a packed format for simple onward distribution. On all order forms there are always special packing and boxing instructions. Most modern distribution is automated and therefore DC's need to be able to handle merchandise quickly.

Unpacking stock for picking and allocation is called 'double handling' and increases cost dramatically. Re-addressing cartons is much cheaper than opening them.

The importance of the DC

Hanging stock

Whether merchandise is being delivered from a home or foreign producer, it is the buyers' and merchandisers' job to make certain that the supplier delivers the product in such a way that it can be *easily distributed into shops or stores*. Each garment is usually hung on a disposable hanger that is given to the customer at the point of sale. There is also a clear plastic cover over each garment to keep it fresh and clean.

The modern DC is now highly automated, with hanging garments carried around on overhead conveyor systems for storage and distribution. These systems have small mobile hanging trucks, known as dollies. On each dolly, between 20 to 40 garments can be automatically carried to wherever they are needed within the DC. Very often there will be a central control room that looks something like a railway signal box to control the movement of dollies. These systems allow huge numbers of garments to be delivered, stored, picked by size and colour and then finally delivered to an individual branch. By delivering garments in hanging format, they remain uncreased and are then ready to put out directly onto the shop floor.

Most fashion chains deliver hanging goods in specially designed hanging format lorries, usually calling at most shops at least twice a week. The routings of these lorries are meticulously pre-planned to avoid wasted journeys and expense. Drivers often deliver at night to avoid the congestion of daytime traffic, the shop staff arrive early in the morning to check off the stock and get it out onto the trading floor. Stock left packed up or placed in stock rooms has no chance of selling. Always expose stock at the risk of selling it!

Boxed stock

Although most deliveries to a fashion store arrive in a hanging format, a great deal of merchandise is also delivered in boxes or cartons. To help the conveyor belt systems cope within distribution systems, these boxes need to conform to certain specifications and not exceed a maximum size that would make them unmanageable for shop staff to handle on delivery.

It is important when boxed stock is delivered to the DC that the merchandise is packed in *logical size/colour ratios*. If, for example, a supplier were to pack one size in one colour way in separate boxes, then there would be a requirement for the distribution centre pickers to unpack stock to put it into a logical size/colour ratio prior to sending out to the branches: this is called 'double handling'. Wherever possible, the buyer and merchandiser will ensure that a large part of any boxed delivery is packed in the required size/colour ratio. Then it is possible to simply put an address label onto the end of a carton for immediate onward delivery to the relevant shop. This enables stock to be turned around immediately and for the merchandise to be put on sale without delay.

The basic order form, discussed in Chapter 5, is pivotal in ensuring that the supplier is clearly briefed by the buying and mechandising team as to how they need to pack stock. Most fashion retailers no longer use their DC as a warehouse. Warehouses are generally for holding stock, whereas their new definition as DCs makes certain that they do just that – *distribute* rather than store stock. Despite this definition, even the most efficient DC will in fact hold back up stocks for weekly replenishment via the automatic allocation system.

The merchandiser is still under pressure to phase in such stock over time, rather than simply taking it as one delivery. This is to avoid clogging up the DC and also, more importantly, leaving unrequired stock hanging up for any longer than is really necessary. Good merchandisers realise that stock hanging up in the warehouse equates to 'dead money': it is simply an investment that is not working for the business. Having too much stock in the DC also has the knock on effect of reducing the overall stock turn of the department and the business.

Stock fragmentation

Even with the best-run fashion business, lines sell out, leaving fragmented residues of stock behind. Often there are broken runs of size and colour left behind in both shops and even in the DC. The problem of fragmented lines is that they create a very poor image in the shops, particularly if they are fragments of what has been a best-selling line. Customers can become very frustrated when they find a style they like, but it is simply not available in the size and/or colour they desire.

To help customers locate a garment that has sold out in a branch, some fashion chains such as Next make a point of interrogating their central stock information system and will often get the required size/colour transferred in from a local branch that still has it in stock. The problem with any form of transfer is that it is very expensive in terms of time and effort. On a direct-cost basis it is likely that offering such a service will usually create a loss on the specific transaction. However, customer satisfaction and likely future loyalty is hard to measure in pure economic and financial terms.

To avoid the costs of individual transfers, it is often more efficient to undertake a complete recall of all fragments of a line from all stores, and then redistribute it in a balanced size/colour ratio, in depth, to the few larger shops where it has the best chance of selling. The decision to recall fragments on a bulk basis is also not cheap, but is a key way to improve stock turn and to make sure that the individual shop offer does not look broken and fragmented. Each different type of fashion business has a different policy on fragmentation, with more up-market shops, selling higher-price merchandise, taking a more proactive stance to keeping fragmentation at a minimum.

Fragments and year-end stock takes

Merchandisers will also find small fragments and residues left in the DC, sometimes as a result of erroneous picking. All merchandisers will regularly 'walk' the DC to ensure that no fragments are left unallocated. Keeping both the shops and warehouse free of fragments makes life so much easier at the end of the trading year, when all retail businesses usually undertake the annual stock check. This confirms that the business has taken in and sold the stock as planned and indicated. Simply taking away the value of sales from deliveries should give you the value of the year-end stock, although there is always some discrepancy.

Stock, as we know, is lost as a result of 'shrinkage' factors. Shrinkage or loss of stock can occur through a number of causes including, stock checking errors, theft by staff or customers and even poor accounting. The causes are many and varied, but needless to say the final level of stock shrinkage in the whole business has a direct effect upon the final net profitability. While buyers and merchandisers are not normally held responsible for shrinkage levels, good paperwork and administration can ensure that year-end stock count errors can be kept to a minimum.

Final comments on stock management and distribution

The very detailed nature of this part of the merchandiser's role should not be underestimated. In many respects, it is true to say that this part of the job can be dull, repetitive and sometimes boring. However, getting the stock flowing into and around the business efficiently yields big dividends for the whole business. It is in this area of the business that rigorous and meticulous attention to detail is vital. Simply failing to adjust automatic replenishment system parameters in one week have lead to disastrous incidents where, for example, all the DC stock has been sent in error to one branch. Sometimes, best-selling lines have inadvertently been left in the DC for weeks on end. Whatever can go wrong has gone wrong – ask any experienced merchandiser.

The future development of more intelligent replenishment systems that can scan and examine stock detail by size, colour, garment category and department by shop is becoming a reality. The vast numbers of calculations needed to monitor this multitude of parameters can now be done in a flash. More importantly, intelligent systems are now making detailed recommendations and suggestions. Nevertheless, it would be naive to assume that any system would be developed without the need for human intervention by the experienced merchandiser or distribution manager.

■ ☑ **9** Retail formats and visual merchandising

The ever-changing face of fashion retailing

This chapter aims to explain how fashion retailing has evolved, and is evolving. It is important to understand the dynamics at work and the changing patterns of trade that are driving the industry. Many of these changes are directly impacting upon the work of the fashion buyer and merchandiser, as well as the way in which fashion is being marketed. Not only does fashion change, but also – more importantly – the way fashion is sold and displayed is now changing at a very dynamic rate.

It is sometimes difficult to understand how much fashion retailing has changed in Europe over the past fifty years. Until the First World War, clothing for a majority of the population, was made to measure. Most people had very few clothes, and those that did, had clothes that were probably handmade by themselves or by a local tailor or seamstress. The concept of factory-made clothing came about from the need to supply millions of military uniforms for war purposes. After the First World War millions of returning soldiers then also required civilian clothing. This demand was the driving force behind such companies as Burton Tailoring, now called Burton Menswear and latterly Arcadia. Burton manufactured millions of garments, in what were known as 'bespoke' or 'made-to-measure' tailoring factories. As fashions became less formal after the Second World War, made-to-measure clothing such as suits have declined in favour of more casual garments.

The fundamental shift towards casual clothing, together with increasing personal affluence since the 1960s, has seen a high street fashion revolution. The growth of large fashion chains such as Arcadia and Marks & Spencer has led to the demise of many smaller independent clothing shops. This pattern is still being repeated across Europe. It can be argued that the loss of smaller independents has created a loss of choice for the fashion consumer. Conversely it could be argued that through economies of scale associated with large-scale buying, consumers have benefited from lower retail prices, although many would argue to the contrary. The level of competition within fashion retailing is increasing dramatically as a result of several internal and external factors. These are shown in – Table 9.1.

It is sometimes difficult for an individual, organisation, or industry to fully comprehend the forces that are impacting on it. The fashion industry has never been under such great competitive pressure. The pressures listed in Table 9.1 can be summarised as follows:

Table 9.1   Current factors impacting upon European fashion retailers

- Increasing foreign competition
- New technologies
- Larger conglomerates
- International branding
- Increasing affluence
- The growth of the individual – no 'followership'
- Move to casual life-styles
- Changing socio–economic trends
- New ways of shopping
- Time starvation
- Improving competition
- New international price transparency
- 'New-value' retailing

International foreign competition

As a result of the internationalisation of fashion caused by increasing personal travel and by the growth of international media, fashion is moving from national to international acceptance. For example, the casual fashion worn by students around the world is now very similar. As a result it has become easier for such international fashion retailers as Bennetton and Gap to increase their total market potential by opening in countries around the world. Many American retailers are now finding that higher European pricing structures and profit levels make European expansion a very tempting alternative to their original home markets. International entrants are putting great pressure on existing European retailers who have previously not been bothered by foreign competitors.

New technologies

Up until the mid-1970s, most retailers had to keep control of their stocks by manually counting every last item and recording the details on paper. As mainframe computers became widely available in the 1980s, only the largest fashion retailers could afford the then expensive technology. This enabled them to gain a competitive edge over smaller less efficient competitors, by using IT to be quicker at spotting best-selling lines, buying more of them and getting the most sales they could from the line: this process is known as 'line potentialisation'. However, as the price of technology has dropped, PC systems and technology are now ideally suited to smaller businesses; the original competitive advantage of the larger fashion retailers has slipped away. Small retailers are now very quickly aware of what is and is not selling. Retail technology is now open to all fashion retailers.

Larger conglomerates

The 1980s saw a great deal of takeover and merger activity create larger fashion conglomerates. The size of these conglomerates gave them larger buying power than ever before. 'Big became beautiful' in terms of the price deals they concluded with suppliers as a result of huge buying power. This meant that large retailers were in general able to offer better prices than small ones. Even now, at the turn of the millennium, we are seeing larger and larger international conglomerates entering Europe. The American Wal Mart has joined with ASDA to enter the UK market. Wal Mart is the world's largest value retailer, committed to giving consumers the best prices in the market. Whether in the long term the consumer will benefit from being supplied by a few large conglomerates is a matter of debate.

International branding

The increasingly international nature of media and advertising has created global brands. Names such as Levi's and Doc Marten have immediate international recognition. Both brands rate in the top ten most recognised brands in the world. Branding has become an increasingly important selling feature of fashion garments, and increasingly across Europe there is an interest amongst younger fashion customers to buy branded merchandise. Often this merchandise is conspicuously branded, with the name emblazoned on it. Some brands seem to have long-lasting appeal, while others come and go within a matter of months. Many larger retailers have deliberately not stocked brands, preferring to promote only their own retail name or unique brand, available only through their own stores. While this strategy has worked for many years, several larger retailers such as M & S are now having to revisit this decision. With consumers now being more knowledgeable about brands and fashion generally, only the bravest retailers will continue selling their own brand to the exclusion of all others. The power of new international brands is creating strong competition to all types of existing brands.

Increasing affluence

Most European countries have experienced a doubling of real personal income since the end of the Second World War. More income than ever is available to spend on clothing and other consumer requirements. However, in real terms clothing has fallen as a percentage of income, as people spend more on holidays and leisure pursuits. As the customer has become more affluent, expectations of style and quality have increased: all around the world, poor-quality garments are simply no longer acceptable. As manufacturing techniques and fabrics have improved, the demand for clothing quality has moved ever upwards. The need to deliver acceptable quality at all levels of fashion retailing puts increasing pressure on those retailers selling at the lower price end of the market.

The growth of the individual

Western society has increasingly become more concerned with seeking personal happiness and satisfaction. Historically, family, religion, government and employers were much more important than the individual. For many reasons, this is no longer the case. The individual no longer has as much 'followership' as they once used to. Fashion has therefore become very individual in its style. Many people are no longer prepared to follow mainstream fashion trends, preferring instead to make their own individual fashion statements. Diverse tastes in popular music are a clear indicator of how society is breaking down into smaller style tribes. Mass fashion was easy for buyers and merchandisers to track and satisfy; with smaller tribal trends, the scale and speed of change is making it harder and harder for businesses to find large-value markets to follow.

Move to casual life-styles

Fashion from the Middle Ages until the early 1900's was mainly the preserve of the rich. Probably as a result of the relaxed post-war influence of American films, fashion has taken on a much more casual interpretation, especially among the young – blue jeans are probably the most obvious example of the phenomena. Although formality does have a role to play in fashion, the number of businesses now encouraging a more casual approach to office dressing indicates that the move from formal to casual is now growing faster than ever, but many fashion retailers and brands have found it difficult to move their ranges and brands towards this more casual emphasis. Some fashion businesses and brands have historically developed with a very formal styling level, and it is often very hard to reposition a business from a formal to a casual target market overnight.

Changing socio–economic trends

Society continues to change at a fast rate. Increasing numbers of women entering the workforce, for example, has created new demands for practical new styles of fashionable work clothes. Children at increasingly younger ages now play a major role in their clothing buying decision process. Parents are now succumbing to what is known as 'Pester Power': children are increasingly involved in the purchasing decision of many more products than previously. Women's dress styles are also becoming more masculine, as they opt to wear trousers in preference to dresses and skirts. Androgynous or unisex dressing is a new force that may have even more profound effects in the future. Increasing differences between the rich and poor in society is also creating a Europe of the 'haves' and the 'have-nots' – large segments of society are becoming poor very quickly and as such will therefore be denied access to fashion.

'Fashion futorology', or trying to guess what will happen next, is a popular pastime of fashion writers. Changes in the way society develops will fundamentally change the competitive stance of the retail fashion business. Societal change always was and always will be a key influencer of fashion.

New ways of shopping

Retail fashion shopping has always been associated with the idea that customers visit shops or stores, make a selection and then take the selected garments away with them. The launch of 'e-tailing' or shopping on the Internet or interactive television shopping channels is now here. New digital technologies may fundamentally challenge the concept of the need to sell fashion from shops. The concept of clothing recycling through charity shops and other types of secondhand retail fashion units is also changing the way many people buy fashion. Second hand purchasing is taking an increasing percentage of the total fashion marker. Purchasing directly from clothing manufacturers is growing quickly: as customers demand cheaper prices and manufacturers seek greater control over the supply chain. Garment suppliers may decide to bypass conventional retail outlets as Internet technology gives them direct access to millions of Internet consumers. Conventional retail shops are now under increasing competitive pressure from new technology.

Time starvation

Despite the increasing affluence for a majority of many fashion consumers, the downside is that people have less time available to shop for fashion as they spend more time at work. The luxury of time to shop may one day be a thing of the past. Again, interactive Internet shopping may be one solution, or possibly mobile shops visiting places of work. Retail shops are competing for the valuable resource of customer time.

Improving competition

Throughout all consumer markets, both small and large organisations are now using increasingly sophisticated business techniques and tools to try and understand the fashion consumer. Market research and loyalty systems are just two examples that are helping fashion retailers to do this. As more businesses apply new business techniques and technologies to understanding their customers better, the more competitive the trading environment becomes. Fashion retailers are always seeking any sustainable competitive edge, although any advantage is usually temporary.

New international price transparency

As more fashion consumers undertake international travel for both business and pleasure, customer awareness of international pricing is a growing phenomena. High-priced international clothing brands have a particular problem, as on-line Internet consumers are able to compare international prices and currencies on screen. With mail order and the international acceptance of credit cards, there is hardly any justification for any international brand or retail business to charge higher prices in any one country. Often European consumers are confused about international price comparison as a result of complex currency structures and contantly changing currency exchange rates. The introduction of the Euro as the single European currency makes price transparency obvious. Differential world pricing may soon be a thing of the past, again putting competitive pressure on retailers and brands, as markets become less able to sustain high prices in individual countries or markets. The ultimate impact will, of course, be reduced profitability, through this increased understanding of consumer pricing.

'New-value' retailing

In any form of retailing, the easiest way to compete in the short term is by reducing prices. This has the effect of increasing the volume of units sold, but also has the effect of reducing the level of profitability on each item sold. In general the increased number of garments sold should enable the retailer to maintain or improve the overall profit level. Over the past five years, there has been a rapid growth in what can be termed 'New-value retailers'. Such retailers are continuously using price reduction, multiple pack offers (e.g. two for the price of three) and many other gimmicky sales promotional techniques. Often buying in special lines at very keen prices, initial offer prices are often artificially inflated, only to be reduced a short time later. These retailers use price reduction as their key promotional tool, unlike most fashion retailers who tend to use price reduction as a means of clearing old stock during the normal twice-yearly Sales.

Specialist factory or 'off-price' outlets have sprung up away from the conventional high streets, which sell branded goods far below normal high street prices. By being away from the normal competition, they enable branded retailers to maintain normal higher price points. In America, 'off-price' retailing is now a major force in fashion, selling something like 60 per cent of all branded garments at below the 'normal' price. This new American style of retailing is gaining momentum throughout Europe. Price reduction as a sales promotional tool is subject to varying degrees of legislation in different countries, but this has not been a barrier to growth within the United Kingdom.

Final comment on fashion change

With all these factors impacting at once, it becomes clear that fashion retailing is not as easy as it first appears. During every reader's life-time, they will remember a fashion shop that they once liked and used, that has now ceased trading. This bears witness to the fact that fashion retailing is not a simple form of retailing. Apart from the continuous change caused by external forces, customers are themselves generally very promiscuous in their purchasing patterns, often switching and changing between fashion retailers at a whim. The changeable nature of fashion garments in their own right, added to all the factors above, all increase the dangerous and volatile nature of fashion retailing.

The changing high street

The inexorable movement toward larger conglomerates of fashion retailers is putting the independent fashion outlets under great pressure. In some European countries, governments have tried to create legislation to keep independent outlets in business – despite this, in France, for example, the independent is still on the decline, unable to fight the market forces and power of large-scale retailers. It would appear that government interference in any type of retail activity generally fails in the long term. Over the past fifty years Britain has lost 250 000 general shops as small outlets in villages, towns and cities have closed as a direct result of the competition from the larger more efficient retail companies.

Despite the fact that nearly 40 per cent of shops have closed, the remaining shops and stores have got bigger, with retail space having more than doubled in the same fifty-year period. Larger outlets generally are more efficient than smaller ones, in terms of higher sales per square metre and lower overall percentage costs: again, the economic principle of economies of scale comes into play. As well as a fundamental shift in terms of overall numbers and size, the likely impact from Internet trading is fundamentally changing the way customers shop and their preferences for the types of shop they want to buy clothes in. The key types of fashion retailers are listed in Table 9.2.

In general, these different types of shops are mainly found in or close to town or city centres, although there is now an increasing move to large 'greenfield' out-of-town shopping centres or complexes. These are modelled on the American idea

Table 9.2 Taxonomy of fashion retailing

Type of outlet	Description
Single independent	Small space, privately owned mainly branded, often in trendy or exclusive location, high emphasis on personalised customer service, unique garment offer.
Medium multiple independents	Small to medium size, privately owned, brands and own brands, 10–20 outlets, generally offering more exclusive and higher styled garments – e.g. Pilot, Oasis, Whistles, etc.
Large national multiples	Medium to large, mainly own-brand plus key brands, 50–500 outlets, Plc ownership, e.g. Top shop, Dorothy Perkins, Burton Menswear, Oasis, etc.
Franchise shops	A larger chain allows private investors to run a shop or group of shops under a known name. The investor puts their money into setting up shop and then buys stock from the brand or retailer. Strong controls as all shops have to appear exactly the same. Best example – Bennetton. Fast way for brand owner or retailer to expand shop chain.
Cooperative shops or stores	One of the earliest mass-retailing formats, created at the end of the 19th century. Originally started by factory workers as way of providing cheap goods, they were originally plain and basic. Although in decline, they still have a sizeable share of the clothing market. Mainly remain today in variety or department store formats. Tend to appeal to older customers – e.g. regional cooperative store groups.
National department stores	Large-scale, fashion + other goods, large space, major centres, own-brand plus key brands, Plc ownership, multi-floor – e.g. Debenhams, House of Fraser, Selfridges and John Lewis, etc.
Local independent department stores	Small to medium, privately owned, sometimes joint central buying facility, often family run, locally-based, sells all types of goods and brands, generally in smaller towns – e.g. Association of Independent Department Stores (AIS).

Table 9.2   Continued

Type of outlet	Description
National variety stores	Medium to large, selling wide variety of goods including fashion, but more limited than department stores, usually sell food – e.g. BhS, Marks & Spencer, Woolworths.
Superstores	Very large space, warehouse-style units located on edge or out of town. Similar to variety stores, but usually carrying food plus a wide range of own-brand and branded products. Strong price promotion often a feature – e.g. Asda, Tesco.
Concessions or shop-in-shops	A brand or retailer 'rents' space to open a small specialist department within a larger store. Usually based on a rental or commission. Often used in department stores to increase range interest. Also cheaper way for brands to get a high street presence – e.g. Alexon, Planet, etc.
New-value chains or 'off-price'	Small, medium and large sites. Mainly driven by strong price reduction and promotion. Often selling well known brands at discounted values. Fast stock turn, quick and reactive buying – e.g. TK Maxx, New Look, Ethel Austin and Matalan.
Factory outlets	Generally large out-of-town warehouse-type outlets situated close to factory. Sell seconds, returns and excess production at very reduced prices – e.g. Mulberry, Jaeger, etc.
Secondhand shops	Small independently run, sometimes called 'second time round', also includes charity shops chains such as Cancer Research Campaign and Oxfam. Increasing share of the market.

of getting customers to drive out of town to custom-built shopping centres with plenty of parking – examples are Lakeside, Trafford Centre and Blue Water Park. The reason for their success is that in the United Kingdom and many other European city centres there is simply no further room for large-scale expansion, within existing high streets. Developed over many hundreds of years, these historic city centres are often made up of smaller retail units, not big enough for today's large-volume retailers. There is debate that out-of-town shopping centres are impacting badly upon smaller rural and suburban town centres as they cause customers to move from their historic shopping areas. This causes great social problems for customers without cars, such as pensioners and the poor.

Wherever a fashion business trades, there is a general preference to have other competitors in the same street or area. By having a selection of fashion outlets in one area, the area automatically becomes a *'fashion destination'* for the consumer. However, there are instances where competition becomes too crowded and the number of clothing shops in one place are simply too many to support the number of customers in the locality.

The siting of new shops and shopping centres is now scientifically planned. Careful examination of socio–economic profiles of different areas is researched in conjunction with car ownership and other transport infrastructures. Key to the equation is how long it takes for customers from different areas to drive to the proposed site – for example, the Lakeside centre in Essex has a catchment area of over 5 million people within a half an hour's drive!

European governments have varying interests in the siting and location of new shopping complexes, although the United Kingdom government is now planning to reduce planning consent for more out-of-town centres in favour of a new initiative to retain and improve town centres and high streets. In America the decline of the 'Main Street' (the UK high street), is causing a big problem, particularly in poorer inner city areas. All international governments are beginning to query the wisdom of large out-of-town shopping centres aimed mainly at wealthy car-owning customers.

A review of changing retail fashion formats

Independents

This sector is currently contracting under competitive pressure from the major fashion multiples. However, in more up-market and specialist fashion fields, such as outsize and maternity wear, there is still evidence of potential and growth. As customers become familiar with repetitive retail offers in each town and country, there are certain observers who believe that independents will stabilise as consumer tastes seek out individual fashion statements. The 'follow-my-leader' approach to fashion, while successful in the 1960s and 1970s, is now very dated. The individual approach to creating your own fashion statement is making the target marketing of fashion more difficult for the larger fashion chains, which are unable to move their product focus quickly. Being agile in terms of buying is much easier for the small independent shop.

Multiples

In the past fifteen years we have seen a great deal of conglomeration of smaller groups into larger ones, Arcadia Plc, the owner of Top Shop, Evans and Dorothy Perkins, has taken over Sears's women's wear. Now Arcadia is also responsible for Miss Selfridge, Wallis, Richards and Warehouse. This new grouping makes Arcadia second only to Mark & Spencer in terms of their share of the UK women's wear market. With centralised management and control, they enjoy considerable economies of scale, but conversely run the risk of becoming homogeneous in terms of the product they offer the consumer. The demise and collapse of the British Shoe Corporation (+2000 shoe shops in 1990) was mainly attributed to the sameness of product and environment and stands as a warning of how easily large shares of the fashion market can virtually be lost overnight. At their peak

British Shoe Corporation represented nearly 30 per cent of the entire UK shoe market! 'Large organisations with varied offers' would seem to be the fashion mantra of the future.

Franchise shops

If a fashion retailer has a good business that requires fast expansion, then there is the opportunity to franchise the name, stock and a way of running the business to outside investors. The investor has a detailed contract to ensure that they run the business exactly as the retailer or brand requires. The investor pays a commission on all the stock they buy from the brand owner. This enables smaller investors to become involved with a leading brand. The retailer or brand can expand its retail outlets quickly and increase buying power over a very short period of time.

Co-operative shops and stores

One of the first large-scale retail formats, created by factory workers to sell goods cheaply for their own use. Originally based on food retailing, they soon started selling basic clothing. Their heyday was at the end of the 19th century and the start of the 20th century. In decline for many years, they are usually regionally based and have a department store or variety store approach. Still strongly based on food, they still have a sizeable share of the clothing market. 'Co-ops' are found to varying extents in several European countries. Their fashion offer is more targeted at an older customer profile.

Department stores

During the early years of the twentieth century, the French invention of the department store acted as the main supplier of fashion to the wealthier classes. Relying heavily on manufacturer's brands, these stores really catered for an older clientele: there was simply very little demand for what is now termed as 'young fashion'. The main driver for the mass availability of young fashion was during the early 1960s, as the young post-war 'baby boomers' entered their teenage years. Fuelled also by American styling brought over to Europe by American servicemen, it acted as the catalyst for the development of young fashion chains such as Miss Selfridge and Top Shop. The department stores found themselves unable to compete as result of owning large, ageing and unfashionable buildings, and throughout the 1960s and 1970s many closed as a result. However, many were taken over by larger groups such as Debenhams, who immediately created a more modern environment, introduced better buying techniques together with younger more appealing brands. This has successfully abated the decline, and department-stores are well poised for the new millennium, in view of the fact that they ideally suit the 'baby boomers', who have now matured and are seeking a more age-relevant fashion environment than, for example, Top Shop.

Variety stores

Developed as an answer to department stores in the 1920s and 1930s, from American origins, they set out to offer a more limited range of goods than the department store, but at more popular prices. Food was added to their inventories after 1945, but they generally did not carry heavy goods such as furniture and carpets. The clothing ranges were not originally that fashionable, as during this period customers had low levels of disposable income. However, in common with all fashion retailers, the variety stores such as Marks & Spencer and BhS have become more fashionable than ever before. In recent years they have found the fashion elements of their ranges very difficult to maintain as a result of the heightened competition elsewhere, and their share of the market has become static.

Super stores

Again from American origins, these out-of- and edge-of-town large-area retailers were mainly focused on the supply of food at keen prices. Originally started by smaller British grocery chains including Asda, Tesco and Sainsbury, these three are now the leaders in the UK. After their food offers had become well developed, they turned their attention to clothing ranges. Originally not seen as a place to sell fashion garments, Asda with its fashionable 'George' range has clearly disproved the doubters. With their high weekly traffic flow, they have an opportunity to sell clothes to a wide age range of customers. The British super store market is also likely to see more foreign groups entering during the new millennium, many of whom will put an increasing emphasis on fashion clothing.

Concessions or shop-in-shops

In large-area retailers where there is plenty of space, concessions are often traded. They appear to be a small shop within a shop, usually carrying the brand in a well designated trading area. Often the concession employs its own selling staff, to ensure that the department is well maintained and managed. For the larger retailer it can provide extra range interest in addition to their existing ranges, and for the brand it enables them to quickly obtain a visible trading presence, without the expense of opening their own shops. Generally the concession pays a percentage on sales for being allowed to trade in the host store.

'New-value' retailers

The newest type of retail outlet to enter the UK European fashion market, these highly promotionally driven fashion retailers aim to give acceptable quality at a keen price. The secret of their success was originally based upon selling what is known as 'distressed' or 'bankrupt' stock from other businesses, that were either failing or simply overstocked. Often ranges were put on sale at highly inflated prices, only to be marked down within a short time to a keener price anywhere between a third and half of the original asking price. Lines move out quickly at low prices, and therefore the high stock turn means that customers see a fast stock change every time they enter the shop. There are few continuity lines and the buyers are continually on the lookout for a better deal than last time. As these chains have become more established and improve both the design and quality of their products, it is likely that they will put other types of fashion retailer under increasing competitive pressure. This more aggressive American-style approach to price promotion will be a growth area for European fashion retailing over the next few years.

Factory outlets

Individual fashion outlets, as well as groupings of factory shops into factory shopping malls, are again an import from America. They offer the brand owners and manufacturers a way to clear excess or 'distressed' stock, without the need to go through jobbers. By selling excess branded stock away from the normal high street, they do not destroy the higher-branded price structures found in normal outlets. Some retailers, whilst not actually manufacturing stock, also open factory-style outlets to clear problem lines as well as overstocked or lines of seconds quality: there is sometimes a blurring of what truly constitutes a 'factory outlet'. In their out-of-town situations, they also have much lower rental overheads than in those of the high street or city centre. They enable the manufacturer to sell directly to the public, by-passing the wholesaler and retailer.

Second hand outlets

The new environmental lobby that emerged during the 1980s has radically shifted the public's views on textile and clothing recycling. Originally seen as a harmless product, the manufacture of some fashion garments can have adverse environmental impacts, chemicals and dyes used in them can be quite toxic and damaging. Also the way in which some natural fibres are cultivated can also be environmentally damaging, especially in developing countries. We have seen a great interest in the recycling of fashion as a fashion trend in its own right: many young customers actively seek out retro clothing from another era, in order to make their own individual fashion statement. Wearing secondhand clothes has less social stigma in the United Kingdom, although acceptability of this fashion concept varies by country. The United Kingdom is unique in terms of a large charity shop sector with over 7000 outlets. This group of shops undertakes major recycling of many good garments that might otherwise have gone to waste.

All the time there is a heave and shift of fashion business from one type of outlet to the next. Types of retail shop, like the garments themselves, tend to go in and out of fashion. The revival of department stores is a good example. The future of conventional shop-based fashion retailing may now be under competitive threat from the new Internet-based retailers or e-commerce, although many experts feel that only basic rather than fashion clothing can be sold without the customer seeing, feeling and trying it on. This is popularly known as the 'touchy-feely' aspect of buying fashion!

Mail order and Internet buying – a retail format or not?

Mail order, and latterly Internet and Direct Response Television Purchasing (DRTVP), are an important part of fashion marketing, but they are not considered by some observers as being part of the 'retail fashion scene'. Originally mail order fashion companies targeted their products at the less well off, allowing repayments for garments by instalment. Using a network of local self-employed agents, they provided a localised selling and distribution network, as well as very importantly providing credit to those with low credit potential.

In general, mail order companies were marketed as a separate proposition, although some were also linked to 'bricks and mortar' retail outlets. The fashion offer originally provided by the early catalogues was quite traditional and safe. With the long lead-times involved in catalogue development and production, it was necessary to ensure that the products offered would not go out of fashion too quickly. Products promoted also had to have what was known as 'page appeal', as the definition attainable in a small photograph was limiting in terms of the garment detail that could be conveyed to the customer. Mail order or catalogue trading also had the advantage that it could provide goods for geographically remote regions. Provided that there is a regular postal delivery service, then goods can literally be sent to anywhere in the world. The famous R.M. Williams business in Australia was founded on the basis of providing durable, practical and hardwearing clothes for itinerant Bushmen. These men worked in harsh conditions, away from civilisation and needed special clothing that could endure the tough life they led. Clothes would be ordered by letter to Sydney and then delivered many weeks later to a small post office in the nearest town for collection by the Bushman, often many hundreds of miles away. Today R.M. Williams is an international business, which while still selling via mail order, also widely trades from conventional bricks and mortar outlets. Here we see an original mail order company diversifying into conventional retailing.

The renaissance in mail order catalogues has also been fuelled by the new 'time poverty' being experienced by many consumers, whose work schedule is so hectic that they simply do not have time to shop. When Next Plc, the famous and successful clothing chain originally launched their mail order catalogue, it was supposedly targeted at the less affluent segment of its customer base, perceived wisdom at the time believed that mail order was still really for them. Interestingly the incredible early success of the Next catalogue indicated that, on the contrary, it was the better-off customers who were availing themselves of the mail order service. Explanations at the time suggested that in fact it was the 'time poor', more affluent, office workers who realised the benefit of the new mail order operation. Over the past five years or so, we have seen throughout the United Kingdom and Europe, a marked growth in specialist mail order catalogues for both men and women. Often dubbed 'life-style' catalogues, name such as Land's End, Racing Green and Cotton Traders offer a wide variety of high-quality clothing. The offers are mainly easy-fit casual garments, often targeted at the more outdoor life-style.

These catalogues have proved very successful amongst wealthier, and generally older customer profiles, who have busy life-styles.

Internet trading has been adopted by many of the mainstream fashion groups, who wish to defend their markets as well as take advantage of the new media trading opportunity. Arcadia Plc has many of its well known brands names such as Evans, Top Shop and Dorothy Perkins already well represented with web sites. At present, the conventional retailers who have developed onto the web still achieve a major proportion of their trade from 'bricks and mortar' retailing. The recent demise of boo.com indicates the early difficulty of Internet retailing.

Changing consumer expectations and the shopping experience

The growing affluence of most developed countries has raised consumer environment expectations. Where they work and live are now furnished and maintained at higher levels than ever before. It is therefore logical that the shopping environment they use has needed to raise its standards accordingly. Modern shops and stores are generally light, airy, clean – and, most importantly, convenient to use. Pictures of old-fashioned shops show small, overcrowded establishments, and often look positively uninviting. At the turn of the twentieth century, smart shops were not open to everyone. In fact, Selfridges, when it opened in 1910, made great play of promoting that it was 'Open to all'. It is hard for us to understand why shops were not open to all, but hopefully this story explains how fashion retailing was once only for the rich.

As well as becoming fundamentally better off (most people in Europe will retire about twice as rich as their parents did!), society is now being educated to a much higher level than ever before. Despite the debate about educational standards, the average customer is better informed about most issues as result of the explosion that has occurred in the media. Advertising and promotion are powerful educational tools in their own right. International brands like Levis and Coca Cola are known in every corner of the world. Consumers therefore enter into fashion purchasing already consciously and sub-consciously armed with vast amounts of relevant and not so relevant information. As a result of this higher knowledge base, today's consumer has an increasing expectation that retail store staff will have good product and fashion understanding. Therefore well trained, knowledgeable and communicative staff are now an essential requirement for any fashion retailer, who now seeks a very high calibre of staff for the vital task of selling to their increasingly well informed customer base.

Having the right stock to complete the sale

Assuming that the retail environment and the sales staff are acceptable to the consumer, the other vital ingredient required to make the sale is having the selected style available at all times. The style must also be available in the right size and colour. Further complications can occur when a style is part of a colour or style coordinated range; again, there is the requirement to keep all coordinated styles in stock together. Keeping in stock at all times is an ideal, but is very rarely achieved in any type of retailing. If ranges are not kept fully stocked in all sizes, colours and styles, then the range is said to be 'fragmented'. Obviously there are different levels of fragmentation, missing one size or colour is only a minor problem. Fashion businesses do not generally run many continuity lines, by virtue of the fact that fashion by its nature calls for continuous change. Therefore fragmentation is a continual problem for fashion retailers. The problems caused by fragmentation are listed in Table 9.3.

Table 9.3   The problems of fragmented stocks

- Customer disappointment – customer unable to find size and colour, rejects alternative colour and unlikely to accept alternative size.
- Slowing rates of sale as lines become more fragmented by size and colour.
- Shop display becomes untidy and cluttered as more and more lines fragment – customer perceives shop as possibly badly run and/or downmarket.
- Fragmentation takes up valuable store display space for new faster-selling lines.
- Fragmented remainders require higher levels of price reduction to encourage customer purchase.

It is virtually impossible for a fashion retailer to sell every range of garments down to nothing. There will always be fragmentation of even best-selling lines. The ways in which retailers deal with fragmented ranges vary, but normally they adopt one or a combination of those shown in Table 9.4.

Table 9.4   Methods for dealing with fragmented fashion ranges

- *Recall fragments* from all stores into the DC, and then send them back in complete size/colour runs to a few larger stores. By re-establishing a complete range the rate of sale normally increases. This is visually better in store and customer perception of shop and ranges improves (*Note*: If timing is too late in the season, such action may be unprofitable).
- Recall fragments and then send the stock out the *following year*. This is a risky strategy for most fashion merchandise, with the exception of basic continuity lines that do not change each year (e.g. basic T-shirts).
- Undertake *regular price mark-downs* as the season progresses. Usually percentage reductions increase as season progresses to ensure high rates of clearance in the short selling period left.
- Recall fragments to DC and sell stock off to a 'jobber'. A jobber is a *specialist dealer in low-priced clothing*, which generally sells onto other wholesalers, market traders or value retailers at extremely low prices. Generally the jobber will be required to remove branding or other identification from the garments, in order to make them anonymous and therefore non-damaging to the full price 'brand image'.

As can be seen from Table 9.4, there is no one way to deal with fragmentation. It is a normal part of fashion retailing, which needs to be dealt with, at no matter which level of the market you are trading in.

The dangers of continuous price reduction for dealing with fragmentation

In order to maintain 'brand integrity' many branded fashion manufacturers and retailers try to avoid discounting their products. When it proves necessary, for example to clear stock, they move stock away from prime sites to alternative outlets including 'seconds' shops, factory outlets or occasionally sell to 'jobbers'. If any product or brand is being consistently offered to the consumer at a reduced price, after a relatively short period the reduced price is no longer seen as a bargain, but in fact becomes the expected price.

Continual price reduction on brands can easily damage their image and *undermine consumer confidence* in them. Often branded manufacturers will 'dump' excess stock in one country, rather than destroy brand values in another. Price reduction, while mainly used for fragmentation clearance, can also be used for dealing with general excess stock levels. Continual price reduction on any brand can have a long detrimental impact on the brand's value in the eyes of the consumer.

Fashion retailing – a fast-changing vista

The increasing appreciation of good design throughout the developed world has also affected the work of store designers. Fashion shops were originally designed more for functional than for aesthetic values. Goods were often kept out of sight, possibly folded or in drawers. Often garments were out of the reach of the customer, sometimes even being kept in a glass case. Retailers were historically possibly less trusting in the past than they are now!

Today's modern retail environment enables the customer to touch, see, feel and try on the clothes. Virtually nothing is out of their reach. This move towards more customer involvement with the garment can also be attributed to the general reduction of shop sales staff in many larger stores; the concept of self-service has been widely embraced by the European consumer. However, in certain countries great value is put in the effective retail sales person. Strangely the United Kingdom has a rather snobbish view towards shop work: social structures, together with a poor perception and understanding of the economic importance of the fashion industry by the media, may be to blame. In the United Kingdom, the fashion industry is the fourth most important sector of economic activity, employing some 400 000 people.

The new retail environments are characterised by twelve key factors:

- Well lit, airy, clean and uncluttered – up-market atmosphere helps to command higher prices; advances in electric lighting create artificial daylight to help enhance product
- Well stocked but not overstocked – customers able to reach garments
- Minimal signage giving clear and easy-to-understand information – signs must not dominate the garments

- Life-style display settings – customers clearly understand what occasion or situation the clothes should be worn in; this can also add value to the product
- Easy to follow colour and style coordinated display groupings – customers can easily see how clothes coordinate and how they should be worn
- Departmental and life-style display groupings, placed logically and geographically adjacent to one another – e.g. swimwear and underwear – customers can then find departments in a logical sequence
- Service points are logically positioned, with a clear space for customer to make a transaction – customer finds it easy to get served, goods paid for and wrapped
- Colour schemes are soft or neutral – in order not to dominate the style and colour of individual garments
- Changing rooms are comfortable and more user friendly and inviting – this aids the selling process
- Garment rails, racks and shelving are conveniently placed, with easy walkway access – this enables customers to move freely between different departments
- Hangers individually marked with the garment size – easy size location is important for customers
- Minimal window displays, with focus on garments rather than on window dressing – allows customers to focus clearly on the product.

The retail fashion environment is a key driver to overall business success. Some of the most successful fashion businesses aim to redesign and refurbish at least every four to five years. A refurbishment (or 'refurb') is a costly business, and retail accountants look for sales to rise by at least 30 per cent–40 per cent against the previous year. Very good refurbishments have occasionally been known to increase sales levels by as much as +100 per cent against the previous year.

The refurbishment or modernisation of a store has the effect of *revitalising customer interest* and dramatically improving sales to a new higher level. Fashion shops, like their products, need to be continually updated in order to keep as fashionable as their products. It is also a matter of practicality that fashion shops in common with any public area suffer wear and tear over time. Sometimes fashion retailers that cannot afford to completely refurbish their stores undertake a minor restyling and redecoration. If done well, this can also dramatically improve sales.

It is important to realise just how vital the *retail environment* is in the whole selling process. While good merchandise will sell in almost any retail environment, the improvement that comes from selling in the right environment is staggering. As customer life-styles improve, they become less prepared to shop in worn-out and down-at-heel shops. The shopping environment has increasingly become a major driving factor in the whole shopping experience. The very nature of the fashion product and the psychological benefits derived by the consumer from purchasing may even require even more attention to detail than shops selling other non-fashion products. One of the major expenditures of any modern fashion chain is the ongoing need for continuous refurbishment.

Home-selling an old but increasingly interesting opportunity

The concept of the door-to-door salesman is an old one. Selling directly to people in their own homes is becoming an increasingly interesting opportunity for conventional 'bricks and mortar' retailers. With many consumers so busy working and so short of time, the ability to take product to them in their own home, or possibly at their place of work, effectively *buys time* for the customer.

Home-selling parties of ladies' clothing have been around for a long time and have proved successful for several operators. Companies such as Ann Summers have specialised in selling lingerie to home-buying parties. Selling suits and shirts to men at work is also proving effective. It is likely that 'bricks and mortar' retailers will increasingly use these techniques as part of a more integrated marketing approach. Direct selling has many benefits, not least that the shopping experience is not immediately comparative against competitors' products. Consumers are therefore unable to undertake immediate competitor price comparisons.

10 Future trends in buying and merchandising

Background

For readers under the age of thirty, it may be difficult for them to understand how fast the modern fashion industry has developed over the past twenty years, without undertaking a great deal of research. The change and loss of fashion retailers and businesses is probably faster than in any other business sector. The fickleness of fashion has had much to do with these changes. However, fundamental improvements in manufacturing quality and design, combined with the development of cheaper international manufacturing sources, have also been important drivers. The offer of width, depth, type and price level of fashion ranges has never been greater, and there appears no reason for consumers not to want this situation to continue. The modern consumer has been weaned on continuous change and increasingly wider offers for at least two generations.

While, from the consumer's point of view, this may seem good, the result for fashion retailers has been the creation of a *hypercompetitive environment*. The original concept that large organisations gained competitive advantage as a by-product of enhanced buying power, owing to size that automatically delivered economies of scale, may now in fact be a fundamental disadvantage. Large cumbersome businesses, in any industrial sector, currently seem to have difficulty in adapting themselves to ever-faster change. With the new emphasis upon flexibility and speed of change, it is becoming increasingly difficult for large fashion retailing organisations to find cost savings and buying advantages as easily as they once did. They also appear to be experiencing difficulty in changing ranges quickly enough to effectively target the fast-changing consumer demand. Size now seems to be losing its once important competitive advantage.

The changing impact of IT on fashion retailing

Large fashion retailers were once the main and virtually only investors in information technology (IT). The high cost of early computers precluded only the largest retailers from acquiring IT. Originally large main frame computers gave an immediate competitive advantage, by enabling large-scale retailers to track best-selling lines quickly and accurately, rather than losing time using inefficient manual-count-based stock control systems. Those large retailers using IT, were able to quickly re-enter markets ahead of smaller competitors, allowing them to quickly buy back into those fast-selling fashion lines that the customers wanted.

In today's world of cheaper and more accessible IT, even the smallest one-shop retailer can easily compete with giant organisations.

Early hardware and software were cumbersome, expensive and certainly not suitable or adaptable enough for small chains of shops. The result of the information age is that IT is empowering smaller fashion retailers, who are now also able to look at selling patterns quickly, enabling them to follow best-selling styles, colours and trends as quickly if not quicker than their larger competitors. The old saying that 'information is power' is very relevant to the modern fashion industry.

The impact of new manufacturing techniques

Alongside the development of affordable IT, smaller retailers are also starting to benefit from the increasing use of quick response – 'just in time' or 'JIT' – manufacturing techniques. These techniques, originally championed by larger retailers and large manufacturers, are now being successfully employed to produce smaller, quickly manufactured runs of virtually any garment type. Economies of scale are now no longer so obvious, as modern manufacturing techniques allow small batches to be made almost as cost effectively as large ones.

Small-batch manufacturing has also been driven as a result of the consumer's shift towards a desire for buying more individualistic garments. Brand proliferation, increased competition and the development of micro markets are having a dramatic effect on all fashion businesses, which are today buying less per line than they were, say ten years ago. For the youth generation of the 1960s, mass-fashion following was the norm, with most of that generation being prepared not only to wear the same fashion statement, but even the same fashion style in the same colour.

With the exception of the 'new-value' discount fashion retailers, the majority of fashion retailers are likely to be buying between 30 per cent and 40 per cent less of a line than they were a decade ago. As a result of faster changes in consumer demand, even fashion chains with expanded numbers of branches are buying less than they were say ten years ago. Smaller buying quantities can also be symptomatic of uncertain buying strategies, where the buyer is unsure of what style, colours and fashions to buy at any point in time. Less confident buyers often hedge their bets by buying more lines in less depth, but buying small quantities of a line can often create a self-fulfilling cycle of failure, as fast-selling trends may not be spotted easily, nor can the overall level of customer demand ever be properly fulfilled. The most successful fashion businesses buy the right quantity first time, and plan ahead with adequate reserves of ready-made garments, spare fabric and spare production in readiness for customer demand.

Consumer expectation of rapid product change and wide line selection, fuelled by the enhanced capabilities of retail IT, combined with more flexible manufacturing techniques, is having a profound effect upon the way in which both buyers and merchandisers now have to work. It is in the critical area of IT that the battle of fashion retailing will be lost or won.

The fashion buyer of the future

The buyer initially held the key responsibility for getting the right goods into the business at the right time and at the right price. In the early, more stable, fashion retailing environments, ahead of the development of good IT and the information it gleaned, it was often difficult for management to see how successfully a line or range was performing. Often the only indicator of success were the sales being achieved. Simply judging buying success on sales, as readers will have already noted, was a dangerous management technique. There is fundamental difference between the *absolute numbers of sales* being achieved on a particular garment and the *rate at which it is selling out* of a business. Smart fashion retailers always make judgement using both criteria. High sales can sometimes be achieved at the expense of spending 'clearance' mark-down, with the ensuing loss of profit that this would inevitably cost. Analysing sales alone, without looking at rate of stock turn and net profitability at the same time, is a recipe for disaster. Buyers using new technology are able to see trading performance more quickly and logically than their predecessors, who were using inefficient paper-based stock management systems.

The modern buyer is now expected to be highly computer literate, in order that he/she can interrogate and investigate all aspects of their buying performance embedded in the retail information system. Many human resource managers working within fashion retailing are in fact currently worried by a major skills gap in some buyers. Many older buyers are finding it increasingly difficult to keep up with the speed of technological advances within retail merchandise planning systems. The buyer of the future will increasingly need to have also developed statistical, analytical and keyboard skills if they are to take maximum advantage of the information available.

Gone are the days that the buyer had time to wait for the merchandiser to 'do the weekly sales figures'; the once long and tortuous manual extraction of weekly sales and stock data from reams of paper printouts is a thing of the past. Good spreadsheet and reporting systems now make analysis a fast process: sometimes reports are generated on an automatic basis, requiring no weekly intervention by either buyer or merchandiser. The new role of the buying team is therefore focused upon the *analysis* of the report and the ensuing action plan, rather than upon its *production*.

Until recently many fashion retailers often had to wait until Tuesday mornings before a full analysis of the previous week's sales and stock performance was available for management and the buying team to act upon. Valuable time could be lost, with the more efficient retailers being able to quickly get back to both fabric producers and garment manufacturers to book repeat production on proven best-selling lines. Getting back into the market ahead of the competition is the name of the game in successful fashion buying.

Today, the best fashion buying and merchandising teams will have undertaken their basic analysis of sales and stock data, in readiness for management review by 10 o'clock on Monday following the previous week's trading. The new challenge for retail IT systems will be the development of '*real time systems*', enabling fashion retailers to interrogate their sales on a minute-by-minute basis. This technology is now widely used by large US retailers such as Wal Mart. Using sophisticated real time satellite-linked technology, they can make *continuous buying and supply chain decisions*. While this technology exists, European fashion retailers are not using it widely, but earlier and earlier capture, analysis and reaction to all types of fashion trend will create competitive advantage for the pioneers in this field.

In fact, the buyer of the future may well take on more of what was once seen as merchandiser's work, especially as a result of the development of 'intelligent' information systems. These use intelligent processes contained within the programmes, to spot minute changes of demand and supply that cannot be easily seen by the human eye and brain – e.g. early small but significant indications of best-selling colour trends. With existing systems, it is often difficult to spot small numeric changes, but these small changes can often have a major and significant impact further into the season as consumer demands gathers pace. Intelligent systems with 'detect and alert agents' will enable both the buyer and merchandiser to quickly spot such minute trends and reactions deeply embedded in the mass of weekly sales data. 'Detect and alert systems' automatically highlight these new events which buyers and merchandisers could easily overlook.

Today's buyer is increasingly expected to be much more *visually and technically literate* than earlier generations. The need to be able to understand consumer requirements has never been greater. With the development and growth of visual media, today's buyer is being continually bombarded with images and information that will be processed and stored in their minds to be later used as an aid to the final buying decision. The buyer is similar to the artist in that the outcome of their selection, like the painter's picture, has to please the eye of the consumer.

The modern buyer requires a mix of skills, spanning the visual arts, mathematics, marketing and psychology, if they are to ensure success for themselves and the business. In reality no individual buyer could possibly possess all these skills. Human resource management (HRM) in fashion retailing has the task of identifying the strengths and weaknesses of each buyer, to ensure that any missing skills or imbalance is corrected through training, mentoring or coaching. More and more fashion retailers will be submitting future buyers to assessment processes that examine their match to the job and person description using a wide variety of techniques.

Already prospective buyers face a range of selection scenarios prior to being accepted or appointed by many organisations. These tests often involve candidates in simulated range selection tests, requiring them to select from previous season's ranges with known sales performance. The main aim is to see whether the prospective candidate has an 'eye' for the type of product that has already sold within the business. Over the next few years, as human resource selection techniques are developed, proven and tested, the buyer of tomorrow will need to accept the increasing use of the selection test. The historic role of the buyer is changing in tune with societal, consumer and technical demands. The implication is that many universities and employers will need to face the fact that existing qualifications and training courses will need to be redesigned to meet the new demands now being placed on the fashion buyer.

The fashion merchandiser of the future

The buyer's clerk filled the first 'merchandising' roles, often a 'Dickensian' figure found mainly in the old department stores. Their job was to simply hand write and despatch the buyers' orders, while at the same time keeping a running manual ledger of the value of stock bought so far. The buyer kept manual records of daily and weekly sales, therefore keeping a record of trade through time. The merging of smaller shops into larger buying groups eventually created the need for a geographically remote buyer, who faced a much more complex record-keeping process. During the post-war years, the American term 'merchandiser' was imported to Britain and Europe. This higher-level role relied mainly on manual-based stock counting systems, requiring mountains of paper and hours of paper-based analysis.

The slide rule and mechanical calculator were in use in the United Kingdom until the middle 1970s, being quickly replaced by the ubiquitous mainframe, midi and personal computer during the early and mid-1980s. Many large retailers such as Marks & Spencer chose to continue manual counts for many years after such technology had become widely available. The increased data processing power and speed of the new technology has fundamentally changed the role of the merchandiser over the past ten-year period. The merchandiser soon took hold of this new-found power to deliver better and faster analysis for the buyer, with which to make better and faster buying decisions.

The way in which retailers now use modern IT for controlling their businesses is still very variable, despite the availability of increasingly smarter stock planning and control systems. There are now many proprietary retail-planning systems enabling fashion retailers to plan their ranges and control them down to the very lowest levels. Planning by style, size and colour options down to individual branch location is increasingly becoming the accepted norm. With such powerful planning systems, the modern merchandiser is able to plan to supply *very unique local demand patterns*. For example, people in different parts of the United Kingdom and Europe tend to be differently sized; immigration into local areas can often fundamentally change the sizing patterns required in a local shop. These are known as *anthropomorphic merchandising demands*.

Other demographic profiles can skew some areas toward a younger, older, richer or poorer profile. These *micro market demands* are now a new battleground. This is where extreme technology, combined with creative merchandise planning and control will allow the fashion leaders of tomorrow to win the final fashion battle by giving consumers exactly what they want at a local level.

Apart from the socio–demographic and anthropomorphic variations at each shop location, the variable shape and size of fashion shops makes it difficult for fashion retailers to ensure that the width of range alternatives sent to each shop can be displayed to its fullest. Often the central buying office sends too many or too few options to fill the available floor and stockroom space. With the development of digital imaging and virtual reality, the possibility of merchandisers being able to visually plan a range into each branch ahead of dispatch, is already being used by American supermarket chains. Planning a range and controlling it by numbers alone is a dangerous way to merchandise, hence the need for the merchandiser to visit branches, to see the fruits of their labour. With fast-changing and fast-moving stock ranges, the look and balance of fashion stock in any business is rapidly changing, and very hard to visualise.

Quite clearly the Holy Grail of merchandise planning is going to be the fully integrated numeric and visual merchandising system that links together stock value, stock units and available stock fixtures back to branch level. At present, merchandise stock planning and control systems are generally run as stand-alone planning systems, with visual stock layout systems running separately. Their full integration into easily understood and managed 'Grail' systems that will draw together all salient information and consolidate it clearly, as well as making recommendations within the scope of previously defined trading parameters are being developed and will revolutionise the role of merchandiser.

Just as the buyer has had to become more numerate, the merchandiser will need to become aesthetically more literate, unable to escape into the detail of numbers alone. Regular and seasonal range reviews may also involve 3D imaging of the ranges in virtual shops, to ensure that the stock numbers stack up, not only numerically, but visually as well. This technological development is going to be a major driver in redefining the skill sets required of the fashion merchandiser. This may be the first true meeting point of art and mathematics. Again employers, colleges and universities alike will need to review and refine the skill sets that will be required to undertake a merchandising job effectively.

The future will undoubtedly require fewer, but better intellectually equipped, buying and merchandising staff backed by more and more sophisticated technology. Just as the paper-based bank clerk has in large been replaced by technology, so will be many of the buying and merchandising jobs of the future.

Likely future technological impacts on the consumer

For buyers and merchandisers, at the 'supply end' of the business, the effect of new technology has already had and will continue increasingly to have a major impact upon the way they work in the future. At the 'consumer end' of the equation, it is also important to try and evaluate how technology might develop and affect the work of the buyer and merchandiser.

We are now facing the prospect of traditional 'bricks and mortar' fashion retailing coming under increasing attack from Internet retailers, or 'e-tailers' as they are popularly known. Internet fashion retailing is happening, but at present the level of market penetration is quite low. Many observers believe that Internet shopping for fashion will be limited owing to the tactile nature of the fashion purchasing process. Pictures can never replace the touching, feeling and trying on of a garment. Also there are still dramatic technical limitations in terms of the difficulty of viewing clothing products effectively.

The convergence of the home PC and the domestic television will soon happen, as a result of the introduction of digital TV channels. This technology will therefore bring home shopping directly to the fireside, rather than to the spare room of the house, where the family PC is located. Higher picture definition and faster picture formation will also allow fine detail to be seen more clearly and quickly. The days of the slow and cumbersome Internet picture download will be a thing of the past. It is also possible that with developments with virtual reality, there will also be possibilities for the consumer to 'virtually try on' a potential garment for purchase. The virtual fashion catwalk has already been developed, and there is now talk that Lara Croft-type 'virtual' models will replace all the real, temperamental, expensive and sometimes neurotic supermodels! These have the immediate benefit of always being available for work at much lower cost.

In the future, the customer may well be able to feed their own 'virtual person' into the garments on offer, even matching their own physical measurements to the actual measurements of the garment. The bother of going in and out of the crowded fitting room will be a thing of the past. It is also likely that the rather frozen picture gallery offer of fashion products on the Internet will develop into much more of a 'virtual shop', where the customer can, from the comfort of their own arm chair, move around inside. Possibly the virtual shop could show exactly the stock, ranges and options available in an actual clothing shop at any point – how often has a reader set out to buy clothes, only to come back with nothing as your favourite shop has nothing that you actually like, or worst of all does not have your size in stock? While this scenario may sound too futuristic to be taken seriously, technology can and will deliver it in the foreseeable future. Fashion shopping could happen on line, but only as soon as the technology gets good enough to deliver realistic pictures of fashion products in realistic and humanistic settings.

Fashion buyers and merchandisers will need to adapt their work to take into account the new information age customers. Possibly the buyer and merchandiser will need to be involved with the detailed design of the 'virtual shop'. As with buyers for mail order catalogues, who need to buy product that has 'page appeal', there will be a new need for buyers of interactive fashion retailers to ensure that products have 'screen appeal'. Whatever happens, new technology will take an increasing share of the fashion market and impact directly upon the buying and merchandising activities of the future.

Other types of fashion retail competition

Although technology is heralded as the most important force likely to impact upon 'bricks and mortar' retailers, there are in fact many other ways of trading fashion products that seem to have been overlooked by many of the more conventional fashion retailers.

These include:

- Charity shops
- Second-time round shops
- Secondhand clothing shops
- Special location retailers – hospital foyers
- Car boot sales
- Direct from factory sales
- Mobile shops
- Office or place of work visitations
- Transport location shops – airports and stations
- 'Black' economy – illegal trading
- Market stalls
- Pyramid selling
- Event shops – pop concerts, rural shows, air shows, etc.
- Garage sales
- Door-to-door selling
- Home-clothing parties – e.g. Ann Summers' home underwear parties
- Hand-me-down clothes – mainly family.

While this list may not sound like a threat to conventional fashion retailers, if the turnover of all these sources were added together, it would represent a sizeable part of the entire fashion clothing market. For example, the United Kingdom had over 7000 charity shops in 2000. Charity shops are probably numerically the fastest-expanding sector of the entire retail sector. Unknown to most full-price fashion retailers is the fact that the total UK charity shop sector sells more clothing units than Marks & Spencer! Sometimes obvious key factors and influences escape the observation of even the most professional marketers. Unlike conventional 'bricks and mortar' retailers, all of the above activities do not carry extremely high rental and other infrastructural costs. Rentals throughout European fashion retailing generally represent one of the highest fixed costs.

More and more fashion retailers will look for new and cheaper ways to deliver product to the consumer. It is inevitable that both buyers and merchandisers will need to adapt to any such new approaches. As with the product, their roles will change accordingly, and equally as fast. Nothing is forever in the world of fashion buying and merchandising.

■ ▼ Glossary of terms

Accessories A range of products that are designed to accompany items of clothing to complete an overall look. Usually intended to be decorative, common examples include ties, belts, bags, scarves, hats and jewellery, although the width of a range will vary among fashion retailers. Retailers that are selling a life-style image will have a wider range.

Agent A person or business, which acts in a selling capacity for another party. Foreign manufacturers will often sell their products in other countries through agent/agencies. Agents are normally paid on a percentage commission basis. Agents will often 'carry' complementary ranges from several manufacturers at one time. They deal directly with the buyer.

Allocation The process of distributing stock to stores. Stock is allocated selectively to stores according to certain criteria, including store size and sales targets. Principal stores will receive 'top store'-only lines together with the rest of a season's styles. Smaller stores will receive a representation of stock to achieve their targets. The allocation process varies according to whether the stock is being distributed for the first time or being used to replace sales.

Allocator Sometimes known as a distributor. This individual will work in a predetermined manner, using available computer systems to ensure that stock is allocated effectively and efficiently to individual shops. The job ensures that available stock is used to its best effect and sent to the place where it is most likely to sell.

Androgyny A reference to the convergence of gender in society. Fashion has reflected the convergence of status between males and females in Western culture in many ways. Clothing, accessories, hair products and perfumes are examples of fashion where strong unisex products have been established.

'Baby Boomers' Generally refers to the large birth-rate bulge that occurred during the late 1940s and 1950s, as result of European servicemen returning home from the Second World War. This is a large section of the population, which is now relatively wealthy. They were the first teenage generation able to buy mass fashion in the high street. They still represent a significant marketing opportunity.

Bar codes (bar coding) Bar codes or bar coding is a unique way to give each fashion product an individual identity that can be read by laser scanner at the point of sale. This ensures that the retailer is then aware of what line/size/colour of garment has been sold. They are found on most consumer products. On fashion products they are printed onto a cardboard swing tag attached to the garment. They are internationally recognisable and have been developed to ensure that retailers are able to monitor sales quickly and control their stock levels accurately.

Base fabric All fabric, woven and knitted, needs to be approved for quality before it is used in garment construction. Fashion buyers give approval at two different stages referred to as 'base' and 'bulk' fabric approval. Base fabric is approved for stability and suitability for end use before the fabric is committed for further development.

'Blue Cross' mark-down A special type of mid-season sales promotion event originally devised by department stores, but now widely used by all types of fashion store. A standard discount is typically applied to selected slow-selling lines that have been identified as needing sales stimulation ahead of the normal Summer or Winter Sale period. A blue cross is used to identify selected lines that carry the price reductions.

Boxed stock/ Flat-packed stock Garments shipped from other countries are usually folded and packed into cartons or boxes. This reduces costs and ensures that fashion products arrive in good condition. Flat-packed/boxed stock will often require 'processing' before being put out onto the shop floor; it will often require pressing.

Branch An individual shop or store of a larger chain. Each branch is usually designated with an individual branch number that can be recognised by the computer for delivery and sales transaction purposes.

Brand In fashion, the term usually refers to the name of a product, company or designer that has a distinctive image and perceived set of values associated with it. A brand will be distinguished from competitors and convey an image that motivates the consumer to respond positively towards it. Traditionally associated with non-retail products, although successful branding of own labels has created strong retailer brands.

'Bricks and mortar' retailing A recently adopted term that refers to any form of fashion or other retailer who trades from a normal shop or store, rather than one that sells via mail order or via the Internet.

Bulk fabric Refers to the completed fabric that is used in the make-up of garments. The fabric is dyed to a specific colour, will often contain printed designs and possess certain 'finishes' which provide it with specific benefits. As such, the approval tests are more focused on colourfastness and the specific benefits provided by the finishing process – e.g. wrinkle free.

Buyer The job of a fashion buyer varies according to the nature and size of a business. A boutique buyer will often also be its owner and will buy branded or designer-label stock to sell to customers. A buyer for a fashion retail brand will be involved in a more complex buying process involving design, sourcing and production.

Buying assistant The most junior role on a fashion buying team. Also referred to as 'buyer's clerk' by some fashion retailers, it is mainly an administrative role concerned with organising records and details of suppliers, orders and samples.

Buying ethics A self-imposed code that ensures that fashion buying is carried out in a decent, moral and honourable manner. It covers such issues as buying bribes, environmental issues and poorly paid or child workers. Many fashion retailers will give buyers clear written guidelines on these issues.

Buying team The team of individuals that is responsible for planning and buying a specific range of merchandise within a fashion company. Usually it consists of a buyer and merchandiser, together with their individual support staff. Normally a buying team is product- or garment-specific, although sometimes a team may be responsible for a range of products.

Category Sometimes called a 'product group', it is used to group together garments or similar lines into one group. It ensures that a fashion retailer is able to quickly see how one type of group of lines is performing as whole. It helps in the monitoring of sales performance and overall stock control.

Charity shop Originated by Oxfam during the late 1940s, they mainly sell donated second-hand or recycled garments. There are currently over 6500 charity shops in the UK and it is a growing worldwide phenomenon. These 'not for profit' charitable organisations donate all their income to charitable causes and it is increasingly becoming an accepted form of fashion retailing.

CIF – Carriage, Insurance and Freight The term refers to the agreement on the delivery of foreign goods that is included within the cost price. The cost price paid by the buyer includes transport of merchandise by vessel to a country specified by the buyer. It is up to the seller to arrange insurance and delivery of the merchandise within the price they agree.

Closing stock The term applied to the retail value or number of units of stock left at the end of a trading period. Trading periods are usually weekly, monthly or annual. Used by both buyers and merchandisers as a judgement point as to whether there is too much or too little stock in a business. It can be of interest at individual line, category, department and total business levels.

CMT An acronym for the words 'Cut, Make and Trim'. Generally used in the production of more complex or tailored garments, where a clothing manufacturer receives fabric owned by the retailer or another party to make up into a finished garment. The price paid for the process is only for the cutting, making up and provision of items used to trim the garment.

Colour way A colour option of a product style.

Commitment The value of stock (usually at selling value) that has been ordered by the buyer, but not delivered or paid for. The term usually applies to firm orders, however sometimes unconfirmed orders may also be included in the calculation.

Comparative advantage An economic term expressing differences between countries' ability to have a competitive advantage over others, through their inherent resources.

Computer tag A small cardboard tag usually applied to fashion products by a small plastic shank. On this label is usually found a unique bar code, the line number, the description, the size colour and the price. It acts as an information carrier for both the customer and the retailer.

Concession A branded shop operating inside another store. The shop will be run virtually in the same way as if it were free-standing outside the store, managing stock staff and its space independently of the host store. The host store will usually receive a premium and a rent from the shop and will benefit from the additional customers it generates. There have to be strong reciprocal benefits for both retailers for it to be sustainable.

Confusion marketing A new term that is applied to any pricing situation that is so complex that the customer has great difficulty in understanding what value is actually being offered and as result cannot make direct comparison with the price of another similar product. Offering complex discounts and 'two for one' offers can be a form of confusion marketing.

Continuity lines A basic style that sells well from one season to another, often undergoing minor updates. The life-cycle of, and degree of change in, a continuity style may vary dramatically between different fashion retailers.

COO – Country of Origin Most products have the country in which they were manufactured recorded on a label attached to the garment. This is not however a legal requirement in the United Kingdom and most European countries. It is a requirement, though, for country of origin to be declared on purchase orders for quota purposes. As garments can be made up in different locations it is the country where the principal process occurred that needs to be recorded.

Cost price The price paid for a product before a mark-up is added to achieve a selling price. Generally the cost price of a fashion product bought for resale by a retailer includes all tickets, hangers, protective covers and packaging. Transport to the retailer will be included according to different cost terms.

Couture Derived from the French word for 'dressmaking', it generally refers to extremely individual and unique hand-made garments made in the studios and workrooms of international *haute couture* designers. Aimed specifically at the extremely rich, it tends to be more usually applied to French design houses, although not exclusively.

Cover A general term applied to how long the stock in store will last based upon current sales performance. Usually this is expressed in numbers of weeks. Cover can be expressed by style, category, department, store and total business. It is a key performance indicator.

Critical path A sequence of steps delineating the development process of a product. It is used to monitor progress and draw attention to critical events where decisions are under pressure of lead-times.

DRTV Direct Response Television – DRTV is applied to situations where the customer is able to respond and buy directly from an advert seen on television. At present the customer response is achieved using a separate telephone line, although future technological developments using digital technology will enable the customer to purchase directly using the television remote control key-pad.

Delivery schedule A timetable scheduling deliveries of products from suppliers. The deliveries into the business occur every week and are updated accordingly, providing a record of outstanding stock.

Department store Large-space retailer, usually with several floors selling a wide variety of goods including clothing and household goods in dedicated areas or departments. Originally a French invention, they are found in most developed countries and normally deliver high levels of customer service.

Designer A person who is involved in a creative process turning customer needs into value outcomes. Outcomes may range widely according to the specific role of the designer, but could include manufactured products, corporate logos or packaging.

Distribution centre (DC) A facility which redistributes products to retail outlets having received them as deliveries from suppliers.

Distributor   The individual responsible for allocating stock to stores. The role is more specifically focused on distribution than the similar role of allocator used by some fashion retailers.

Dummy branch   A term used to describe a branch number for a branch that has not yet opened, or one that may be in the process of refurbishment or modernisation. Used mainly by merchandisers to ensure that stock packages are built in readiness for the opening or the reopening of a shop. Generally the dummy branch stock is held in readiness in a special area of the DC.

e-commerce   Any form of commercial activity over the Internet, where some form of transaction takes place. It can also describe commercial activity undertaken via Direct Response Television (DRTV).

EDI – Electronic Data Interchange   This occurs when two businesses exchange any form of information electronically. It generally replaces information sent by paper and often involves the transmission of weekly sales information from the retailer to the supplier. It helps to speed up decision-making throughout the supply chain.

EFTPOS – Electronic Fund Transfer at Point Of Sale   This is the process and systems used for checking and transferring money from the customer to the retailer at the point of sale. This confirmation is made over a telephone wire link connected from the shop to the bank. It is usually known by the customer as a 'credit card machine'.

EPOS – Electronic Point Of Sale   This refers to the equipment and systems used on shop counters to register sales information automatically to a central computer system. Usually an EPOS system takes the form of a cash till with a memory that is able to communicate with the business's central computer, in order to pass specific details of the transaction to head office. Details of the value and the specific line size and colour will be passed to the main computer that will then automatically reduce the stock level information accordingly. It enables fast processing of sales information in order to speed up new stock replenishment to the shop from the distribution centre.

Elasticity of demand   An economic theory explaining the relationship between changes in price and demand. When demand is 'elastic' an increase in price will result in a fall in the quantity that is demanded, whereas a decrease in the price will result in an increase in demand. Conversely inelastic demand means that a price increase will result in a fall in demand but the price increase compensates for the lost sales. Equally a price decrease has a minor affect on demand, making the price reduction costly and ineffective. Price elasticity is measure by the formula:

$$\frac{\% \text{ change in sales demand}}{\% \text{ change in sales price}}$$

Where the outcome is greater than 1, demand is elastic and where it is less than 1 demand is inelastic.

e-tailing   Any form of retailing activity undertaken over the Internet.

Factory outlet   A distribution channel located at manufacturing facilities and used by brands to sell off end-of-line products. The products are usually sold at a significant discount to normally distributed retail goods.

Fashion Traditionally defined as the current style of dressing or appearance that is adopted by the majority of people. Although more commonly expressed through clothing, hairstyles and other aspects of individuals' appearance, fashion is increasingly concerned with other 'visible' aspects of peoples' life-styles. Home interiors, gardens, plants, cars, mobile telephones and club memberships are all influenced by fashion trends.

Fashionability An industry term to refer to the way in which a particular season's fashion is expressed in products. In garments, the fashion trends may be reflected through the manipulation of silhouette, fabric, colour, print, patterns and trimmings.

Fashion buyer The job of a fashion buyer varies according to the nature and size of a business. A boutique buyer will often also be its owner and will buy branded or designer-label stock to sell on to customers in a similar way to that of a department store buyer. A buyer for a fashion retail brand will be involved in a more complex buying process involving design, sourcing and production.

Fashion merchandising In buying and merchandising terms it refers to the analytical stock control and distribution role accompanying buying in fashion retailing. Other definitions can refer to the presentation of stock in stores.

Fashion multiple A fashion retail company that has many branded stores.

Fit Refers to the suitability of the shape and size of a garment to a person. Principally concerned with comfort and appearance, although the latter can be very influenced by styling trends.

Fit model A model, usually a size 12 in women's wear, who tries on fit samples in order that garment technologists and buyers can make appropriate adjustments to prototype garments as part of the quality control process.

Fit sample A prototype of the garment style booked for production. Accurate in fabric and to the design specification dimensions of the garment, fit samples are not accurate for colour, print, pattern and trimmings. Any adjustments made are communicated to the supplier who sends an amended version, which is sealed once considered to be satisfactory.

FOB – Free on Board This is a cost–price term which does not include complete delivery to the buyer in the cost price. The cost price includes delivery onto a vessel at a port in the country of manufacture. Subsequent insurance and transportation of the merchandise from the port to the final destination is the buyer's responsibility. Many fashion retailers prefer to buy FOB as they can control the cost and lead-times associated with shipping to their country.

Forecast A view of where the business will be in the future based on the best known historic and current information. It can be applied to subjective issues such as fashion trends, but is more usually applied to the forward view of likely sales or stock levels. Forecasting is a regular merchandising task that helps to ensure that the business has the right balance and level of stock delivered in readiness for anticipated sales.

Forward buying Relates to the process of buying ahead to meet anticipated future sales and stock levels. The degree to which a buyer forward buys depends very much upon the length of the manufacturing process from conception to delivery.

Forward demand factors   Relates to the likely level of stock or deliveries to store that will be needed to meet anticipated forward sales demand. Prior to seasonal trading peaks, the forward demand factor is normally higher on seasonal products. During slacker forward trading periods, the forward demand factor will be lower. It can be expressed either as percentage increase or decrease, or as a ratio.

Fragmentation   The term refers to a state where a particular style no longer has the full complement of sizes across the size scale in which it was originally bought. This is usually the result of a disproportionate level of sales in selected sizes arising from the style being bought using incorrect size ratios.

Franchise(ing)   A method of retailing that involves the retailer licensing an individual or company to purchase and sell the retailer's own products in an identical way to the retailer. It will involve the franchisee in creating an identical shop environment as the parent retailer, as well as forcing them to buy all their stock from the retailer directly or through the retailer's recommended suppliers. The franchisee generally pays a percentage of sales back to the retailer for this right.

Free stock   Stock available in a warehouse or distribution centre that is available for allocation.

Garment technologist   A technical role concerned with the quality, technical construction and performance of fabric and garments.

GATT – General Agreement on Tariffs and Trade   A global agreement regulating trade of goods and services between member countries. It is the major trade agreement that incorporated the Multi-Fibre Arrangement (MFA). GATT has now been superseded by the World Trade Organisation (WTO).

Globalisation   An all-encompassing word used to describe the increasing internationalisation of all types of fashion business. With increasing levels of foreign travel as well as improved communications the business world is becoming more homogeneous in terms of garments, styles and the ways of transacting business.

Grey market   Particularly refers in the fashion business to the trade of branded goods in any market or country from unofficial sources. Branded suppliers often try to maintain higher differential price structures in certain markets or countries to optimise their revenues. Grey market trading usually tries to break these price structures by bringing in merchandise from another lower-cost country or market.

GRN – Goods Received Note   A record of goods received by a warehouse or DC. Generally, no stock can be allocated unless the DC has recorded the delivery on a computerised system. To do this, the goods are quality checked and any surpluses or shortages against the order are noted.

Gross margin   The difference between the price that a fashion business buys and then sells its stock at is known as the gross margin. It is usually expressed as a percentage, although it can also relate to an absolute financial value.

£ Retail selling price (RSP) – £ Cost price (CP) = £ Gross margin, or

$$\frac{RSP - CP}{1} \times 100 = \% \text{ Gross margin}$$

Hanging stock   Most garments delivered to a fashion business arrive from the manufacturer on hangers. This enables them to be immediately put out on the sales floor. This eases handling when delivering into the DC and then on to the shop. It has the advantage of reducing garment creasing prevalent with boxed deliveries.

High street   An industry term to refer to the middle-market fashion retail sector typically represented in main urban shopping areas. Traditionally the centre of a town was referred to as the 'high street' and this was the location for the major retailers.

Information jockey   An American term increasingly being used to describe that person responsible for the dissemination of all types of information throughout the company.

Initial allocation   The first allocation of a new style to stores. It is usually followed by replenishment allocations of stock.

In margin   Another term for gross margin, before discounts are added and mark-down deducted: the profit on the goods at full selling price.

Intake   A term relating to the amount of stock delivered or planned to be delivered into a fashion business. Intake is phased into the business just ahead of anticipated sales/demand peaks. Intake control is the responsibility of the merchandiser.

In-stock percentage   A percentage figure which describes the stock position of a branch in relation to the stock it needs to achieve its sales targets. The ideal level of stock would be 100 per cent, with stock surpluses and shortages reflecting variations above and below 100 per cent.

Inventory   A detailed list of stock or goods held. Inventory is sometimes used instead of the word 'stock'.

Jobber   An individual who buys faulty stock at a greatly reduced price for resale. Stock which is 'jobbed off' by fashion retailers generally falls into two categories: that stock which is rejected owing to quality control faults and that which is returned by customers to the stores. The stock can be sold in the domestic country or internationally, but will have identifying labels, tickets and hangers removed.

Junior buyer   The buyer for a product area with a small budget, or an assistant buyer who has buying responsibility for a limited range within a department.

KPI – Key performance indicator   A measure of business performance, which a fashion retailer considers to be particularly important. KPIs include, Like for Like (LFL) sales, NAMAD, Stockturn, Linear footage sales and Cover.

KVI – Key value item   This is a best-selling continuity style, which is core to retailers' product sales. Usually priced to represent value and reflect high-volume sales.

Lab-dip   A piece of fabric dyed to a particular colour specification and submitted to buyers for bulk fabric approval.

Lead-time   The period of time from design conception to delivery into retail stores. The definition of a lead-time may vary according to the particular stage in the supply chain which is being considered. For example, some buyers may refer to a manufacturing to store delivery lead-time, while another may refer to the shipping lead-time.

Letter of credit   A form of payment where two parties, a buyer and a seller, use a bank as an intermediary to implement payment on the submission of specified documentation. The documentation must include evidence of the merchandise having been loaded onto a vessel.

Life-style   A general description of how an individual person chooses to live, in terms of where they live, their type of work, the way in which they spend their spare time, as well as their general hopes and aspirations. All of these have a direct impact upon how the individual dresses and their general view towards fashion.

Like-for-like (LFL)   A term used to describe an exactly comparable situation or number. Often used in sales definitions it ensures that two sales numbers are being compared logically. When accurately comparing a sales increase year-on-year, it is essential to exclude any new opening stores that did not trade last year that may have traded for only a limited period this year. Such a direct comparison excluding new openings would give a LFL sales comparison.

Line number   A unique number that is automatically given to each line as it is purchased. The central computer normally generates the line number. It helps all functions of the business to track and monitor the progress of the line from inception through to final sale to the customer. It is found printed on the swing tag attached to the garment or item. Prior to computers, some fashion businesses (especially the shoe business) would give names rather than numbers to help staff easily identify individual lines. The number is broken down to represent the line's department, style, colour and season.

Linear foot   The total length of hanging rail space, expressed in feet. The total length is constituted by the variety of fixtures held in a store. It is often now expressed in metres.

Made-to-Measure   A self-explanatory term that differentiates garments from those that are bought 'off the peg' or ready-made. Prior to the development of mass-factory production of clothing all garments were made-to-measure. Also referred to as 'bespoke'.

MFA – Multi-Fibre Arrangement   This is a global agreement between textile-producing countries to limit the sale of textiles and clothing products from cheap-production countries to the developed world.

Management Information System (MIS)   Describes any system whether computer or paper-based that records and provides management with information that can be used for decision-making. Many systems are becoming highly sophisticated and now help merchandisers to model future sales and stock demand to high levels of accuracy.

Margin   Another word often used to describe the overall profit of a fashion operation. It can be expressed as either a sum of money or as a percentage of profit to sales. See also Gross margin and Net margin.

Mark-down/Mark-up   Indicates a price movement either downwards or upwards. Prices are reduced to make slow-selling merchandise sell more quickly, while price increases tend to reduce the rate of sale. Fashion businesses alter prices regularly to ensure that stock sells out at the planned rate. Fashion businesses keep an on-going record of all mark-downs/mark-ups taken throughout the course of the season/year. It is normally expressed as a percentage:

$$\frac{\text{Value of all price movement upwards} - \text{Value of all price alterations downwards}}{1} \times \frac{100}{1} = \% \text{ Mark-down}$$

Too high a mark-down may indicate poor buying and usually leads to reduced profitability.

Marketing The management process of identifying and satisfying customers' needs and wants through profitable exchange of value. In fashion retailing, the term has been customised to refer mainly to the narrower role of promotion.

Marketing mix A set of tactical tools that are integrated to achieve marketing objectives. Also referred to as the 4 Ps (Product, Price, Promotion, Place) or 7 Ps (including process, people, physical evidence) depending on the level of service attributes included in the 'augmented product' offer.

Market position The position that a business is perceived by its customers to hold in a market compared with competitors. Fashion retailers will use a combination of price, fashionability, attitude, range width and depth and product quality to manipulate customer perceptions.

MDA number A computer-generated number that is given to a supplier by the buying and merchandising team to authorise delivery into a DC or warehouse.

Merchandiser The role of stock planning, management and control. In larger multiple retailers the role is more specifically concerned with planning, analysis and profit maximisation of stock, with a distribution manager controlling the allocations to stores. However, in smaller retailers a merchandiser may well have complete responsibility for allocations as well.

'Mods' The term refers to branches that have been temporarily closed for shop refits and thus are taken off the allocation system until they reopen.

Mood board Boards created by fashion designers to illustrate the main inspirations and key themes behind a specific season.

Net margin (NAMAD) Net achievable margin after discount. The final net profit after trade discounts and settlement terms have been added and markdowns/mark-ups have been subtracted. It is the measure of actual product profitability.

'New-value' retailers Used to describe any type of fashion retailer that uses continual price reduction and reduced price multiple purchase offers as their main promotional tool. Their objective is to sell high unit volumes at low margin in order to make an acceptable overall profitability.

On-trend Any fast-moving trend defined by style, colour or fabric that emerges within a season. There can be several trends emerging concurrently at any point in the season.

Opening stock   A term used to indicate the value at selling price (sometimes the number of units) held in stock at the start of any trading period (week/month/year). Used in conjunction with the planned closing stock value and the planned sales value, it enables the merchandiser to calculate the required stock intake pattern necessary to provision the business adequately.

$$\text{Opening stock (first period)} + \text{Intake} - \text{Sales} = \text{Closing Stock (first period)}$$
$$= \text{Opening Stock (period two)}$$

Open to Buy (OTB)   Usually termed intake, this describes the amount of buying money available at any point in time:

$$\text{Opening stock} - \text{Closing stock Sales} = \text{Open to Buy}$$

It is based upon the open-to-buy calculation that is being consistently reviewed as a result of current sales performance. Buyers need consistent open to buy available if they are to ensure that the range is kept interesting with new fashion products.

Option   A product style in a colour way.

Order   The contract between a fashion retailer and supplier for stock.

Out of town   Describes any form of retail shopping centre that has been specially constructed away from historic high streets and town/city centre shopping complexes. Such specialist shopping zones have plenty of car parking and easy road/bus/rail access from nearby conurbations. Generally shops and stores built in these areas are very large as a result of the cheaper land prices away from city centres.

Own label   A retailer's own range of products. Increasingly the term relates to products of branded retailers.

Parallel importing   Relates to imports of branded goods that are not brought into a country through the normal channels of distribution. Existing agents and wholesalers are not used, as they will normally sell the brand on to retail customers at higher prices than the parallel importer, who buys in lower-cost countries. The aim of the parallel importer is to sell high volumes of the brand at low prices through cheaper retail outlets – e.g. market stalls. Discounting can destroy brand values and is discouraged by the brand owners.

Payment terms   Every fashion company will stipulate a preferred method and time scale of payment. To ensure prompt payment, many suppliers will offer a sliding settlement discount, which acts as a payment incentive.

Pen portrait   A written description of the personal profile and life-style of a target customer, used by fashion retailers to focus design, buying and marketing activities.

Pilling   A fabric problem resulting in the appearance of small unsightly balls of fibre on the surface of a garment, usually caused by rubbing and abrasion.

Plan   A clear and defined view of the future defining exactly predetermined objectives, usually expressed as numeric measures of business performance – e.g. planned sales, planned stock levels.

Planning – Bottom-up/Top-down   The overall business plan of a fashion business if imposed downwards by top management without discussion, is known as 'top-down' planning. Plans that are created by junior management and then passed up to top management for approval is known as 'bottom-up' planning. Normally most businesses use a technique that is a combination of the two. This makes for good, sensible and achievable plans.

Point of sale Any customer–retailer interface, although most commonly the shop floor. Also refers more specifically to the till area where transactions occur.

PR – Public relations One of the promotional tools available to marketers. Commonly used in fashion to raise awareness of products and brands through publicity.

Preferred supplier A core or key supplier who provides for a number of garment-buying departments. Usually it is a supplier with a proven track record of good stock deliveries of high-quality merchandise.

Premiere Vision Arguably the largest fabric trade show in Europe, where fibre and fabric manufacturers exhibit to buyers. Originally considered to be the first sight of colour and fabric trends one year ahead of a season, but now more a part of the establishment as other fabric fairs show earlier for the same season.

Price architecture Structured price points for similar styles to provide customers with choice. The same product category, such as a dress, will be on sale in different styles at different price points usually separated by logical price gaps – e.g. £5, £10, etc. The lowest-priced style is sometimes referred to as a market entry-level item.

Price points Varying retail prices for different products. Retail prices frequently end in psychological points – e.g. 0.95p, 0.99p – which some retailers believe increase perceptions of value.

Product benefits A generic term focusing on the benefits sought by customers in the products and services sold by businesses. Marketing theory states that customers seek benefits from products and services rather than the attributes themselves.

Product review Once the season has started trading, there are usually monthly progress review meetings that are held between senior management and individual buying teams to accurately review sales and stock delivery performance. These require samples and merchandising paperwork to support the review process. Action plans to buy more or less stock, or take other remedial action, are derived from these important meetings.

Quota A specific number of garments or square metreage of fabric that has been set by international agreement between two countries. It defines how much product (in specific and agreed protected categories) the importing country is prepared to accept from the exporting country over a defined period. Normally quotas are set annually and they are aimed at protecting the importing country's home industry from being swamped by cheap imports in the short term.

Range planning The process of ensuring that each shop or store has the right range delivered to it during a season. The range plan checks that the right number of lines, in the right quantities, at the right price is delivered at the right time. The variable physical sizes of shops and the variable nature of local markets make this a very important seasonal process for the buyer and merchandiser. The range-planning process is the main guide for the buyer as to the width and type of range that they will need to purchase for any chain of shops.

Range presentation   At the start of the seasonal buying process, the buying and merchandising teams will present the proposed range to senior buying management. It is the formal process of having the range agreed and requires sample garments together with all the numeric merchandising plans to support the logic of the range.

Range width and depth   'Width' refers to the number of product lines or categories on offer to customers, and 'depth' refers to the amount of stock held by style, colour and size options available within product categories.

Rate of sale   A measure of the speed that an item is selling out of the business. It is the number of weeks forward that the existing stock will last in the shop assuming that it is not replenished. It is usually expressed as the number of weeks' forward cover in stock:

$$\frac{\text{Unit closing stock at end of week}}{\text{Unit sold during week}} = \text{No. of weeks' forward stock cover}$$

A long or large weeks' cover figure indicates a slow-moving line, a small or short weeks' cover figure indicates a fast-selling line. Relevant action will need to be taken by the buyer and merchandiser in each case.

Ready-to-wear   A term first used in tailoring once made-to-measure suits went out of vogue. It relates to any mass-made factory garment that is not made specifically for the customer. Customers now select a suitably coloured/sized garment from the wide ranges held in store.

Recommended Retail Price (RRP)   For many years branded clothing manufacturers were legally allowed to dictate at what price a retailer should sell their products. This limited retail competition dramatically, and was abolished by an Act of Parliament. However, many branded companies still try to suggest or recommend a price at which merchandise should be sold, but they have no legal recourse should the retailer wish to sell it at a lower price. Withholding of supplies to cut-price retailers has been used as a weapon, but is considered unethical. The law varies internationally and can be a legal minefield. European law appears to support price control by brand owners rather than retailers.

Repeats   Once a line or range has been delivered into store, fast- or best-selling lines are immediately identifiable as a result of short forward stock covers/high rates of sale. The buyer and merchandiser will of course try to repeat buy the line in order to try and maximise sales. Repeat buys are made each week as soon as the previous week's sales figures have been analysed.

Replenishment   Refers to stock sent to a branch in response to a sales reaction to an already delivered line. It is usually based upon an agreed or preplanned forward rate of sale.

Retail selling price   The selling price of the products sold to end-user consumers through retail outlets. Also refers to selling prices of products sold via catalogues and the Internet.

Rolling margin   The profit that any fashion business makes on each line varies around a preplanned percentage set at the start of the season. It would be impossible to make exactly the same margin on every line as this would lead to odd retail selling prices. Therefore to ensure that at all times the business is aware of the average margin (or gross profit) that it is making, it averages out the margin that it is making on all deliveries that come into the DC. This average achieved margin continues rolling over time and gives the business its best measure of the overall buying profit that it is making.

Sales density   A way of expressing how many sales are being generated on a specified area of shop floor. Sales in fashion retailing are usually expressed in £ per sq. metre or £ per sq. feet. It is used as a comparative way of measuring selling space efficiency. It can also be applied to stock held on the shop floor. Again this is usually expressed in value against a specified area, although numbers of actual units held in a space may also be used on some occasions.

Sales reactive   An automatic means of allocation where the computer system selects an appropriate stock holding for a style based on the branches' rates of sale.

Sample   Usually a prototype of a product or key product component such as fabric or trim, which is submitted for approval by the buying team. Also a finished product which is used in promoting the range.

Sealing sample   A sample which has been approved by the buying team. It will be used as a standard reference to compare that future deliveries have achieved the required standard.

Season   A trading period which is usually defined by the climatic seasons. Traditionally divided into Spring/Summer and Autumn/Winter, but increasingly broken down into several sub-seasons based around user occasion themes.

Seasonal postmortem   At the end of each season a report is produced outlining the lessons learnt from the previous season's trading. It will highlight the good and bad aspects of line and range performance, as well as examining how well the suppliers performed in terms of price, quality, delivery and percentage sell through. This document is useful to refer back to when planning the next equivalent season, ensuring that weaknesses are avoided and strengths capitalised.

Segmentation   The process of sub-dividing a market into groups of consumers with broadly similar needs. The segments are then targeted with specific marketing mixes.

Sell through percentage   The percentage of a buy that has sold at full price. Typically, the rest is sold at mark-down or ends up as terminal stock.

Shrinkage   Relates to any form of stock loss from store or DC, whether caused deliberately or accidentally. Staff and customers are the main cause of shrinkage, usually as a result of deliberate theft. All along the supply chain there are always individuals trying to take stock without paying. Some shrinkage may be accidental owing to damage – e.g. flood or fire damage. Some shrinkage can occur owing to simple administrative pricing errors. The retail value of missing stock at the end of a season is usually expressed as a percentage of the season's sales. It is normally revealed as result of a regular stock taking exercise.

Silhouette   The outline shape of a garment.

SKU – stock-keeping unit   This relates to the lowest level at which a fashion retailer would like to keep control of their total stock. Most fashion retailers will want to count and keep detail of every different style of garment down to individual size and colour. One specific garment in a specific size and colour is considered to be one SKU.

Smoothing factor   A weighting, which is activated on a computer system, to manipulate future stock allocations. 'Auto-allocations' react to the previous week's rate of sale. If those sales were influenced by an unusual event, a smoothing factor can be used to take proportionately less significance of the sales so that the allocations are not distorted – e.g. unseasonally hot weather may increase demand for summer-weight garments in early Spring.

SMT – Senior Management Team   The normal definition for the key executive team, involved with managing the buying and merchandising function. Usually takes a strategic perspective as opposed to an operational day-to-day role.

Sourcing   The process of selecting suppliers for manufacturing and delivering products and their components.

Specification sheet   The blueprint of a garment used in production.

Square footage (square metreage)   The total selling area, excluding stock rooms and service areas.

Stock   A generic term to describe products for sale.

Stock pattern   A breakdown of a stock holding for a single style across relevant sizes that is held on a computer for the purpose of stock allocation. The computer will hold a number of patterns for the same style at different stock holdings that are generated by varying rates of sale. The higher the rate of sale, the higher the stock holding generated and pattern used in allocation.

Stock take   An audit of stock levels – usually in stores but also in warehouses and DCs.

Stock turn   A KPI referring to the number of times that a stock holding is sold in a specified period of time – usually a year.

Strike off   A sample of a print design submitted on fabric for approval.

Style   A line or group of similar lines in a colour way.

Supply chain management   The active, efficient and effective control and monitoring of stock into the business. It starts from basic raw materials, right though manufacture up until delivery into the retail outlet. This relatively new management discipline aims at focusing management attention onto the total efficiency of how stock arrives into the business. It aims mainly at getting the best value to the customer, as well as delivering better levels of service.

Supplier   Any individual, agent, branded house, designer, wholesaler, jobber, factory, manufacturer or other organisation which supplies stock to a fashion business.

Tariffs   A type of tax imposed by one government on the exports from another country. Tariffs are usually mutually agreed, although if imposed without agreement and acceptance are contrary to the spirit of global free trade.

Terminal stock   The stock remaining at the end of the season that cannot be sold during the following season. It mainly consists of garments of the wrong seasonal material: either too heavy for Spring/Summer or too lightweight for Autumn/Winter. It is usually an indicator of overbuying in the previous season and has the effect of tying up money in the form of 'dead stock'. It is usually expressed in retail selling value terms, expressed as a percentage of the season's total closing stock. Most fashion businesses will have some terminal stock, as it is impossible to sell all seasonal stock. The lower the percentage, the better.

Trade show   A generic term to refer to a meeting place for buyers and sellers, usually manufacturers, wholesalers and retailers.

Transitional   Refers to ranges or garments of a fabric weight, style, colour or construction that can sell well between the end of one season and the start of another.

Trend   A seasonal fashion theme that can be interpreted across yarns, fabrics and products.

Trial line   A line or style that has been bought in a relatively small unit quantity, usually sent only to a small number of stores for the purposes of experimenting with new styles, colours, brands or fabrics. Trial lines are often early experiments in possible new fashion trends and thus are bought in small quantities to avoid the risk of being left with unsaleable stock.

Trimmings   Functional and decorative features on a garment, such as buttons, zips, toggles, linings, embroideries and appliqués.

Turnover   An abbreviation for 'sales turnover'.

USP (Unique Selling Proposition)   A unique package of product benefits positively distinguishing the offer of one fashion business from its competition.

Value added   Increasingly knowledgeable and demanding customers want more for their money when they buy a fashion product. Any extra attribute or service device that adds to customer satisfaction can be described as 'adding value'. Adding value helps to differentiate fashion retailers from the competition.

Variance   Usually refers to what percentage a business is away from any preplanned sales, stock or intake level. Normally this is expressed as +/- percentage number. Variance from last year's trading performance is also part of the normal merchandising process.

Variety store   Usually refers to large-space retailers selling clothing, household and food-related products. They do not carry as wide a range as department stores. The term is more widely used in the United States.

Visual merchandising   The creative display of goods in-store and in windows. Historically, the term was specifically associated with window display. Atmospherics and visual marketing using sound and interactive technology have increased the overall sophistication of visual merchandising.

Wholesaler   An individual or business that buys merchandise in bulk for resale to smaller retailers. Usually these are smaller retailers who are able to benefit from the economies of scale enjoyed by the wholesaler. It is becoming less used as a result of the increasing dominance of larger fashion chains.

WSSI Often pronounced 'Wizzy', this is the fundamental buying and merchandising control document that tracks the weekly sales, stock and intake performance figures against a previously agreed plan. It also contains a facility to insert regular forecasts that then allow it to be used as a decision support document for senior management.

◼ ⁝ Further reading

Anstey, H. and Weston, T. (1997) *The Anstey Weston Guide to Textile Terms*, Weston Publishing Ltd.

Christopher, M. (1986) *Strategy of Distribution Management*, Butterworth-Heinemann.

Christopher, M. (1998) *Marketing Logistics*, Butterworth-Heinemann.

Cox, R. (2000) *Retail Management, Financial Times*/Prentice-Hall.

Diamond, J. and Pintel, G. (1997) *Retail Buying*, Prentice-Hall International.

Hines, T. (2000) *Supply Chain Management: A Strategic Approach*, Checkmate Publications.

Gattorna, J. and Walters, D.W. (1996) *Managing The Supply Chain: A Strategic Perspective*, Macmillan.

Kunz, G. (1998) *Merchandising, Theory, Principles and Practice*, Fairchild.

Markham, J. (1998) *The Future of Shopping*, Macmillan.

McGoldrick, P. (1990) *Retail Marketing*, McGraw-Hill.

Omar, O. (1999) *Retail Marketing, Financial Times*, Pitman Publishing.

Packard, S., Winters, A. and Axelrod, N. (1983) *Fashion Buying and Merchandising*, Fairchild.

Stone, E. (1994) *Exporting and Importing Fashion: A Global Perspective*, Delmar.

Walters, D. (1994) *Retailing Management: Analysis, Planning and Control*, Macmillan.

Walters, D. and Cook, D. (1991) *Retail Marketing: Theory and Practice*, Prentice-Hall.

Walters, D. and Laffy, D. (1996) *Managing Retail Productivity and Profitability*, Macmillan.

Wills, J. (1999) *Merchandising and Buying Strategies: New Roles for a Global Operation, Financial Times*, Retail & Consumer.

■■ Index